Praise for

Thumbs Up Australia

"*Thumbs-Up Australia* is Tom Parry's gripping, funny and enlightening account of an 8,000-mile hitchhike around Oz. In tow is his reluctant French girlfriend Katia, who would much rather be travelling in a 'Jagwar' than an endless assortment of road-trains, camper vans and Landcruisers. However, the people they meet provide a fascinating and highly colourful insight into the harsh Outback."

Daily Mirror

"A very readable and enjoyable tour of Oz that will only inspire the adventurous traveller to get off the well-trodden path and explore the wilderness that is one of this country's greatest assets. And if you're planning on a spot of hitch-hiking, then the advice given here is not to be missed."

Ian Waller, Editor of *realtravel* magazine

"Tom Parry took on one of the marathons of hitchhiking – the round Australia route – and he has written a colourful and amusing account of the journey."

John McCarthy, *Excess Baggage*

'Traversing 8,000 miles of Australian outback with a reluctant French girlfriend makes an entertaining read."

Traveller

"Parry is a great recorder of on-the-road conversations and does a pretty good job of capturing the Aussie vernacular."

Sydney Morning Herald

For Katia and Louis

Thumbs Up
Australia

Hitchhiking the Outback

Tom Parry

NICHOLAS BREALEY
PUBLISHING

BOSTON • LONDON

First published by
Nicholas Brealey Publishing in 2006
Reprinted 2007

3–5 Spafield Street
Clerkenwell, London
EC1R 4QB, UK
Tel: +44 (0)20 7239 0360
Fax: +44 (0)20 7239 0370

20 Park Plaza
Boston
MA 02116, USA
Tel: (888) BREALEY
Fax: (617) 523 3708

www.nicholasbrealey.com
www.thumbsupaustralia.co.uk

ISBN-13: 978-1-85788-390-X
ISBN-10: 1-85788-390-X

British Library Cataloguing in Publication Data
A catalogue record for this book is available from the
British Library.

Printed in Great Britain by Clays Ltd, St Ives plc.

Contents

1

Where Woop Woop Begins

P ort Wakefield: 98 kilometres north of Adelaide, not far from what I once heard one Aussie call "the great bugger all". Even that apparently derogatory phrase, I recall, was pronounced with fondness; he was proud to tell me there is absolutely nothing happening in the heart of his country. He treated it like a loveable village idiot.

That attitude partly explains why more than eighty per cent of the population live on the coast. There are a host of similar terms – woop woop, the back of Bourke, beyond the Black Stump, the never never, the bush and, of course, the outback. Woop woop derives from the slang title given to the man who carried fleeces in a sheep-shearing shed, after the sound he made as he rushed about. The Black Stump is a fictional place in the middle of nowhere. The never never because its inhabitants never wanted to go there, but once established, they never wanted to come back. Just as the Eskimos have manifold words to describe snow, Australians have a lexicon for lifeless land.

"You blokes should go straight up the Track to Alice," the man behind reception at the motel said. "Why don't you get a bus ticket direct for a few hundred bucks? There's nothing between here and there. That's what most backpackers do."

The Track is the colloquial name given to the Stuart Highway, the vital road that bisects Australia, named after John McDouall Stuart, the first man to cross Australia from south to north.

Stuart would have told the motel guy to "rack off", I'm guessing, if that Aussie insult existed when he was around. Soon after he disembarked in Adelaide in 1839, the 23-year-old Scotsman headed straight out into woop woop. In the empty inland, he found a purpose that eluded him in his native Dysart, Fifeshire. Stuart recognised something exceptional in the outback. Whatever it was kept him returning again and again, till he was almost blind from taking sun readings, sick with scurvy and dangerously thin from malnutrition. Stuart rode into the desert because it was there.

The motel manager's right though: most independent travellers only make the recommended stop-offs on the 3,000-mile trek up to Darwin. I decide to ignore him.

So for us – my girlfriend Katia and I – Port Wakefield, hardly anything more than a few bungalows littered either side of the highway on initial inspection, is the ideal start-ing point. It's a proper Australian place, a former squat-ters' outpost, and as anonymous as the scrub that encroaches on it. There's no specific reason to come here. And there are heaps of reasons to keep going. But I'm con-tent. The absence of human clutter is what makes Aus-tralia so intriguing, that's why I've come back.

When I was 18 I spent many happy months wandering aimlessly around the bush, and after years of pestering,

I've finally persuaded my reluctant girlfriend to accompany me on a six-month trip Down Under. My ambition: to find the real Australia and the real Australians that you don't meet on the backpacker trail. We're planning to hitchhike over 8,000 miles across the outback, loosely pursuing the routes carved out by the legendary explorers who first traversed the great continent.

We have a room in the motel, with a large double bed, an invigorating shower and a full range of television channels. There are soaps in sealed packs with the logo of the motel chain printed on them. If we had a car, there would be ample space outside our unit for it; but we don't. This room even has a trouser press. Our tent is spread on the carpet, drying after being stuffed in its bag while still soggy.

I can hear Katia whistling in the bath, maximising the availability of the creature comforts that we have to leave by checkout at 11am. I've told her about the rigours of the bush, so she wants to start today ultra-clean, as she would in her native France. She switches to a French nursery rhyme from time to time – *Une Souris Verte* – to remind herself of back home.

"*Je suis trop bien, quoi,*" she calls out – this is too nice. And then in English, she adds, "I don't want to leave 'ere."

"We'll go soon though," I cry out. "It'll be great."

"Oh wow, just *trop* cool. Standing by zer bloody road in Port Wakefield. *Formidable.*"

It's hard to argue with sarcasm, especially when it comes from someone speaking their second language. So I shut up. Katia starts whistling jauntily again.

Right now, it's shortly before nine. I'm impatient, sitting on the edge of the bed with my tattered old map of

Australia before me. I bought it on my first journey around this country. A slither of its torn edge crumbles off as I open it out. The whole nation spreads out before me – creased, dusty and faded. I draw an imaginary loop with my finger, stretching north from Adelaide into the Simpson Desert, wiggling through the Northern Territory, swooping below the Gulf of Carpenteria to Cairns, zigzagging down the East Coast to Sydney and back to Adelaide. Last night I sellotaped the map back together. It has grown worn along the folds from being reopened so often in my bedroom back home.

Stuart blazed the trail, so we're almost stalking him, in an imprecise kind of way. His presence looms large over my shambling route. I've always been inspired by one-dimensional, unhinged lunatics who screw up everything else in their life to achieve their goal.

Fidgeting with my hands, rolling my thumbs like my grandfather used to, my unsubtle body language says I'm ready to go, desperate even. I'm crap at disguising impatience. There's a yearning inside me, an irrational pulse that has nothing to do with going anywhere in particular. It has to do simply with moving for movement's sake. For the last few years I have blocked this restless impulse, contained it. But I can hear the metallic swish of three-truck roadtrains outside as they turn out of the roadhouse in front of us. I have to go.

I want to hitch the whole route I've just described, from today onwards. This is why Katia is taking her time in the bathroom. Thumbing lifts is new to her.

I have an incurable obsession with the Australian desert. It's so bad an accidental repeat viewing of

Crocodile Dundee can prompt flashbacks, even though I can't watch the film all the way through. While other people are blasé about the country and my own mental souvenirs of nearly a decade ago are fractured, for me it has never lost its allure. Australia always heads favourite destination polls in newspaper travel supplements. It is accessible enough for European rugby fans to go there just to watch a single game in the World Cup. Backpacking in Australia is hardly adventurous. Yet I'm stuck with my obsession, bewitched.

I have mementoes I want to confirm. Is Australia as special as I remember? I recall standing by a prickly sprouting of spinifex grass in the barren desert of silky ochre sand that bestrides the vast interior, and thinking: I could be the first person in the world ever to put my foot in this exact spot. I want to feel that solitude again. With Katia beside me, of course.

To me the Australian bush evokes so much. It is watching a herd of Western Grey kangaroos skip gracefully across the arc of a bald Clare Valley hill at dusk. It is the spectacle of parakeets heading to roost in a Brisbane park, dashes of red, lime and gold against the cobalt sky. It is sizzling forks of ivory lightning appearing above the weatherboard bungalows of Katherine in the dramatic wet season. It is the haunting apparition of silhouetted gum trees looming with zombie arms in the near-darkness of dimly lit Cooma. It is the cleansing, medicinal aroma of eucalyptus that heals you as you inhale. It is the tremor of a roadtrain rushing past on the uninhabited Barkly Highway, and then the gap of utter silence that follows. It is the baked-clean freshness of Alice Springs in the morning before the sky,

5

always cyan blue, cracks with dry heat. And it's the unfailingly optimistic smile of the bartender who opens your Victoria Bitter stubby – a crisp rush of hissing air – and enquires, "How ya going, mate?"

These souvenirs are a continual distraction. They divert me from sensible life choices whenever I'm confronted by the ugly twins of career advancement and location commitment. Despite devoting nearly a year to thumbing lifts around its ungainly highways once before, Australia remains the unconquered wilderness I still want to explore. I can't kick the habit. I'm drawn like a Pine Creek mosquito to the milky light of the Southern Cross. Others might go for unlimited sunshine, sea and surf, I'm here because the upside-down land is where the unexpected happens. At least, that's how I remember it.

In a way, then, I've got a purpose this time around. Not much of one, I admit. The quest is sketchy at best and the pot of gold at the end of the rainbow could be anywhere on my mildewed map. That's the lot of Australian explorers: John McDouall Stuart's first commission was to track down a mythical inland sea that didn't exist; Burke and Wills failed to see their goal – the Gulf of Carpenteria above the north coast – after months of torrid trekking; and Aborigines go walkabout down an invisible dreamtime path with nothing to guide them but handed-down totemic stories.

At least I have more of a clue than I did the first time I came here. I was *really* directionless then. Down here, in this part of South Australia, I went back and forth up the same stretch of highway seven times. This time, there's a loop. We're going to hitchhike in a circle around this landmass. By my standards, that's serious forward planning.

Katia likes the idea of Australia, but it's the kind of idea one sees in glossy brochures – barbecues on the beach beside azure palm-ringed lagoons. You know the drill. She doesn't yet share my unruly predilection for the barren interior, the guts of the country, as blokes who've worked on cattle stations refer to it. Koalas and kangaroos are the only overt Australian symbols drawing her here. Ever since we arrived at Adelaide airport, she's been scouring gum trees for grey koalas chewing eucalyptus leaves.

"They're really hard to spot," I say.

"*C'est nul ici*," she replies, implying Australia is crap thus far.

In France, unlike Britain, there isn't the same background awareness of Australia. The stereotypes – blokes in singlets with corks dangling from their hats cooking damper on campfires, Rolf Harris playing a didgeridoo – haven't permeated the national consciousness. No one in her family has any particular opinion about Australia. In the guidebook they bought her – the only one we possess, thankfully – the cuisine section occupies more pages than I would have dreamed possible. That's French optimism.

Katia's opinions haven't been wholly positive so far. The Barossa Valley isn't a patch on the Bourgogne, she claims. And she's certainly not taken with Port Wakefield.

Port Wakefield was one of the first towns to be established in the fledgling colony of South Australia, so for these parts it's truly antiquated. It was named after Edward Gibbon Wakefield, one of the architects of the enormous state. He wrote an ideological pamphlet proposing the population of Australia by free settlers buying small pieces of land, instead of convicts being forced here. South Australia was the first province to employ his thesis. Yet Wakefield himself never set foot in Australia. His dissertation was composed in a prison cell in Britain.

Here in 1802, at the mouth of Gulf St Vincent, another of Australia's foremost white pioneers, Captain Matthew Flinders, landed on Her Majesty's sloop *Investigator*. Flinders did the first real surveying in this region, charting the coastline. He was a brilliant navigator; like Stuart, one of the true heroes of the new colony. He was the first to suggest the name Australia. Over the following two years he became the first person to circumnavigate the continent successfully – an epic voyage.

Last night we stumbled on the original settlers' jetty by fortuitous accident. We walked past quaint colonial bungalows with their wide verandas and flattened pyramid corrugated-iron roofs till the road stopped at a weed-strewn beach. The glimmer of stars on the shallow mudflat lagoon at low tide betrayed this ghost town, the relic of a once bustling port. Bullocks would transport copper ore extracted at Burra, east of the Clare Valley, to Port Wakefield. Later, when the copper ran out, wheat was ferried here by a tramway. But the town lost out to other sea ports. On the estuary, one could see that ships would have run aground regularly. Only fishing dinghies bobbed in the narrow channel.

"Are you ready yet?" I shout. "If we don't go soon, we'll miss the trucks going north from Adelaide."

Katia groans from within, still not infected by my all-consuming bug. She swears in French, far more convincing than the English curses she's picked up over the years.

"*Laisse-moi tranquille,*" she demands, "*tu m'énerves*" – leave me alone, you're pissing me off.

"Come on, babe, I didn't come here to lie in bed all day."

"You're just so impatient. Why can't you just relax for five bloody minutes? I mean, what difference is it going to make if I dry my 'air or not?"

"I know it won't really change much, but it's best to start early when you're hitchhiking."

"Yes, we all know about your 'itchiking, don't we? Oh yes, because you've 'itchiked all over zer world. Ooh, what a tough guy."

This comment prompts more mocking laughter in the bathroom. Katia doesn't buy my rambling romanticism. Her coming here was prompted only by my insistent clamouring; otherwise she would have stayed in her rewarding teaching job, in which she was having unprecedented success, another promotion beckoning.

We left behind a cardboard-box-sized semi-detached house in Lincolnshire, England. Picturing that place now, it's a perpetual Sunday afternoon. From far off comes the murmur of traffic on the dual-carriageway bypass that smears the playing field behind our back garden. The climate is gloomy, burdened by oppressive fog and lazy drizzle leaving a greasy film on the pavement. Sunlight pokes through at frustratingly intermittent intervals, and then vanishes behind a scurrying cloud when I open the front door. I can hear boy racers' screeching brakes outside the Burger King roundabout.

Just before we left, kids poisoned the local river with mercury, so fish floated on the surface. The mirage of the distant-remembered outback was a catalyst for flight. So I elbowed Katia into unstitching our domestic cushioning. This morning, I think she's regretting that resignation letter she left with the headteacher.

She emerges from the bathroom, fragrant with Thierry Mugler Angel. She's ready, two hours after me.

We cross the road to the ugly Shell roadhouse canteen. This is Port Wakefield's premier eatery. There is another place called Tucker Time, but it was shut last night; and it's shut now. The Australian service-station staples of meat pies with tomato ketchup, Dim Sims (a mass-produced version of Chinese dim sum dumplings) and Chiko Rolls (a deep-fried spring-roll-type snack with boned mutton, vegetables and rice in a dough tube) all fester beneath the heat plates. There's flake (shark fish) in batter with chips. If you request it, you can be served a pie floater (meat pie in a green-pea soup).

"Couldn't you go a Chiko?" a poster on the wall demands. It features a leather-clad blonde model straddling a motorcycle holding a Chiko Roll near her crotch.

Brash, tangy, deep-fried flesh smells emerge from the kitchen. Standing in the queue triggers a tingling flood of Australian roadhouse reminiscences: my first steak sandwich with "the lot" – beetroot, pineapple and cheese; pitching my tent in the rock-hard sand at Coolgardie; playing two-up – an Aussie coin game – with locals in Shepparton. The intervening years are abruptly filed away.

A Greyhound bus pulls up opposite us. Nobody alights. Against the bus's windows are pressed the incurious expressions of its passengers, maybe hoping the driver won't pause here too long.

They'll miss out on this roadhouse. That's why I insist to Katia that hitchhikers unpick the closeted secrets of a country better than bus travellers. Hitching teaches you to make the best of wherever you are; it becomes your *modus operandi*. I don't use those words, of course. I tell her we'll get dropped in places most Greyhound passengers never see.

"Good for zem," she replies, looking disdainfully at her dank toast.

As we hand in the motel room keys, the man at reception is keen to re-establish the earlier rapport. He knows the highway, he tells us, the movements of the road-trains, the best places to ask for a lift. Now he's established that we're not going to buy a bus ticket, he desperately wants to help.

"If you walk round the back of the roadhouse, you'll find the truckers having their smoko," he tells us sagely. Smoko is Aussie slang for a teabreak. "There's a good chance half of those blokes will be heading to Port Augusta this morning. You kids will have no worries."

He winks kindly at Katia. "Good luck," he adds.

It's been a long time, but the street-smartness remembered from years of hitchhiking prompts my first decision of the day – ignore him.

"Shall we go and speak to zer truck drivers?" Katia asks me, as I load her rucksack onto her back.

"No chance," I reply. "It never works. When you're hitching you have to make an effort; that's why people stop for you. Otherwise it's just laziness."

She breathes in deeply, raises her eyebrows and scrunches her mouth to the side; we haven't even started and I'm already bugging her.

"I wish you'd stop being so stressed about zis," she says. "Oo cares?"

But I have been visualising the beginning of this quest for so long that I want to get it exactly right. I never asked around for lifts before and I'm not about to start now. Only people who've never hitchhiked believe you can make headway like that. They're totally wrong. You have to stake a claim, you have to find the best place to stand, and you have to sell yourself to oncoming motorists – present an image.

Haulage drivers regard people who harass them for a ride while they eat breakfast as pests. They don't want to feel guilty about refusing a request first thing in the morning. And regardless of the inconvenience, truckers rarely pick any hitchhikers up anyway. They work for companies with strict rules about extra passengers sitting in the cab, and if they're caught out they can lose their licence.

So, on my resolute insistence, we walk north up Highway One, the road that coils loosely around this unmanageable country.

This very road, which feeds onto the Stuart Highway, tore off a chunk of my stability the last time I was here. Its bitumen surface propelled my hitherto disguised wanderlust; it is the source of my incurable itchy feet. Indeed, the route between Darwin and Adelaide has snaked itself permanently into my consciousness. Much has happened in the interim, but this morning I feel I've never left.

John McDouall Stuart's susceptibility to outback wanderlust was of an altogether stronger magnitude. He barely stopped exploring the bush for 22 years. In all, he led six major expeditions, four of which were aimed at forging a viable route for a telegraph line across the continent. There was nothing of the conventional hero about him: he was a diminutive, frail individual, too short to be accepted for military service, with a disabling fondness for whisky binges. Legend has it that he boarded the *Indus* bound for Adelaide in a fit of pique. He mistook his fiancée's goodbye kiss to a trusty friend for infidelity, and left Scotland immediately. On the voyage over he was seasick and heartbroken; hardly adventurer material. Years later, he learned of his appalling error by letter.

But he found his calling when he joined a survey team mapping the unknown territory beyond Adelaide. As a natural loner, it was perfect for him. Once he mounted his horse and followed his compass north into the bush, the dour Scotsman transcended himself. Stuart combined dogged resistance to the recalcitrant landscape with meticulousness. I've got nothing on him; he's the kind of person who makes me feel unworthy. We don't really need any of Stuart's exploratory discipline to travel up his eponymous highway.

At least by hitchhiking, I'm inventing an unnecessary challenge. I mean, what else is a travel writer supposed to do these days?

By the time we reach a mechanic's yard at the frontier of this linear town – only a few hundred metres – I make a stupid compromise. I decide we've walked far enough.

At first it feels peculiar to be sticking my left thumb out. I haven't tried this properly for several years. In the meantime I've had a company car, my first speeding fine and a seasonal rail card. By default, I've become a conventional traveller, using the modes of transport relied on by the non-hitchhiking population. So I feel like a middle-aged man going back in time to snogging girls behind the bike sheds after a long, unhappy marriage; a paroled prisoner squinting into daylight after a ten-year sentence. I must be annoyingly giddy.

Many of the vehicles going in our direction tow caravans. These are predominantly occupied by so-called grey nomads, a race of retired office professionals, miners and shearers whose labours created Australia's wealth, and who have now decided *en masse* to see what they were missing all those years. They might be British-born Aussies who migrated here in the fifties and sixties, the ten-pound Poms, so named because their assisted passage to the new country cost only that. Or they might be Poles and Germans who fled from ravaged Europe for South Australia after the Second World War. They have devoted their lives to Australia out of gratitude. The caravan dwellers have paid their dues, and are at the vanguard of a new phenomenon – the geriatric gap year.

Some smile, others deliberately pretend to be looking elsewhere when they get near us. I imagine they would be naturally amiable in any other context, like the kindly old ladies who served us tea in the Germanic wine-making town Nuriootpa a few days ago.

As the first hour passes, I wonder if we are unwelcome in Port Wakefield; perhaps the friendly Australian bush has changed from my halcyon days as a single traveller. That could totally undo the premise on which I've sold this trip to Katia; as well as the koalas, she's also been inspired by my portrayal of Aussies as the most altruistic race in the developed world. Her reference point is the *bonhomie* displayed by people living in the same crescent in the television soap *Neighbours*. There were no Australians against which to measure this stereotype where we lived in Lincolnshire.

Just as I'm dipping towards mild pessimism, a white-haired, elderly woman who drove past us in the opposite direction comes back up the highway. She gets out with a paper-bag package.

"I saw you standing here when I came past," she says. "I've brought you some Lamington cake. You must be starving."

"Not many people in South Australia want to pick up hitchhikers now," she adds. "You want to be careful."

"Oh right," Katia says, giving me her stand-at-the-back-of-the-classroom eyes as she turns to the woman. "Why not?"

The woman in the flowery dress founds her scare-mongering on the grisly murders in the little township of Snowtown, half an hour north. These killings were discovered two years ago, at the end of a year-long police missing persons' investigation. It was the most shocking piece of news to ever trouble these parts and has left a permanent scar. Snowtown was Australia's worst ever serial killing. Eleven lives were taken. Thick true-crime books have been written about it. The world's press descended on Adelaide in the following weeks.

Thankfully, the woman spares Katia the murder details. The victims' remains were concealed in a disused branch of the State Bank of South Australia. Behind the vault's metal door, investigating officers discovered six black plastic barrels. Inside were the chopped-up body parts of eight different people. Three people were arrested in Adelaide's northern suburbs the day after the appalling find. Police soon unearthed two further bodies buried at the home of one of the accused, and another elsewhere. Astonishingly, the motive for these brutal murders was simply to continue withdrawing the victims' social security payments, nothing more sinister than that.

Before leaving, the woman tells us not to gamble with our safety by taking lifts with strange people. She leaves us to eat the cake – an Australian speciality of sponge covered in chocolate and dried coconut – washed down with the coffee she also gives us in paper cups.

Katia glares at me. "You never mentioned anysing like zat, did you? Oh no. I'm definitely going to be scared now."

Once she's formed an opinion, Katia is always difficult to sway. My task of bringing round a reluctant hitchhiking partner has just been made that little bit harder.

"Look, they've got the murderers, so we'll be all right," I reply, unconvincingly. Now is not the time to let serial-killer scare stories get in the way of our journey.

"Are you sure?" she demands.

Of course, I say. No worries. Psychos don't stop for hitchhikers. Secretly I think of myself, "You liar."

I am positive we haven't walked far enough. We're only fractionally past the last roadhouse on Port Wakefield's periphery, opposite the sign welcoming southbound visitors to sample greasy fare.

"But what if we get stuck?" Katia complains. "Zen we'll have to walk all zer way back. I bet 'e was right, zis man.

You're just so stubborn about 'itchiking. I tell you what, no joking about zis, I'm going to make the most of Australia; not stuck in bloody places like – what is it – Port Wakefield. *Non, non et non.*"

The mechanic from the garage behind us emerges. He has a long goatee beard and receding hair tied back in a straggly ponytail. Tattoos are taut over his gym-hardened triceps. He grins broadly.

"I just thought you fellas might like to know that the highway splits about one and a half clicks up that way," he says, pointing out an intersection. "A lot of the traffic coming through here is heading down to the Yorke Peninsula. Once you get rid of them, everyone's going up to Port Augusta."

I thank him and then swear under my breath. I feel badly prepared. Soon we're tramping further towards the outback. We outstretch our arms for vehicles coming up behind us, but they don't stop. As a tactic, it rarely works. People like to see the faces of the people they could be spending the next five hours with, not the backs of their heads. The principle is identical to that of job interviews; the protruding thumb is a statement of intent, like a CV.

By the time we reach the fork, both Katia and I are singing.

"*Ai li, ai lo, on rentre du boulot...*" That's the Seven Dwarfs' song from *Snow White* in French.

Now I'm not bothered by the trickle of sweat running down my back. Nor am I concerned about the lost hour spent outside the garage.

It must be something about the space. Yesterday, riding down the hill, Katia pointed out where the truly untamed bush begins. Now, after just a short walk from town, we're right in it. The rugged wastes of the Australian landmass open up before us. Trees are sparse. The fenced boundaries of the sheep paddocks are far apart. Cereal crops struggle to sprout through the ageing soil. Dust spurts off passing vehicles' back wheels.

The mechanic was spot on in his assessment. Most of those caravanners – so populous before – turn off for Port Victoria, Yorketown and Coobowie. We are left with people making serious, professional journeys. These are the most likely candidates to pick us up, even though the grey nomads have all the time in the world and more space in their vehicles.

Within ten minutes we have our first lift. The protocol comes back to me in a flash. "Thanks a lot for stopping," I shout hurriedly while picking up my gear. "That's really good of you. Where are you heading?"

"Way up the Track," the driver replies, "past Port Augusta." And we jump in.

I recall diplomatic hitchhiking pleasantries. It's the kind of patter that becomes second nature after a few rides, in the same way that cold-call telesales people churn out saccharine drivel to entice new customers.

"We were just starting to think we would be stuck there all day."

"No dramas," he replies. "How long have you been waiting in Port Wakefield?"

"It must be nearly two hours now," Katia says beside me. "Yes, two hours."

If she feels unsure about the driver, we have worked out a code of practice: she squeezes my hand and I make up an excuse so we can get out at the next settlement. Of course, I know deep down this is never going to happen. I mean, let's face it, if my optimism is ill founded and we do get picked up by a deranged lunatic thirsty for blood, request pauses are unlikely to be on the agenda.

"Jeez, mate," the driver says, "there's heaps of cars passing through, ay. I reckon you must have picked a bad morning. The name's Jeff Kerr, by the way."

We introduce ourselves. "How far are you actually going?"

"I'm driving all the way to Roxby Downs, which is way out in the desert near Marree. You blokes probably won't have heard of it. It's actually less than a hundred clicks out of Pimba, which you'll pass further up on the track."

"What's life like in Roxby Downs?" I ask.

"Mate, it's a hell of a place to live," Jeff exclaims. "The town didn't exist until 1988. Now there's a whole community and everyone works down the copper and uranium mine. It's called the Olympic Dam Mine. What's good, I reckon, is that everyone knows each other."

"You must like your neighbours." That's Katia.

"Ah yeah, buddy, unreal. I tell ya, when we had the big drought last summer, the temperature was bloody unbearable, so we had to support each other. The temperature reached over 50 degrees Centigrade out there."

He waits. I say, "God, that's amazing," which I think is what's required. It is.

"You just couldn't bloody move. I guess you two missed the drought if you've just got here."

"Right, yeah, everyone was talking about that in Adelaide."

"Well, they reckon it was the hottest summer on record," he continues. "One day we went out playing cricket in that bloody heat. You had to drink a cold beer every over just to stop yourself dehydrating. The stubby was warm by the time it reached your lips. Ah yeah, and the rubber on the handle of my bat melted on my hands. God that was full on, a real tragedy for the cattle stations out there."

Jeff provides an intimate portrait of life in the Olympic Dam Mine, the self-proclaimed "largest mineral ore body in the world". He works as a mine engineer, spending his days travelling around two hundred kilometres of underground roadway, inspecting machinery in basketball court-sized caverns.

I turn to Katia and she smiles. She never disguises her feelings. She must be at ease.

I am happy sitting in the front of a ute – slang for utility truck, the archetypal outback vehicle – watching the gum trees that border the highway become sparser. A corroded, grilled smell seeps through the windows, overpowering the agricultural aroma of before. Cracks appear in sand, for unfilled channels. The undeviating road has a slim stretch of stones and red earth on either side, as well as the inevitable litter thrown from car windows. Then it's endless unruly scrubland. To the right are the rippling foothills of the Flinders Ranges.

I want to take in every nuance of the barren land I've been gravitating back to for so long, but the conversation restarts and I dutifully join in. In Australia there are few roadside distractions to occupy a motorist's mind, so many people pick up a hitchhiker for one reason only: to either talk at or listen to. They also want to display generosity towards strangers, their national trait.

Jeff is transporting a flat-pack shed and a fridge-freezer unit on the flatbed of his ute. His two-day round trip to Adelaide and back is 1,128 kilometres. There is nowhere else nearer to Roxby Downs where he would be able to get hold of the same product at a decent price. Taking two days to obtain a fridge is nothing exceptional if you live out there, he explains, gesturing at the stunted wattle trees that puncture the landscape.

"Wow, zat's just amazing for us," Katia comments.

"That's just Aussie for you," Jeff replies.

I remember a lift in 1993 from Kulgera, in the Northern Territory, with a plumber. He drove slowly. It was Sunday. We covered 250 kilometres. I asked him the reason behind his trip. "Being from overseas you probably wouldn't know this," he replied, "but Marla actually has a swimming pool. It's only small I guess, but you can swim lengths there for as long as you like." He was heading straight back home after towelling himself dry.

We arrive in Port Pirie, Jeff's hometown. I was here last time. I got a lift with a Presbyterian grandmother who insisted on taking me to her house for tea and biscuits before I hit the road again, a typically magnanimous gesture to hitchhikers. Her bungalow was decorated with Toby jugs and photographs of cats.

"Do you two mind if I show you round Pirie?" Jeff asks, clearly proud of this little port. We both shake our heads. "I hope you guys like her. We do."

We receive a guided tour of the main attractions. Foremost of these is the world's biggest lead smelter, with its chimney towering on the shallow skyline. This is the Australia that isn't promoted on massive posters world-wide. It's Hicksville – out in the sticks.

At a servo on the edge of town, Katia buys a carton of chocolate milk for Jeff. I saw the advert for this brand on television in Adelaide. The slogan was: "If it's not choco milk, it's nothing." And although I offer to buy anything by way of refreshment, choco milk is all he'll accept.

Jeff drops us off at Stirling North, just short of Port Augusta. He has to pick up his family, whom he dropped off for shopping. He helps Katia with her bags. Unknowingly, he has provided the perfect first ride of this trip.

"Zank you very much. Zis is so nice of you. You are really kind."

"No dramas," Jeff replies.

2

The Overland Telegraph Song Line

We stroll across the highway at Stirling North with less trepidation than would be required on a minor cul-de-sac on a housing estate back home. There would be time for a fag break between cars. No vehicles approach in either direction.

Toyota Land Cruisers and white camper vans are parked against the eroded kerbstone on the main high street, which turns off towards the Flinders Ranges. Stirling North is a small, dusty town of 350 people. The pub is a functional, oblong building, offering West End Draught and TAB betting. Trails of laid-back conversation emanate from inside. We reach the outer limits, over a railway track, in less than two minutes.

The heat blanket that presses on the centre of this awesome continent like a steel shroud is nearly upon us. Flecks of warmth filter through palms and eucalypts on the shady side of the road. I am reminded of Mediterranean villages at siesta time during August, such is the torpor of this late morning. Stirling North feels like part of a separate nation to yesterday. I spy my first cockroach scampering across the brown sand layby and point it out to Katia.

"Aie, ça, alors, c'est dégoûtant," she says. To express disgust only her native tongue will do. "I didn't know you got nasty creatures like that in Australia."

"Of course, I saw flying cockroaches last time I was here. They were everywhere. One landed in my ear."

"God, zis is 'orrible. All zees beasts. I wish you told me."

As we're here, we may as well spend a few days in the Flinders Ranges, of which I have fond memories. That hadn't really been the intention this morning. The loop streams northwards, and the mountains are to the east. Yet one of the most satisfying aspects of hitchhiking is arbitrarily ending up where you didn't plan to.

I whistle a tuneless ditty. In doing so I remember a knapsack-toting hobo in a black-and-white film I once saw, clinging to the shade and whistling jauntily. American hoboes have fascinated me ever since I heard about hopping on boxcars. I loved the notion of leaping into the empty wagon of a slow-moving locomotive as it pulled out of a yard. There might be other hoboes inside; or there might be a merciless security guard, a "bull". Railroad-riding hoboes crossed the country in search of work on the flimsiest of recommendations. Their migrations were incessant. They braved the risk of falling under a train's wheels for a free ride. Significantly, hoboes objected to being described as vagrants because their propensity to move set them apart from their more stable counterparts in the big cities. Social commentators of the time thought that wanderlust afforded them a noble stature.

After riding the railroads, hitchhiking in automobiles was the logical next step; security was almost impassable in city rail depots. It was during the mass movement of unemployed men in the Great Depression of the 1930s that thumbing first became popular in the United States. In Britain during the Second World War it became common to see soldiers hitching rides from one end of the country to the other while on leave.

In the formative years of hitchhiking, practitioners were actual hikers who marched along a road and put their thumb out when a car approached. Such was the scarcity of vehicles on some routes that hitchhikers would walk their whole route. The post-Second World War economic boom changed that. More people had cars and the wherewithal to embark on vast journeys. Not long afterwards, hitching became synonymous with Jack Kerouac and the beatniks. A cultural movement was born. From then on, obstinate thrill seekers like me deliberately stuck their thumbs out by the road instead of boarding a bus.

Tramping ahead, I find us an umbrageous red-barked gum tree to sit under. Katia is really enthused after Jeff's lift, which relieves me.

"He was a really nice guy, zis one," she states, reinforcing her point with the translation, *"un mec cool, quoi."*

Katia always goes on first impressions. If Jeff had been a screwball – and despite what I anticipate there will surely be a few, hopefully harmless examples on this trip – I might be digging out the wretched bus timetable already. She has been patient of my whims before, but this, I guess, is a real test. Prior to our arrival there were summers when we camped instead of staying in a hotel as she prefers, but we've never done a long journey together.

This trip is a bridge of sorts, a walkway between two aspects of life I've cherished most: on the one hand hitch-hiking alone through the desert, and on the other having the person who means most to me in the world to clutch. I'm greedy: I want to be a lonesome traveller, but in company. I want a wandering lifestyle, without having to suffer the gloom that settles on middle-aged adventurers when they return home and realise they want neither to set out again nor stay put.

The leaves of the gum tree make a crinkling noise as they swish against each other in the breeze. All is still otherwise. The unmistakable aroma of eucalyptus is a pad-locked bastion of happy memories, like the first mown grass of summer in shady lanes where I used to cycle. I could breathe it in all day. To the west, the cirrus clouds that hug the coastline disperse strand by strand.

Katia takes the bottle of blue Powerade I purchased at the roadhouse in Port Pirie.

"Blue drink!" she says. "What's zat?"

"No idea. Why not?"

She snorts derisively at my stupid answer, which provokes a brief conversation about the absence of blue in natural food produce. Hitchhiking allows time for such nonsensical banter.

I watch a flock of pink galahs waft upwards like a safari flamingo cloud. An approaching car rumbles. The gears whine. Katia gets up to signal for a lift for the first time. The car, a heavy white Holden estate, screeches to a halt. The driver brakes dramatically, wheels spinning across the gravel. But there are no net curtain twitchers to aggravate in Stirling North.

Leonard reaches over for formal handshakes. He bears a sceptical expression, like an interviewer grilling campaigning politicians.

"Let me guess where you're from," he announces rhetorically. "I reckon you're both from Europe and this is your first time in Australia. Am I right?"

He doesn't wait for an answer. "Well, let me tell you about this part of South Australia, which of course has a totally different name to the real locals."

"What's that then?"

"Well, it's not really a name for the place as such. They call their heritage Yura Muda."

"Yura Muda, zis is a weird name," Katia pipes up from the back of the junk-filled vehicle.

"No, that's the white fellows' way. It's not Yura Muda, it's Yura Muda."

"I see," Katia replies, but in the mirror I glimpse her perplexed expression. I too can make no distinction between her and Leonard's pronunciation.

Leonard has the pasty skin tone of someone of European origin. He wears a brightly coloured shirt emblazoned with dreamtime prints: snakes, dingoes and bush tucker berries. When I ask where he is from, he is evasive, refusing to name an actual place. He talks about the Aborigines as though he is a member of the indigenous population; perhaps he identifies with them so much that he wishes he were, like white blues musicians from Surrey wishing they were black and from Alabama.

He even warns, "Don't call us Abos."

"Okay," Katia says. "Do you live with Aborigines?"

"Hey please, indigenous peoples," he reprimands.

"Yep, I work for a cross-cultural group out near a place you won't have heard of called the Nepabunna community. Yous going to Wilpena?"

"Probably for a day or two."

"The problem with Wilpena Pound is they haven't brought in enough indigenous workers," he tells us. "I mean, these people need to integrate the traditional land owners. This is something I know a lot about because my wife's from Nepabunna. You two wouldn't know it, but it's a dying community because of the white man. They all move to Port Augusta these days. White tourists like you should get to know about this."

"Sure."

"The only real travellers are the nomadic tribes of this world, which you as a white man could never be part of."

At one point Leonard pauses on the crest of a hill. I enjoy the lull in his monologue. We can see right across the flat, sun-bleached territory leading to the Spencer Gulf. Discarded frontier properties are riven in two by the harsh climate. Their decaying frames bend to the ground. The sky is spectacularly wide and, now unhampered by the coast, a rich, dazzling indigo blue. To our right, across the horizon, is Devil's Peak, an outcrop of beige boulders beautified by lonely cycad plants and bushy grassland.

John McDouall Stuart might have passed this way on his first forays into unexplored South Australia. His formidable character was formed in the furthest outlying settlers' camps, using his surveying instruments to chart potential grazing ground for livestock. After several years with the Survey Department, with which he became a valued draughtsman, in 1844 he gained a post on the expeditionary team of surveyor general Charles Sturt. As well as having remarkably similar surnames, Stuart and Sturt were also kindred outback spirits. Sturt was leading a party towards the continent's geographical centre. No one had done it before.

The expedition's impetus arose from a perfectly rational premise of the time: the main rivers appeared to curve away from the coast, therefore there must be an inland sea into which they all drain. Sturt actually commissioned carpenters to build wagons that could be converted into small boats when they found this mythical southern-hemisphere Mediterranean.

Clearly his theory was garbage.

As the intrepid explorers ventured inland, waterholes became increasingly scarce. They came unstuck in one of Australia's most blistering hot, arid wastelands, an area in the top right of South Australia today called Sturt's Stony Desert. Only by sheer chance did they stumble on a sequence of billabongs, which were named Cooper Creek. Most of the crew crawled back to Adelaide, just skin and bone, happy to admit failure.

The expedition was unsuccessful, but Stuart had revealed an exceptional aptitude for survival. Sturt was so impressed that when the chief surveyor James Poole died from scurvy, Stuart, until then a junior member of the team, replaced him.

"I guess neither of you have read much about Aborigines," Leonard says before he lets us out at Quorn, where he is pausing to talk with his "indigenous mates" who take groups out on guided five-day tours through the Gammon Ranges and out into the Strzelecki Desert. He advises us to do this rather than hitchhike, which he says is not educational.

"How would you know zat?" Katia asks. Leonard pretends not to hear.

Quorn is a Wild West frontier town abandoned after an incursion by marauding cattle rustlers. I imagine Clint Eastwood striding through, his spurs clinking on the pavement. There is a faint breeze that would catch the tumbleweed were there any here. The main street is wide enough for four cars. No surprises: there isn't any traffic.

Along one side are the wide balcony terraces that typify the saloon-style roadhouses of the outback. Their awnings, with sturdy nineteenth-century supporting columns, possess an anachronistic charm. The Transcontinental Hotel is a gigantic edifice for such a small settlement. It has a wide gallery running right round its four walls, with the upper floor painted a different colour. Upstairs hotel rooms lead out to the balcony, which is in almost permanent shade because of the long reach of the steep sloping roof. Paint peels from the frontage in long chunks. On the side of the Bullion Hotel and Motel one can just about make out old advertisements from the days when mining prospectors and drovers first populated Quorn.

In the near-derelict yard of the railway station ghost gum trees peel ivory bark, as though giving up on growing. These native Australian trees are like snakes, constantly shedding and renewing their outer skin. Dead bark complements the unkempt charm of Quorn.

It is difficult to imagine how the station was once a major hub for the Flinders. But when Quorn was officially proclaimed a town in 1878, there were high hopes. The first trailblazers to stake their claim here were optimistic farmers, following in the wake of Stuart and then the Overland Telegraph Line. Like the homesteaders who bought plots on the Montana badlands in America, their dreams, stoked by government assurances, proved to be misguided. The outback was unforgiving. Better off by far were those who settled in the wine valleys, where the benevolent climate rarely falters.

During the Second World War, the railway was transformed into a vital link for transporting soldiers. The agricultural boom was literally burnt out, charred by bushfires. Thousands of troops would stretch their legs here as their commanders shuffled conscripts between billets. A brown heritage placard mentions the pristinely preserved town hall and picture house.

Today the Pichi Richi railway line is a tourist steam locomotive route to Port Augusta. Trainspotters make the journey especially.

Over Pinkerton Creek, which bisects Quorn, is a sculpture for the Serpentine Trail Project – "art linking the outback". In Quorn the focus is the yellow-footed rock wallaby, which lives in nearby rocky gorges and comes down to creeks late in the evening to drink. A man parks a hire vehicle by the road. His female partner walks up to the sign by the sculpture to have a read. When she's finished she looks around, as though for yellow-footed rock wallabies. They leave.

I love Quorn's deserted atmosphere, the dilapidation, the rust on the old locomotive. The place will remain unalterably adorable because we'll be moving on, having to trust our memories. Hitchhiking is a procession of unplanned-for epiphanies, discovering pockets of delight on every highway – like a late-opening takeaway at the end of a night bus journey.

"It's a bit dead 'ere, isn't it," Katia says.

"Well I think it's got charm, do you know what I mean?"

"Yeah, whatever, you always 'ave to disagree wiz what I say."

"No, but I like dead towns."

"Blah, blah, blah, blah, blah."

There is hardly anywhere open to buy food. Make that one place: a tiny grocery store hidden in the township grid that sells pasties. A musty odour rises from the paper bags. The pasties taste revolting, as though they were actually made in heritage times. They deserve their own brown sign. We throw them away and move towards the green distance panel for the next lift.

I read some ancient graffiti carved into the back of the sign to gauge how much longer our hitchhiking predecessors waited. These tales of woe are a common feature of thumbing dead ends the world over. Often someone will etch the length of time they've been waiting, with a suitable complaint like: "Three hours – fucking hopeless." Or the epigram might be more optimistic: "The best view in South Australia."

Quorn's tag is succinct: "Jon was here 1995." Jon's reconnaissance trip is a comfort. His message means people have hitched up this road since I last passed through.

A rickety brick-red ute swerves onto the dry dirt in front of us, as though remote controlled by my limply raised thumb. Instinctively, I jog towards the vehicle. It is essential the hitchhiker adopt an appearance of eagerness. The driver, looking in his wing mirror, will want to pick up a person with a genuine desire to move on. Like a first day at work, any slouching will be noticed. For wary motorists, a lethargic attitude might convince them to accelerate off, offering evidence that you're not a serious hitchhiker.

On the back of the ute are the classic Australian bush accoutrements: two bales of hay and a terrier dog. A call comes from within: "Just chuck your stuff on the back, you'll be right."

The dog is unmoved by our sudden intrusion on its territory. As I hoist the rucksacks onto the sawdust-strewn flatbed, it looks at me disinterestedly, without even a growl. Once the disturbance is over, it returns its gaze to over the roof of the little truck, like all the farmers' sheep dogs you see on gravel tracks around here, below the coast-to-coast dingo fence.

As we climb into the cramped cab of the ute, we are greeted by a broad, boyish smile. It belongs to Gordon, a silvery-haired Aboriginal man with world-weary wrinkles. His deep-set eyes have a cheeky twinkle, but his stare is probing. He studies us carefully before driving off.

"So what are your surnames?" he asks – a strange question. When Katia tells him, he is curious about the etymology of her family name, Garnaud.

"Now, what part of France does that one come from?"

Katia isn't sure. Gordon carefully enunciates his own name: "Well, I'm Coulthard, like the racing driver, you know, David Coulthard."

He moves methodically through the gears, in no rush. He asks us to place groceries that were on the front seat in the back. These are items he bought on his latest shopping trip to Port Augusta: house plants, a loaf of bread and dog food. I guess there can't be many shops where he lives. If you carry on this road to its conclusion, you will never stumble across a supermarket.

"I live in an old settlers' homestead between Hawker and Wilpena Pound," Gordon says proudly. "A place by the name of Arkaba is what it's called. This is an old sheep property that goes back to the 1850s. They still shear sheep there on the station. But I live by myself in a little house, with ten ponies and that old dog."

There is a soothing quietness to Gordon after bullish Leonard's sloganeering. He is not desperate to impress us. Hitchhiking intensifies encounters that you experience less frequently if you use other modes of transport. At best, it's a crammer course in humanity: a year's worth of memorable characters in a week, a fantasy dinner party.

"So what do you do wiz all zose ponies?" Katia asks.

"What I do, mate, is take tourists out on some of the old dreamtime trails in my people's country."

He leaves this sentence hanging pendulous in the air. The matter-of-fact manner in which he says dreamtime, a white man's translation of Aboriginal tribes' metaphysical creation beliefs, is enticing, like a wily teacher teasing enthusiasm from his pupils.

"Where are your people from?" I enquire.

"I'm from the Flinders," is all Gordon will say. He reaches down into the glove compartment above my knees and gives me a brochure for his horse-riding treks. It says, "Come and Experience the breathtaking scenery of the Flinders Ranges on Horseback." His services would usually cost $20 an hour.

He is immensely proud of all the nationalities that have ridden his horses. "I get young people from overseas, like yous; pay me money every week to ride on my horses. I've got English, Germans, Austrians, Canadians, Swiss and a lot of Swedish. But Swiss and Swedish is the same, isn't they?"

I don't correct him, nor does Katia. Why the hell should Gordon know about European geography? Out of the window his tribal country spreads gloriously as far as the eye can see with no sign of habitation. His people's country probably contains several Switzerlands.

"You must enjoy telling people about your land?"

"Mate, I love horses, ever since I worked on a station."

I ask about his passion for this sacred turf. Is it innate, in the blood?

"These are big, dry old mountains," he says cryptically, sweeping his hand across the landscape. "I understand them is the oldest ranges in the world. I cannot say why this should not be true."

The mountain ranges beyond, on both sides, are indeed arcane. In fact the area's geological history goes back 700,000,000 years. Seismic plates shifted and through the gaps in the Earth's crust the mountains we see before us pushed their way through. That's the accepted scientific explanation. The dreamtime creation tale is more extraordinary still.

Whichever story is right, the tawny bluffs that rip across the mesmerising scenery tower over the rotten fenceposts of the first European settlers. These mountains preceded the dinosaurs and will certainly supersede us. In the foreground, the empty plains are given definition by a little copse of mulga, saltbush and hummock grass that looks like a lonely oasis. There is an occasional movement, possibly of a kangaroo or an emu, which swirls the stubble into fleeting dust clouds. Scars of human habitation are visible, the dilapidated remnants of where some gold-seeking dreamer laid foundations for a fortune that never came and an entire derelict mining ghost town. These haunting landmarks are signposted by the ubiquitous brown heritage sign.

"You see the old wreck?" Gordon asks, pointing to some abandoned ruins. "That used to be a pub. The story is that the fella who ran that place fell off the balcony. You can see the gravestone behind the pub. I don't drink," he adds by way of a postscript. "I just have lemonade."

He points out where a Canadian company is testing for minerals and another spot where diamonds were found. Canada is a major source of interest for him. He tells us it was the model for the handling of indigenous matters in Australia. "I met some of their people, the Inuits, when I visited Canada," he adds.

It turns out Gordon is the chairperson of the Adnyamathanha Land Council, the body representing indigenous land claims in the region. He has fought against multinational uranium firms like Southern Cross Resources and battled against proposals to discharge radioactive waste onto sacred sites. Making a native title application for the Wooltana Station, he took on the South Australia Farmers Association in federal court. I struggle to imagine this pacific old man banging his fist against the witness box.

A startling sunshine that makes my eyes ache streams in through the gaps in the windows. And as the far-off ranges become redder, more mysterious, Gordon becomes more willing to talk about some of the traditions of the Adnyamathanha people. I know we are only receiving a much edited version, but nevertheless it's an unpaid-for privilege.

I ask Gordon if he can pick out sacred dreaming sites for Katia and me. He nods vaguely, then points to an undulating sprawl of rocky hills in the distance. These are the Elder Ranges, which fringe the natural amphitheatre of Wilpena Pound.

"What does that one look like?" he asks.

I squint. It's like picking faces out of the clouds. Katia does the same. She says she can make out a man lying down.

"That is right. That's very good you see him so quickly. Him is an old Aborigine lying down, this one. You can see his nose."

He stops the car to look. We have our picture taken before two other peaks that, he informs us, have sacred meaning. In the dreamtime, the Aborigines' God-like spiritual ancestors created these features, giving order and form to the world. Gordon is in no hurry, so we spend ten minutes picking out what are just rock formations to our European eyes, but to him each has its own creation story. He expresses animistic beliefs, explicitly connecting geographical features with the omnipresent dreamtime. Although he's a modern rationalist, he gives the impression of believing devoutly in mythical forefathers who literally sang the world into existence.

I once read a book of Aboriginal stories. One such explained how the wind of the Murray river in Victoria was created by a mythical reptile, Whowhie. This fearsome creature was four times the length of a man, with the body of a goanna and the head of a frog. After it killed off hundreds of the local inhabitants, hunters crept into its cave lair while it slept and speared it. Aboriginal tribes in the area tell how when the wind whistles, it is the spirit of the Whowhie still roaring in pain. Those tales were written like amateurish children's fantasy stories. But in Gordon's masterful narration, each symbolic notion becomes intelligible.

He moves on to rock paintings. "This one young man said to me my people did the paintings for entertainment," Gordon states. "That is not my view. These paintings were like signposts for men walking the land. If I painted a red cross on this road, it could mean I'm going to Wilpena. A white circle would say I was going to Hawker. This paint was made of ochre and animal fat so it could not be scraped off."

"*Bah oui*, sorry, wow, zat makes sense when you sink about it," Katia says.

"Of course," Gordon agrees, "it is very simple."

There is a wistful pause when we reach the turning for Gordon's isolated dwelling. The homestead is nestled beneath a ridge littered with red boulders, perfect for rock wallabies. Now it is owned by a couple with ties to nineteenth-century frontiersmen who claimed Gordon's tribal land for themselves. They offer paying guests the chance to experience the lifestyle of a working sheep station. Gordon bears no grudges towards the current-day landowners, at least not outwardly.

The Adnyamathanha still speak in their native tongue. Although dispossessed of his heritage, Gordon seems dogged enough to be wrestling it back from pastoral prospectors. His horse trails operate alongside tourism ventures. Despite his age, he is overspilling with youthful optimism. With the engine still running, he talks of how his parents handed down dreamtime stories. "I just try to keep these things alive for the kids," he says. "This land is where they belongs."

I am sad our ride has come to an end, even though my buttocks are numb from squeezing on one seat with Katia. Comfort is never the prerogative when hitchhiking. In fact, not having to grimace through temporary hardships makes travelling all too much of a breeze, I think. When you stroll from airport departure lounge to arrival lounge, there's not enough perseverance involved to make an imprint on your memory. During one ride on my last outback trip, I was lying on toolboxes and wooden planks with my face towards the roof. It was like being in a coffin in the rear of that station wagon. But I remember it.

From nowhere, a cloud of dust whisks from the crest of a hill adjoining Arkaba.

"That's the four-wheel-drive tour," Gordon exclaims. He pauses for a second and scratches his chin. "I'll take yous kids down to the gate so you can meet them on the way out. They'll give you a lift all the way to the camping at Wilpena. Just mention my name to the driver."

We leap back in, and Gordon drives us to the end of a dirt track. There is no time for a proper thank-you, as we have to catch the fast-moving truck as it accelerates down hill. Gordon departs with a smile as broad as the one he greeted us with, and wishes us good luck.

Sure enough, weaving along a dirt furrow through a natural avenue of coolibahs is the four-wheel-drive tour bus. We flag down the Aboriginal driver, who seems not in the least perturbed by our appearance at this isolated spot. The passengers eye us with apparent unease. They have seen nothing but cockatoos, hopping euros and snakes all day. We are not on the list of common flora and fauna. One guy sitting on the back seat helps us lug our bags down the gangway and squeezes next to a plump, rosy-cheeked woman for us to sit down.

"Well g'day," he guffaws. "What the hell are you blokes doing this far out beyond the Black Stump?"

The people at the front are whispering, trying to ask the driver who we are perhaps, but he simply ignores them.

"We were just hitchhiking and the bloke that lives on the homestead down there spotted your vehicle," I explain. "He said the driver could give us a ride."

"Pleased to meet you," the man says, and introduces his companions. They're a family from Adelaide and are on the second day of their authentic bush tour.

Today's "Top of the Mountain" trip includes outback damper and snags cooked over a campfire. The single day alone – part of a four-day round trip from Adelaide – costs several hundred dollars, he explains. Tomorrow they are going up in a light aircraft over Wilpena Pound itself.

"They say it's a beautiful view," the female companion butts in. "We're just happy to see the outback and to help all these lovely people understand the great culture of Australia. You must try the tour yourselves. It's just a beaut way to see this fabulous country."

She offers us sweets and something to drink; very generous considering her guided tour has been hijacked by hitchhikers.

"It's just a grouse place, isn't it mate?" the friendly guy continues rhetorically. Grouse means something is very good in Aussie slang. I find out he works in an Adelaide bank when he's not wearing his Akubra hat. They proudly point at the little planes on the tiny airfield outside the Wilpena Pound complex.

"You really should come with us tomorrow," he adds.

But I know that however spectacular the twenty-minute excursion is, I'd rather be squashed up in the cab of a ute listening to Gordon Coulthard's snippets of wisdom.

3

Outback Rules of Thumb

I unzip our front door, trying not to rouse Katia. I rub my eyes. The view is enchanting, an unexpected bonus after pitching the tent in the dark.

We are positioned at the top of a forest that slopes down to a valley creek. Tents and camper vans dot spacious clearings. The forest-floor leaf litter is fine dust, decorated by newly fallen jade-coloured gum leaves. Splinters of sunlight pierce through the meagre foliage shading our pitch, the rays already harsh enough to burn the skin. Here you don't get the gentle early-morning warm-up that precedes a midday blaze. You are bundled blindly into it from your bed.

I watch a kangaroo grazing by the boundary path. It hops lazily forwards, slurping up as much yellow grass dust as it can. The long, dirty black tail flops behind, an annoying extra appendage. It looks like a Western Grey, one of the most common species in South Australia.

Here in Wilpena, kangaroos are partially tamed by the ready availability of food offered by National Park users who ignore signs asking them not to feed wild animals. Admittedly, it's hard to resist. For all foreigners, kangaroos are an amazing curiosity, the very symbol of the weird land

Down Under. You never believe they'll eat from your hand. Properly wild kangaroos are very reticent.

Last night a whole family of Western Greys came for our leftovers. One greedy female stuck her head into an empty soup tin. The animal reared up on her hind legs, prompting our camping neighbours to run for cover. They are intimidating beasts up close. Their pluckiness is the bane of many farmers' lives.

To stockmen kangaroos are a pest, munching on cereal crops and sheep pasture. Farmers assist the "sustainable control" of Australia's kangaroo population – which numbered between 20 and 25 million in 1999 – with rifles. Around five million kangaroos are shot per year for their meat and skin. But according to the authorities, such is the adaptability of the most versatile marsupial that this barely makes a dent in their growth. A female kangaroo has a gestation period of only 33 days, after which her joey can climb from her uterus into her pouch.

Silky-feathered black birds – possibly cockatoos – squawk in the boughs of a she-oak gum as I walk over to the toilet block. Crows caw further up and dazzling lime and yellow rainbow lorikeets dart between the branches. The water I throw on my face in the bathroom is refreshingly icy. It smells of moss-covered mountain rocks. My stiff back creaks into action.

I can hear the leader of an all-inclusive South Australia bush tour addressing his backpacker customers when I walk out. I assume he's party leader because his bush hat has the widest brim in the group. The tents are arranged in a circle about a kindling fire being built by another guide.

"Okay you guys," he calls out, "let's get this tucker down, go to the dunny and head off. We've got heaps to see today. Strewth, you blokes are lazy, ay! All-right-ee, let's see if the sheilas can be ready first today," he adds.

Hearing this, our lack of itinerary soothes me. By the time I return to our tent, passing a cute, cream-furred wallaby assiduously munching, I feel ready for the outback. Katia is awake and contemplating her shower.

In 1993 the Wilpena Pound complex was a log cabin selling camping essentials like gas cylinders and guy ropes. Now it's a recreational concept. Gently piped New Age music featuring a token didgeridoo flutters through the store as we stock up with supplies. Kangaroo meat jerky is available in an array of packs, at prices that suggest it's a gourmet luxury.

Coach parties peer at panels describing local dreamtime traditions before walking to the restaurant for a three-course meal. Most people stay overnight in the resort's deluxe suites or motel rooms. Campers are a minority. Old women with name badges check a panel advertising times for an Aboriginal corroboree performance on the veranda. A real corroboree is a sacred assembly strictly for tribal men.

I convince Katia we should attempt the most strenuous hike of the marked bush trails. Instead of the undemanding two-hour loop to Wangarra Lookouts, we head for St Mary's Peak, the highest summit in the Flinders Ranges. Walkers are advised to allow eight hours.

The route takes us first through flat forest. The sand at our feet is iridescent scarlet. Large spiders scamper across their thick, complex webs at our approach. The creeks below are dried up, and the yellow wattle trees that line them stoop down towards the empty watercourse.

As the incline grows steeper, Katia's sighs grow more profound. She is about to stop when a grey snake slithers past, centimetres from her feet. It pauses to sunbathe on a boulder. Faced with the possibility there could be more behind, she quickens her pace.

Eventually a broad vista opens up to the east, and we can see where the weathered peaks of the range peter out, moulding into the pancake-flat desert. The sight marks the end of the fertile valleys that deluded early immigrants. Directly in front is the semicircular mound of St Mary's Peak, which looks like the scaly, ribbed back of a dinosaur.

I look at the path and then at Katia. She's not going to like this. The route is treacherously steep, rocky and exposed to thundering gusts of wind that fizz across the ranges.

"*Merde, c'est dur*," she says through gritted teeth. Complaining is better in French too.

But from somewhere deep inside, she summons up the will to move on. Her steely resolve is such that she refuses my offer of a break. She won't buckle so I can feel superior.

"Why do we always end up walking so bloody far wiz you?" she demands.

"It's only a little way further. I can see the top. Look!"

She stares reproachfully at the peak.

"Okay, let's go back then."

"Don't be stupeed. We've come zis far."

"So what's the point in complaining then?"

But we get there. And when we do, it's one of those disappointing would-be sublime moments blotted by a profusion of fellow walkers, all wanting to be alone like us. Their smiles are bittersweet; inevitable in a crowded world, I suppose.

We can clearly see the colossal crater of Wilpena Pound. Its rim, on which we sit, is actually the stump of what was once an epic dome pushed up from the ocean, equivalent in height to the Himalayas. All that remains is this severed caldera. The crest of the Pound is daintily trimmed with yacka grass trees, spiky palms and pampas grass.

The path takes us down into the wooded interior of the extinct volcano. Accessible via only one narrow gorge, the eleven-kilometre plain is an ecosystem shrouded in secrecy by the Earth's ruptures. It is like a completely sheltered reserve, accidentally formed, the Lost World of Arthur Conan Doyle.

Out of the quiet we feel the ground vibrating, a low bass thump growing gradually louder.

"What's zat?"

"Not sure."

The forest floor is definitely shaking. Katia grabs me and we stand behind a wide trunk. The noise is directly in front, rising towards a crescendo. We hold hands instinctively. Earthquake, I wonder? Can't be.

The source of the thudding emerges – a herd of emus. There must be ten of them, led by two birds at least a foot taller than me. They sprint past at a dizzying speed, knocking the undergrowth flying. The power of their stick-thin legs is extraordinary, like pistons connected to the ground.

The stragglers are just inches from our faces, their gawky eyes fixed directly ahead. We freeze, hold our breath – and just as rapidly the emus disappear into the darker corners of the forest. How the hell do they avoid bumping into trees?

"Mon dieu, c'était fou ça," Katia says – my God, that was mad. She adds that she's never seen anything like it in her life. Me too.

I feel like I've just swerved around a car smash on the motorway. Had we been standing behind a different tree, we'd have been flattened.

The real bush, away from the leisure facilities, is a dangerous place. Tame kangaroos at the campsite are a decoy.

We would have a perfect view of approaching traffic. Yet again, there is none. On the rare occasions a vehicle emerges from Wilpena Pound there is ample time to prepare a suitably respectable hitchhiking manner. Yet the stony expressions of unwilling motorists deflect our good humour.

We throw stones at a tree trunk in a plundered patch of forest behind. Katia is the best shot. I give her marks out of ten for various ballet movements. We holler favourite tunes standing in the middle of the road. We complete a game of chess on our travel-size board (the only worthwhile luxury item we packed). Katia sketches the landscape in front of us on the back of a magazine. It would be wrong to say standing by the side of a road is boring; far from it. Long pauses are as integral to hitchhiking as moving.

A herd of tall Big Red kangaroos bound out of the Spartan bush country and hop across the airfield. They find better grazing in patchy grass beneath a bloodwood tree.

For once we are doubling back, to Hawker so we can connect to the famous unsealed Oodnadatta Track up through Leigh Creek and Marree. At William Creek, we will hitch a ride on the unsealed connecting route back to the Stuart Highway at Coober Pedy. Enough people use it for us to get a ride, I assure Katia.

North from here is Blinman, close to Stuart's base camp on his first ever expedition as leader. After a fruitless decade of unprofitable sheep farming and opening up new lands for stations, his real expertise was once again called upon. Wealthy businessman William Finke, together with entrepreneurial brothers James and John Chambers, wanted Stuart to eke out more useable pasture in the Flinders Ranges, going beyond the massive salt lakes discovered earlier by Edward Eyre. Private financing was the only way to get an expedition off the ground after Sturt's expensive failure. The government wasn't interested.

Stuart departed from Oratunga Station, the Chambers brothers' main property, on 14 May 1858. Accompanied by a white man named Forster and an Aboriginal youth, he set out on his first self-governing quest. From Blinman the trio skirted to the east of the cracked, moistureless bed of Lake Torrens. They had six horses and one month's supplies.

A National Park maintenance truck approaches us. The driver points to the right to indicate he will be turning off shortly, so there is no point in picking us up. This courtesy makes a huge difference when you're hitchhiking. It's a gesture no one needs to make, but when people do you no longer feel like an irredeemable highway parasite. The truck stops two hundred metres further down towards Hawker. I see a figure jumping out, followed by what looks like a giant black holdall. The guy waves at the truck as it speeds off and stands there.

After fifteen minutes, he stumbles up to us. His kit bag really is about three times his size and weight. To watch him with the cumbersome piece of luggage is a refreshingly impractical sight. The people we met buying round-Australia bus tickets in Adelaide all had ultra-lightweight, adjustable-strap backpacks, even though they would hardly need to walk.

"Hi," he says, grinning. "I thought I'd better come to say hello."

He speaks with a sugary Welsh lilt. We introduce ourselves.

"Where are you trying to go to?" Katia asks.

He has a similar plan, up the Oodnadatta Track from Hawker.

"I've hitched absolutely everywhere since I arrived in Australia," he tells us. "I was in Sydney at Christmas, and since then I've just kept going. It's so easy to stay in hostels and hitchhike here. Smashing, isn't it?"

Meeting a replica of one's former self on an empty road in the Flinders Ranges is bizarre. It's like the last eight years have peeled away. Spookily, his name is Stuart. He is 18, as I was when I came here before. I envy him. I never thought it would be so long before I returned. We discuss tactics for a while and then he returns to his waiting place. He says it's only right to observe hitchhiking etiquette.

Stuart remains in gesturing distance for the next hour. On several occasions his imprecations provoke stalled engines from hired 4×4 drivers, perhaps shocked by two sets of hitchhikers on this vacant thoroughfare. The occupants look at us disdainfully. But I'm surprised they don't fall for Stuart, because he's alone and has a cherubic face.

The sun's glare disappears behind the mountains. A disconsolate walk back seems inevitable. Five hours have passed. A large hired camper van approaches, one with a dining table in the back. I regard such a vehicle as a virtual non-starter. My hitchhiking plea is only half-hearted. But the van stops.

Inside is a German family, all equally blond, with the dad, Gunther, behind the wheel. He is arguing with his wife as we stumble in. She sits on a sofa with her two cowering children. Although she smiles for us, you could cut the tension with a knife. Our bags take up too much space on the already cluttered floor. The wife tuts. Katia joins the children at the rear, while I take the front passenger seat. No sooner are we moving than Gunther spots Stuart and asks if he's another hitchhiker.

"I suppose I must stop too," he says formally. His wife says something angrily from behind. I don't speak German, but fury needs no translation.

Stuart squeezes into a gap on top of his sofa-sized bag. He hunches on the floor, out of earshot. Gunther, who has spectacles and the remnants of a mullet haircut, tells me he can take us to Hawker before they divert to Broken Hill. The family have spent a month travelling around in the van and now they're on their way back to Sydney. He was granted a sabbatical by his IT firm in Frankfurt.

Unsurprisingly, Gunther is a former hitchhiker who once cadged lifts around Europe. His wife never hitched and does not want complete strangers in the vehicle with their children.

"Shit happens, *ja*," Gunther says.

We make an unusual trio, Gunther, Stuart and I: one married and looking back wistfully on his bachelor hitch-hiking glory days, one on his way to being married and trying to hang on to the lifestyle, and one just setting out on his first big trip with unclouded optimism.

Several times at Gunther's insistence we pause for photographs in front of burnished hillsides and barren semi-desert. His wife is apathetic and the children are immune to the splendours of the scenery. Perhaps he just wants to show his mates back home the day he picked up hitchhikers, to prove he isn't totally henpecked. I still make the choices, he'll say.

He lets us out at Hawker and pauses while our bags tumble out of the camper van. Thanks to Katia, who can usually defrost the most hostile people, the wife has warmed to us and waves from the back with her sleeping children. Or maybe she's just glad we're gone.

"I feel sick," Katia says, and promptly is, round the back of the little roadhouse toilet cubicles. There was me, so content with our lift that I forgot to check on her during the whole ride. She is really pale actually.

"I sink it was because I was seeting zer wrong way in zer van," she says afterwards. She's abstracted from this place, and I know all she probably wants is to lie down somewhere. But as always, she perseveres for me. How many stubborn hitchhikers could find a companion like

Katia, willing to go on after spending half the day throwing pebbles at trees by the road?

Stuart bids us goodbye for the time being. He agrees to stand further up the road again. "Hopefully I'll make it as far as Leigh Creek," he says.

We watch him struggle up past a row of trees through a yard full of rusting, warped machinery. He looks like a Steinbeck character in a bleak mid-Western dustbowl town with not a cent in his pocket, nor a care in the world.

In the general store an Aboriginal woman buys sweets and crisps. Outside, some kids play with a grey snake that had found its way into the boot of their vehicle.

What a beautiful evening. The crepuscular sun is setting over the abandoned railway yard in front of us. We walk a few hundred metres to a side road lined with clapboard kit bungalows and a place selling agricultural equipment. We're not at Hawker's periphery, but it's far enough.

A truck slows down. "I'm turning off down here," the driver shouts after winding his window down. He gives us a wave. Nothing else comes for nearly an hour. Thousands of pink galahs heading to roost in the trees behind add to the cerise spectacle.

Katia's feeling better and starting to curse at the drivers who turn off. It's a good sign.

"Eh, you little buggeurs," she cries with heartfelt Gallic ire. "Ee is nasty, zis one. Zis one could have easily taken us."

I have a short-lived desire to snuggle down for the night and forget about moving on. That's the difference between me now and the impulsiveness of my last Australian journey. I'm sure it's prompted by the cushioning comfort of having Katia with me. I'm juggling two lives really, I have to be honest about it.

I can just see Stuart, or rather his bag, on the horizon. A stuttering van comes past and the driver shrugs his shoulders as he passes us. Yet he slows down for Stuart. I watch him clumsily hoist his load inside and then tumble in. That's it: there goes me eight years ago. Behind, my potential future self, Gunther the father, must be struggling to provide his wife with solace as the kids cry for their bedtime story.

Sitting in the bar at the Hawker Hotel Motel, we overhear this conversation.

"Ah yeearh, she'll be right," a man's voice pines. "You've always been a decent sheila to me."

As he listens to the reply, he burps and greedily slurps back what must be most of a schooner of West End lager. He butts in. "Ah, please, darling. Give your bloke a break. I reckon I deserve it after three months shifting sand out in the fucking desert, ay."

From his attempts to interrupt the mystery woman in her next retort it's clear he's losing. He huffs and swears throughout. Finally he gets another word in. "It's just no dramas, darling. No bloody big dramas. I'm coming over to Whyalla to see ya. I want to have a bloody look at my place too, all-right-ee. It's no dramas."

No dramas: that is his refrain for most of the next twenty minutes. This simplest of Australian phrases, diplomatic and universally understood, becomes slurred to the point of meaning nothing at all. We hear the phone drop to the floor and him saying, "Ya can stop whingeing, I'm not hearing you any more."

I'm still thinking about that conversation in the morning. We head back to a point slightly further out of town than where we were, beside a scrapper's yard.

The drunken caller's car is about the third to approach and it pulls up some metres in front, sweeping carelessly across the stones. The car is a battered Holden, in such a brittle condition it would never be deemed roadworthy in Britain. I guess it isn't roadworthy here either. The brake lights don't come on, one of the tyres is either deflated or flat, and the rear windscreen is so thickly coated in red sand that there's no possible way the driver can see out of it.

"G'day," he says, stretching across to open a passenger door that limps off a rusty hinge. "How the hell are ya?"

"Good thanks mate," I reply, using the Australian standard response to the question, rather than the British "not bad". There is nothing signifying the differences between our two respective countries better than this straightforward replacement of a negative with a positive.

"Yous better chuck your bags somewhere in the trunk," he commands. As I tentatively lever the boot, he says, "Good on ya."

"Good on ya" can be used in just about any situation – when someone buys you a beer, when someone scores four runs, when someone still manages to be a good bloke after having his legs bitten off by a shark or a croc – and it never sounds phoney with an Aussie accent.

The driver introduces himself as Wayne, after I've offered my hand. His breath reeks of stale beer despite the bulging wad of chewing gum hidden in his cheek. He is careless in his appearance, a true "bushy", a "larrikin". He must be in his late fifties, but has retained the unironed appearance of a bachelor. He wears dirty jeans, with engrained stains, a sweatshirt that looks decades old, and underneath that a lumberjack shirt. Contrarily, he sports a distinguished-looking moustache, the kind favoured by members at Lord's cricket ground.

Katia clambers into the rear seat, stepping over a foot well that is ankle deep in junk. There is no sign of a map or any of the usual car accoutrements. But what she does find on the seat are several dog-eared porno magazines, one left open on a particularly explicit gynaecological shot. Dangling above her, hanging from a string mobile attached to the roof, is a double-sided photograph of a topless model. Wayne makes no effort to apologise for the porn, nor indeed to remove it.

He describes himself as an "earth mover". I have to ask exactly what this entails, even though I guess he would have told us anyway.

"I reckon I spend most days working a digger through the bloody Flinders, ay," he says. "Me and the other blokes in the team build roads over whole mountains, you know. Big bastards too. We make new tracks for tourists like yous two as well."

Technically Wayne is a grader, a job that entails levelling out the corrugations on dirt roads. Yet as he expands further on the risks involved in upgrading unsurfaced tracks, his life sounds like that of a crack SAS commando in the wilds of Afghanistan. By his account, the job entails plunging down sheer-sided ravines behind the wheel of a mechanical bulldozer at dawn. To my untrained eye, however, there aren't many large-scale civil engineering projects in the vicinity of Hawker; at least we didn't see any Alpine-type passes on our way through. Maybe, as he accidentally confesses, "it's just moving heaps of shit, ay."

Wayne brings up the thorny issue of Aboriginal land rights while still narrating on the general theme of "earth moving".

"I get on well with the fucking Abos," he informs us. "But I'd love to shoot the bastards' fucking legs off." He scratches his chin sagely. "They're bloody whingeing bastards. If I wanted to build a road across that empty field over there, they'd say it was a fucking sacred site."

I mention Gordon Coulthard, wondering whether they might know of each other in such a vast, yet tightly knit community.

"Yeah, well to yous kids Gordon could be an interesting fella, but for us blokes that have to make a bloody living out here, he's a clever, scheming bloody blackfella. I guess he just gets in the way," Wayne adds, in lieu of any genuine complaint. He has no personal grievance.

"The trouble with the Abos," he concludes, "is that they want bloody everything. They want the bloody land because they say it's theirs, but then they don't do any racking thing with it."

I keep my counsel, guessing Wayne wouldn't like a devil's advocate in his passenger seat. A hitchhiker can be no more than an empty receptacle, nodding appreciatively to the ugly prejudices spouted by some drivers.

He has something of Crocodile Dundee about him, Wayne. He's a concoction of bullish vulgarity, understated charm, intuitive kindness and pig-headed male chauvinism.

Like Mick Dundee, Wayne acknowledges the "Abos" are the only ones who will ever properly understand and persevere in places like the Flinders Ranges. And also like Mick, Wayne is tamed by nothing – except the "lady friend" in Whyalla.

The journey trembles along, pitching into potholes where Wayne and his earth-moving colleagues have not finished their job. We cover one hundred kilometres in nearly two hours. Wayne forgets we are out-of-towners and makes reference to the less than riveting social goings-on of Hawker, with its population of less than a hundred.

Katia asks Wayne where he has travelled, I presume in a desperate attempt to shift the conversation elsewhere.

"What the hell would I want to do that for?" he counters. "I've never been anywhere north of Coober Pedy. I've only ever left the state once; that was when I went down to Victoria. I spent a few days in Melbourne. Couldn't stand the bloody place. I've never been overseas and I can't say I want to. This country's got everything."

With this précis of his worldview, Wayne reiterates an outlook I encountered many times while thumbing in Australia. Aussies who share his opinion have no desire to visit other parts of the globe. Many, I've noticed, use the generic term "overseas" for all foreign countries, not caring to make a distinction between Iceland, Tanzania and Nicaragua. "Overseas" is a catch-all word I've heard most often when people speak about their foreign holidays, whereas if they take a domestic break they are more precise. "We're going to this beaut little place on the coast of northern Queensland. It's just down from Port Douglas. If you follow the Captain Cook Highway to the turning for Mount Molloy near the sugar cane farm..."

Wayne is far happier talking about the lack of water in the Flinders following the drastically hot temperatures earlier in the year. "You can see there's been no rain out here," he indicates, pointing an accusing finger at an empty creek. "Jesus, do we need some rain! That's the reason you see all the kangaroos by the side of the road at night, because the water drains off the highway, which means things can grow. Stupid bastards end up getting hit by roadtrains though."

At Port Augusta he says he will have to jettison us. "I hope the lady friend is ready for me," he comments, staring regretfully towards the dock jetties. I guess he's wondering what he said to her last night. We could help him out, but he'd probably think we'd been spying.

Instead of advising Wayne, we laugh generously when he chuckles through a crap self-made one-liner, probably one he tells strangers every time he goes drinking in Port Augusta.

"Whenever I go to Whyalla, I say I'm going overseas," he says and laughs out loud. "Do yous get it? We've just crossed the sea."

We cross the Port Augusta Bridge traversing the concave mouth of the Spencer Gulf estuary. Wayne pulls over at the beginning stretch of Route 87, the Stuart Highway. He is taking a turning to the left, on to the coastal Eyre Highway skirting Whyalla. As he swerves off, he crunches his gears awkwardly. Something about the damaged look on his face as he waves tells me the machismo attitude could be bullshit. He looks apprehensive.

Later, on a bench outside a golf course, a local eccentric clasping a transistor radio to his ear the wrong way around sits opposite. There is a special phone-in on the subject of remembering Australia's fallen war heroes from the First and Second World Wars. Why? Well, yesterday was Anzac Day, one of Australia's most important national holidays.

Duh! Everyone knew that except me – which explains why no one stopped for us. Anzac Day is probably one of the quietest travel days of the Australian calendar. It is the one solemn occasion when the whole population pauses to remember and sets aside normal activities. Even in the outback, few people would be making long journeys.

The host asks people whether Anzac Day and Remembrance Sunday should be combined. Anzac Day marks the occasion when the ANZACs (Australia and New Zealand Army Corps) properly entered the First World War with the Gallipoli landings in Turkey, after it allied with Germany. On the day itself, 25 April 1915, strong winds forced many troops to the wrong landing areas. They made easy pickings for the Turkish shore batteries. Following months of ugly fighting and no real military gain, 7,000 Australians and an equivalent number of New Zealanders lost their lives.

Anzac Day is revered because it marks the slow separation from Britain. Rather than acknowledging indebtedness to the mother country, Anzac Day is a commemoration of Britain and Allied Europe relying on Aussie back-up.

"I reckon our own blokes deserve heaps more attention than they already have," one caller comments. "You can't stop having parades for these fellas in Adelaide just because of some ratbag politician."

Few people want Anzac Day to be downgraded in any way. Increasingly, Anzac Day parades have greater prominence than those on Armistice Day, 11 November.

"The country should come to a total standstill for the ANZACs," the final caller concludes.

Note to self: always check what's going on in the outside world before thumbing lifts.

4

Breakdown on the Gibber Plain

The road that leads north from Port Augusta is daunting. Not long after you've left the comfort shade of the local power station chimney stacks, the scrubby, untransformable inertia of the desert looms. Ahead are rows of flattened tablelands, encroaching on uneven plains that contain only sporadic gidgee and mallee trees; the former a crooked, spiky lump of vegetation and the latter a skeletal eucalypt with hair-like foliage at its spindly branch ends. No paddocks now, just gargantuan cattle stations – an interminable blank canvas.

The existence of this town beyond the docks depends entirely on the outback's long, clawing reach. Look at the map: one can't really miss out Port Augusta on any serious journey around Australia. The Ghan railway from Adelaide to Alice Springs passes through, the route to Perth across the Nullarbor Plain twists left from Port Augusta, the Stuart Highway starts properly here and Adelaide is three hours south. An enormous placard reads Port Augusta: Cross Roads of Australia. It's the kind of place in which haulage men have a favourite service station – or servo, as they might say – but they have no knowledge whatsoever of the town centre.

Historically, Port Augusta was a vital cog in the wheel for many of the great overland explorations. Flinders carried on here in search of a source of fresh water before the circumnavigation. In 1839, before Stuart, Edward Eyre set out north from the town to discover South Australia's great salt lakes. After Stuart, the southern section of Charles Todd's overland telegraph line party made the port its first target.

For Europeans like us, it is the juncture where the distances grow unimaginable. There is a green distance marker road sign that reads Alice Springs, 1222km. Above Alice Springs are listed Woomera, 176, Andamooka, 281 and Glendambo, 283. None of these settlements is much to shout about. What a wonderful amount of vacant, and unuseable, land lies between us and Alice Springs. To me there can be no more tantalising thought. Nothingness is a big draw.

"*Mon Dieu*," says Katia.

"Why do you say that?"

"*Il n'y a rien*" – there is nothing.

"But we've come here for *rien*."

Instead of commenting further, Katia takes a picture of me standing under the sign with my thumb stretched out.

A man driving south pulls up opposite. "Yous would be better off walking up to the truckers at the stop about half a click up the track," he calls. "No one's going to stop here."

Katia gets one arm under a rucksack strap and is about to topple over, when a car does stop for us. The bonnet flicks open in preparation.

"Woohoo," she shouts, and lets the bag drop.

The driver has a cigarette hanging out of his mouth. He wears a blue vest bearing a logo for the Ord River Dam Project (an irrigation scheme in Western Australia). He wears hole-ridden jeans and steel-toe-capped work boots. His skin is freckled. On his left arm is a Hindu-design tattoo, the kind a footballer would have without knowing what it symbolises. Although his receding hair is freshly shaved, he has a full gingery beard, making him look like a monk.

"G'day buddy," he says, "the name's Shane. And her in the car there, that's my girlfriend. She's Yvonne."

Yvonne ignores us and fiddles with the radio tuner.

Shane assures us he'll find a place for our bags as he rummages in the boot already stuffed with their possessions.

"Right, we'll just push all this shit down and chuck it inside," he declares, adding, "I know what it's like when you're hitching and bastards say there's no fucking room."

Somehow he closes the boot. We squeeze into the back of a geriatric, cream-coloured Commodore automatic. The overburdened car doesn't purr, it growls, like a wounded bear.

Once inside, the first thing Shane says is, "I hope you've got some tapes because I'm getting fucking bored of the ones we've got."

I assure him that we have, but they're in my bag.

"Well mate, we'll just have to open it up again," he responds. So we do.

In the meantime Katia says hello to Yvonne, who retains her low profile in the passenger seat. It turns out she's from Belgium. Katia leans forward on the pale brown leather upholstery to start up a conversation in French. Plastic bags full of unseen goodies tumble off the back shelf.

"I don't speak much French," Yvonne says. "I'm from the Flemish part of Belgium."

She displays the gritted teeth of someone who's just been in a steaming row. Slithers of angry words hiss out between her pursed lips. That's why Shane's so keen to hear my tapes, I think.

"Don't spit the dummy in front of these people," he instructs Yvonne as he gets behind the wheel. "Spit the dummy" is another great Aussie phrase, meaning to have a tantrum.

After the initial flurry of rattled-off introductions, conversation dies. Our hosts simmer separately. Succinctly, Shane tells us he's from the Blue Mountains. He talks about smoking "heaps of mull" – marijuana – at the last farm they worked at near Beechworth, Victoria.

"And then some bloke offered me this car," he adds.

His words trail off as he recognises one of the tracks on my tape. The song captivates his interest.

Shane and Yvonne's 3,000-mile journey to Kununurra, home of the Ord River Dam Project, is prompted by a promise of melon-picking jobs. In Australia there are thousands of people who follow the fruit around. With the difference in climatic conditions between the north and the south, it's possible to have work all year long. There's a handbook that tells you which farming towns to be in at what time of year. I picked melons and grapes when I was here last.

To be honest, it's pleasant to have the music so loud that we need not bother talking. Unobtrusively, the landscape shifts to absolute desert. Thorny saltbush sprouts out of the reddening sand. Sprawls of root berries lie in tangled knots across the ground. Tufty, withered acacia shrubs provide the only shade. Time passes, and the cassette winds over to the second side. I put my arm around Katia. We gaze at the monotonous yet spellbinding scenery of the outback.

"It's incredible 'ere," she says. Well, at least that confirms it, I think. It's not just me being too obsessive. We both look, pointing things out.

"*Tu as vu ça?*" – Did you see that?

One of the most incongruous sights on this endless, drought-stricken, pock-marked plain is a faded warning sign marking the boundary of where the British Government once tested twelve nuclear weapons. This is the edge of Woomera Rocket Range, a spectre in Australia's ecological history. Hundreds of miles to the west, but still contained within the Woomera Prohibited Area, is Maralinga, the site of atomic blasts. After the bomb tests in the 1950s, radioactive weapon components were exploded on the test ground. Accounts I've read make it sound like a schoolboy experiment in the park: "I wonder what happens if I light a box of matches under this?"

Needless to say, the Poms didn't do their reputation with the Aussies any good at Maralinga. Over 200 Australian servicemen believe they were deliberately exposed to radiation out there. They claim to have contracted cancer and other illnesses from radioactive fallout. And Aborigines, whose ancestors roamed this sterile region for centuries, claim they were given no warning of the mushroom cloud. In the 1980s, a Royal Commission was appointed to investigate the allegations. After eventually receiving secret documents from Britain, the inquiry couldn't confirm the cancer links, but it did result in the Aborigines receiving millions of pounds in compensation for being ejected off their lands.

On my old map, a vast quadrant of land is marked with a fleshy pink to indicate it is prohibited. The forbidden zone appears larger than England.

The Americans took advantage of this empty landscape too, constructing a satellite tracking station within the Woomera zone. Although they've closed it, the infrastructure can be glimpsed from the highway.

Shane shouts, "You fellas really screwed this bloody place, ay."

I attempt a reply, but he sticks the volume back up.

Straggly wire fence gaily festoons the featureless plateau. It's the kind of apocalyptic environment where a mushroom bomb crater would add some aesthetic variation.

We stop at Pimba roadhouse. Shane and Yvonne actually talk to each other.

"I'm going to the dunny, you dumb bitch."

"Go fuck yourself, you bastard."

With us they are just about convivial, however. We offer them food; they choose a bottle of blue Powerade and meat pies, with red sauce on top.

On the next stretch to Tarcoola, there are astonishing topographical phenomena to distract us. On both sides of the highway are the washing-powder-white plains of the dried-out beds of salt lakes. Sheer, almost triangular pinnacles rise abruptly from these lunar seas. Only sand sep-arates us from the unearthly scenery. We are all whipped into a frenzy of acclaim. The tape stops and nobody notices. Even Yvonne gets enthused.

Adding to the desolation are the frequent corpses of kangaroos in the shallow road gutter. Some stretches of the highway are like mass graves, the roadkill victims rot-ting where they were struck. Large wedge-tailed eagles hover over the crystal seas for carrion. Once they've found meat, they chomp steadily on a carcass until an oncoming vehicle is almost on top of them. Some are so engrossed in their feast that their claws become stuck in the decaying flesh.

Our steady progress is slowed for Yvonne to take photo-graphs of these visceral sights. She runs down the highway to get a close-up of a particularly obese eagle. It glares at her and then lifts gracefully into the air. These birds have wingspans of several metres. We watch this manmade food chain from a roadside stop, where there is an absurdly optimistic freshwater tank.

Soon after, the car engine starts to splutter. We jolt in the back seat, as though being driven by a learner who hasn't grasped how to use the clutch. A new rasping noise, like someone in the preliminary stages of whooping cough, comes from the engine. The jolts become more insistent.

"Don't die on me, you bastard!" Shane screams, now oblivious to the calm occasioned by the entrancing scenery. He caresses the dashboard, as if to soothe the aching insides of the long-suffering car.

"I think there's a problem with the transmission," he shouts above the whirring noise. "What d'ya reckon?"

I nod my assent, as if I have the faintest clue what he's talking about. Another advantage of hitchhiking is that you're rarely called on to have even the barest knowledge of engine mechanics.

For several kilometres we continue in a violent stop-start fashion. Shane fiddles with the gear stick, shifting from automatic to manual.

"I bought this heap for seven hundred and fifty bucks two weeks ago and the fucking mechanic promised me I didn't need a new transmission," he complains.

He bangs the steering wheel, imploring the old Commodore to restore itself. But there's obviously no hope. The temperature gauge is sky high, flickering around the maximum. I look across to Katia. She has a concerned look on her face, her backseat driving look. She's anticipating the worst.

Usually I'd say "don't be so pessimistic", but this time she's only being realistic.

Without any warning, the engine cuts out completely. Shane bunny-hops on to a patch of flat rubble. As he puts the handbrake on, an angry cloud of steam billows from the engine. There is a brooding silence. I don't know quite what to say. A new sound, a persistent drip, keeps time over the deathly desert quiet. It is the swift trickle of the radiator, leaking its contents on to the ground.

"Fucking fucker," Shane says. "Fuck."

On examining the damage to the radiator, we discover a hole big enough to put a fist through. In a heroic attempt at salvaging the car, Shane wraps his shirt around the radiator cap and yanks it off. This achieves two things: a scalded hand and a new hole in his tatty fruit-picking vest.

His dispute with Yvonne reaches new levels of bitterness.

"You were the one who wanted to buy this heap."

"Ya don't know what ya were talking about. I've never had dramas before. Ya wanted the car instead of taking the bus."

On the sharply defined, shimmering horizon, I can pick out vehicles coming our way. I remember the camaraderie that exists between motorists crossing the desert. Someone is bound to ask if we need any help.

Katia and I gaze ruefully at the dusty ground while Shane and Yvonne scream at each other. She believes that the bloke in Victoria ripped them off, getting such a massive mark-up on their old banger.

We are standing on a strip of sand and boulders, perhaps one of the most unwelcoming, blank horizons the Simpson Desert region has to offer; and we are gooseberries at a full-on domestic dispute. We are stuck with half a bottle of mineral water and no mobile phone. The land all about us is frightening. There are no trig points, no landmarks. If you went off at right angles to the highway without a compass or a guide you'd fry, no doubt about it. Directly in front, I see utter desolation. This is the great Gibber Plain, a term pilfered from the Aborigines to denote untold miles of rocky rubble.

Stopped in a landscape that most people sensibly drive through at seventy miles an hour, the perils of normal life for desert Aborigines become even more mind-blowing than when you read about them. So-called "civilising parties" found small groups of indigenous people out there, still cut-off from white colonisation, as recently as the 1960s.

As far as the eye can see, there are only a handful of shrivelled mulga bushes and stubborn clumps of spinifex, the last vestiges of desert vegetation. Spinifex, also known as porcupine grass for its prickly appearance, resembles a spiky green dome. It is one of the hardiest species on the continent. Black mirages that look like oil slicks pepper the pinkish sand among stones, boulders and debris. The vista here is extraterrestrial. On second thoughts, Mars might actually appear more inviting.

The scorched plain before us is what undid Stuart as he chartered new lands for the Chambers brothers on that first expedition. Initially, his progress had been marred by the distraction of locating a fertile area, which the Aborigines he encountered along the way referred to as Wingillpin. In his diaries he records, "We came across some natives, who kept a long distance off. I sent our black up to them to ask in which direction Wingillpin lay. They pointed to the course I was then steering and said, 'Five sleeps'." The expedition never located Wingillpin.

As the three haggard men headed northwest from Lake Eyre, the land grew increasingly malignant and the promised oasis seemed as mythical as the inland sea. But Stuart did discover a stretch of permanent water he later named Chambers Creek after his benefactor. He would be able to report potential grazing land. Pinpointing the water source would also be vital in his later expeditions higher into Australia.

From the creek they soldiered on towards modern-day Coober Pedy, the opal-mining capital of Australia. Before it was too late and the supplies ran out, Stuart realised there was little chance of finding anything to eat here on the Gibber Plain, describing it as "fearful country". Reluctantly, he decided to retreat south, two months after leaving Blinman. The burning flinty stones that carpet the desert had inflicted the horses with so much pain they could barely move. "These pebbles were as firmly packed as if they had been put in with cement," Stuart logged. He later added, "All the horses are now so lame that I shall require them to rest before I proceed." Yet due to his navigational skill, the party eventually made it to the coast. He was honoured by the Royal Geographical Society with a gold watch.

I interrupt Shane's sulking by pointing at a large mobile home camper approaching at a leisurely speed. "Do you want me to flag them down?" I ask.

Shane, however, wants to take responsibility. He is ashen faced.

The mobile home pulls into our layby. Its occupants are in their sixties, clad in all the latest outdoor gear. The man erects a fold-up table on the gravel and his wife follows with a flask and two tea cups. Shane wanders over.

"No worries," the man says. "Give us ten minutes for our tea though. Do you want a biscuit?"

Later, as the mobile home eases gingerly back on to the highway, Shane raises a middle finger towards Yvonne. I wonder if we'll ever see him again. I am not sure of our precise location. My estimate is that we are still one and a half hours drive south of Coober Pedy.

There is little to do but wait. We are left with only Yvonne's gloom-ridden company – and millions of flies.

Oh yeah, I forgot to tell Katia what the flies are like in the desert. It's not a sensation one can describe easily. Being pestered by a few wasps while eating outdoors is the closest I've come in recent years. But here one is perpetually dive-bombed. It is as though each of us is enclosed within our own personal cloud of zippy bugs. My hand alternates back and forth like a windscreen wiper as I try to swat them away. There's no point. I remember why I wore a fly net over my pride-and-joy suede bush hat while thumbing rides last time.

Katia, new to this experience, can't cope with the irritating flies. "Zis is really annoying me," she says. She is the same with cold temperatures or when there's something in her eye: she can't just forget it. So she finds a spare top in her bag and wraps it over her head like an Arabic headdress.

Nothing prepares a newcomer for Australia's extraordinary fly population. Everyone's heard about koalas, wallabies, wombats and the like, but the flies don't get the publicity. In many ways, flies have influenced Australian culture more than any other creature. For example, linguists have suggested the Aussie accent comes from outback dwellers breathing through their noses to prevent flies entering their mouths. The fly flick-off outback Aussies perform effortlessly has become known as the Australian salute. And then there's the ultimate Aussie accessory, the cork hat – designed to ward off flies before the advent of aerosol sprays.

We spread blankets in the limited shade of the smouldering car. No wonder the radiator blew, the temperature must be above 40 °C. With Yvonne in such a foul mood I stare ahead, trying to pick out the movement of a lizard or a snake in the rocky foreground. Nothing else would live here. I have no compunction to speak with our hitchhiking host. Our predicament relieves us of the normal obligation.

Katia, however, struggles with the silence. She needs to talk. She often gets into conversation with people sitting next to her on a train. This is a definite asset for us as a hitchhiking duo. She simply bulldozes her way through awkward silences. Or doesn't even notice there is an awkward silence. So she engages Yvonne in conversation.

And the more Yvonne says, the more likely it seems that Shane will abandon the car and cut his losses. Apparently they split up romantically at his behest, but he agreed he would still sleep with her without the need for total fidelity. Our plight is an unfortunate by-product of their emotionally severed relationship.

I look at my watch. We've been here over two hours. The brutal sun grills the flammable vegetation. Waves of heat dapple the blistered ground. For the first time, I have to admit I do feel anxious. I look across at Katia, who puckers her lips and widens her eyes to signal her unease. It's that look again, like I'm holding a glass of red wine over the carpet while drunk.

"Do you 'ave a pack of cards?" Katia asks Yvonne.

"No, but we've got Yahtzee."

Yvonne looks reanimated by the suggestion. Maybe she's thinking her boyfriend will abandon us too. We clear a circle on the blanket on which to throw the dice. Soon all of us are absorbed. I let the flies surround me without reacting. So does Katia. It takes a special kind of apathetic patience.

Katia storms ahead with her dice rolling. She has cast aside her fears about our parlous location. I shouldn't be so apprehensive. Considering our position, she would be justified in cursing this hitchhiking odyssey. But instead she enjoys our desert floor game.

Our absorption is such that we only notice the tow truck as it swings to a halt virtually on top of us. Yvonne throws the paper with our Yahtzee scores into the dust, ignoring Katia's victory. When Shane steps out of the cab, she hugs him fraudulently. Or was the bitterness a sham?

From the driver's side of the little cab emerges our rescuer. I reckon he must be in his 50s, but his wrinkles are caked in grime so it's difficult to be precise. On his feet are flip-flop sandals, known as thongs in Australia. He sports a ragged hoop-striped T-shirt and sun-scarred pink Bermuda-style shorts. Perched on an uncombed outcrop of grey hair is a yellow baseball cap with the words Bulls Transport printed on it. His lips are curled in a permanently wry sneer. The last time I broke down, a hyper-efficient chap from the AA wearing a uniform better pressed than my own work suit clambered out of a gleaming vehicle. Just as he was a caricature Pom, this bloke is his cartoon equivalent for outback Australia. One could not invent a better stereotype.

He lights a cigarette as he walks towards us. So far, he's said nothing. He peers at the stricken car professionally and scratches his chin with his free hand. "Yeah mate, she looks pretty much fucked," he says to Shane. Then, peering underneath the bonnet, without straining himself too far from a standing position, he adds, "Yep, the radiator's buggered. I might know a few blokes in Coober with a radiator for a Commodore, ay."

The truck is an extra sturdy jeep, with a winch fixed on the flat-panel rear. On the side, in hand-painted block capitals, is "DIAL-A-TOW 24HR SERVICE".

The driver, Joe, leans into the cab of his truck and raises a stubby of Coopers Bitter to his lips, the last dregs. "I reckon I'll just have a smoke and then I'll rig her up."

Shane and Yvonne are having an emergency confab out of hearing distance. Joe chuckles to himself as he smokes. Answering a question that hasn't been asked, he adds, "No, yous wouldn't be the first backpackers to spend a night in the Simpson Desert. But hey, I reckon yous kids would have had plenty of flies to eat if you got stuck out here."

Katia sits on my lap in the little truck, squashed between the window and the still sullen Shane and Yvonne. The extra expense of the breakdown truck has compounded their mutual loathing. Yvonne tries to wriggle free. I'm happy up front, leaning forward to peer at the plaster-coloured sand hills and stranded plateaus, listening to Joe's non-stop monologue. It's great knockabout stuff. He needs no encouragement.

"Did yous lot know there are 47 nationalities in Coober Pedy? In fact, it's actually the most cosmopolitan place in all of Oz-traae-lya. Yep, that'd be right. There's more races out here than there are in Sydney. The barber's from Russian-Japanese stock. He has to stand on a stepladder to cut your bloody hair, ay. We've got French, Greek, Japanese, all sorts, even the fucking Abos, ay!"

Joe is a born raconteur whose act is as well prepared as a stand-up comedian. I ask how he arrived here.

"I came out here after the Vietnam War," he says. "It seemed like a good idea at the time. Me and my mate drove up from New South Wales. We spent five years drilling for opal and we never found a bloody thing. It was bloody hard yakka, I can tell yous kids."

Katia looks at me quizzically. "Hard yakka?" she whispers.

"*Plus tard*," I reply – I'll tell you later.

"Then we found a beaut seam," Joe goes on, "it was jam-packed with pure opal, the best stones on the market. We sold the stones for two million bucks. Ah mate, it was fair dinkum, I tell ya. But of course, I blew the whole bloody lot on wine, women and horses."

He sniggers though the tiny gap in his mouth and simultaneously takes a long drag on the cigarette wedged between his front teeth. Even Shane manages a laugh. As if to preface his next anecdote, Joe nods, grins, and gestures out of the window.

"Ah yeah, people go mad out here, ay," he reflects, almost ruefully. "I knew a bloke who shot his wife and kids just so he could get locked up in the prison. That way, he knew he could guarantee a bed and three good meals a day.

"I used to be one of those crazy young blokes too," he continues. "I bought a racing car with a V8 engine to do this race, the bloody Cannonball Run it was called, like the film, ya know. It went right up through the Territory. There's no speed limit up there, ya see. Mate, I was doing over two hundred kilometres an hour all the way. Anyways, it all ended when some stupid Japanese bastard ran over the safety marshals. Could have got me killed too, I reckon."

As we get within commuting distance of Coober Pedy, we pass decrepit pick-up trucks with drilling equipment fixed on the back, leaving town. These belong to the opal miners for whom the place exists. By the roadside are triangular mounds of dug-up pink and red rubble, some taller than houses. The hitherto somnolent landscape is now scarred by ugly gashes, impromptu opencast mines. The fortune-seeking opal prospectors look tiny, gambling their future in this merciless setting.

After keeping silent for more than thirty seconds, Joe explains. "See, a bloke can set himself up with basic opal mining gear for three hundred bucks. It's not much when ya think about it, ay. Ya have to pick up a digging licence, but that's no dramas. Then you're ready to go."

With every kilometre the sight of rusty winches and ungraded tracks heading to mine shafts becomes more commonplace. On both sides, the accumulation of unregulated caverns polka-dots the desert. Massive excavated shelves have overtaken spinifex grass as the dominant landscape feature.

Joe's exuberant depictions of life for the hopeful opal miner no doubt add layers of embellishment to the reality. He tells us how anyone can dig up to thirty metres down using an auger bucket and drill. He gives technical details about modern mining machines with revolving cutting heads. He talks about the hundreds of scavengers, known locally as noodlers, who pick up unseen opal from the waste left behind by miners on their claimed-for fifty-metre square patch of land. As someone who generally hates guided tours about subjects I'd never usually have the faintest interest in, Joe makes me intrigued.

All too soon the haphazard outskirts of the town can be seen on the right. Joe waves to practically every driver coming in the other direction. What a way to arrive in this bedraggled place, I think, in the company of one of its foremost bullshit artists.

The sun is setting over the corrugated back streets of Coober Pedy. But it's underneath them that the real town exists. Apart from opal mining, the town's main claim to fame is its subterranean houses.

"My home's below that little building over there," Joe indicates. "It's beautiful under there. I've got a huge place, ay. And the temperature never changes, even when it's fifty degrees outside. I tell yous, this is God's country out here. The stars are clearer than anywhere else in the world."

He points at a wind turbine towering over the low-level houses. "Hey, I told a couple of Swiss backpackers like yous lot that thing was a fan to cool the townsfolk down when it gets real hot. Ha!"

*S*hane reaches over for his ninth bottle of Victoria Bitter. He gazes ruefully at the cracked kerbstone, smeared with pink dust. We are around a picnic table outside Radeka's Underground backpackers' hostel on Coober Pedy's main street. Opal dealers make up most of the retailers. There are clouds above, the first time we've seen the starry night sky obscured in many weeks. A half-eaten pizza from the local Serbian takeaway lies on the table.

As I drain the last dregs from my final stubby, Joe's tow truck drives past at funereal speed. The cream Commodore is strapped on the back, ready to join Coober Pedy's rust-heap cemetery.

"Useless bloody car," Shane sighs. "I'm going to need to drink a lot of piss to get over this."

He is resigned to losing the vehicle now. The tow truck bill alone was two hundred dollars and he'd need at least another four hundred to have the car repaired. He and Yvonne are catching the bus tomorrow.

A hooker from the local brothel, not far from the underground Greek Orthodox Church, approaches our table. She must be in her mid-40s, but attempts to disguise her age with bleached-blonde hair and stilettos. Disregarding Katia and Yvonne, she asks Shane and me: "Do yous blokes want to see the town?"

We decline and she totters away, pirouetting awkwardly into potholes.

In front of us are a group of dishevelled Aborigines clustered around a cask of wine. They wear cast-off winter coats and torn jeans. They let the flies crawl into the corners of their eyes and over their bare feet without the slightest murmur of annoyance. They are completely hammered. "Hello, 'ello, 'ello," one old woman screeches at us. She pleads for grog money. Another grey-haired lady, probably even older, is slumped against a slither of concrete pavement, passed out.

These are the indigenous people who provided the name Coober Pedy. Kupa Piti it was originally called – literally, white man's hole. The white population can get paralytic in the fresh underground, while the wailing

Aborigines are shooed from scalding kerbstone to back alley.

At the end of the main street is the Old Timers' Mine and above, Coober Pedy's most prominent landmark: the Big Winch. Standing on a little manmade hillock beside it, you can see right out into the 360-degree panorama of lunar rocky plains. Below is a futuristic excavating machine that looks like an abandoned *Star Wars* droid carrier. Yesterday I found a glimmering lump of opal in the dust. Katia insisted I take it to the jeweller, who confirmed it had absolutely no value.

Determined tracks off the main street lead to the rusted garage doors of underground homes. Abandoned mining machinery acts as a substitute for garden furniture. And beyond that is the immutable peach-coloured desert. Coober Pedy is a testament to mankind's stubbornness, a tentative human stain on a callous landscape, a magnet for greedy, unsentimental loners who are prepared to live underground on the off chance they might strike it lucky.

Another group of backpackers discuss the day's guided tour. They visited Crocodile Harry, a legendary Coober Pedy character famed for listing all of his female conquests on the wall of his subterranean nest. They also went fossicking – rummaging for worthless scraps of opal in slagheaps like the desperate noodlers. Tomorrow they're going to the Coober Pedy Opal Fields golf club, dubbed "one of the ten most unique courses in the world". The greens are made of black tarmac and the fairways are flattened stretches of previously mined desert.

We retire to our bunks in a dormitory three floors below the Earth's surface. It is cool, almost chilly, and too cold for a wine cellar. I miss my footing and fall onto some-one's bed. The unseen occupant groans at my disturbance. Katia hisses her disapproval. I can see her head shaking from side to side. Down the room I hear Shane, who's even more pissed than me, miss his bed too.

Once the creaking of my mattress has ceased, there is silence. I gaze at the red streaks in the rock above my head, trying to concentrate on a fixed spot to keep my mind from spinning. There is no decoration here; we are stacked up above each other prisoner-of-war-camp style. But it's cheap.

Someone snores, then silence again, a collective intake of breath. Suddenly I hear an excruciating creak from the surface, a scrapyard sound of metal tearing on metal. A loud clatter follows. Joe is keeping his promise, ripping the Commodore apart limb by limb for what good parts might remain. The desert has claimed another victim.

5

Sacred Sightseeing

Erldunda has made the flourishing fly population its claim to fame. In the roadhouse bar, you can buy stubby holders bearing the message "Erldunda – Centre of the Universe. 10 million flies can't be wrong!"

The community boasts an "ideal location" between Ayers Rock and Alice Springs, a mere 253 kilometres from the former. This is the gateway to the spectacular, world-famous natural landmarks of Australia's red centre: Ayers Rock, known also by its Aboriginal name of Uluru, and the neighbouring Olgas, traditionally called Kata Tjuta.

There is a line of tour minibuses parked outside the roadhouse for a toilet stop *en route* from Alice Springs. An Explorer Tours 4×4 overland truck stops just behind the caravan. The passengers, as young as I was last time I was here, jump out like kids on a school trip, yapping excitably.

"Hey Jeremy," I hear, "look at this, it's absolutely so cool."

A girl looking at a poster in the window of the souvenir shop shouts, "Oh wow, you guys, look at the size of the snakes on this picture. I just can't believe we're going to be camping out there."

Her friend, equally shrill, screeches, "Oh God, I've so got a bad hangover after that drinking game last night." Her voice pitch rises at the end of the sentence, like urbanite Australians. "I'm so not going to drink tonight," she adds. That's the lexicon of the sitcom *Friends*, misappropriating the word "so" in every sentence.

Under its bold red and gold logo, the Explorer Tours truck has its itinerary emblazoned in desert-coloured lettering along the side: Uluru, Olgas, Kings Canyon and the Western MacDonnell Ranges. Standing next to the sturdy truck are two guides. They wear the full bush uniform of long shorts, lightweight boots, matching khaki green bush hats, and the ever-comical mid-calf-length socks, surely a British Empire throwback.

Get-on–get-off tours are now one of the most popular means of seeing the Australian continent. They allow people to have their white-water rafting, diving and bushwalking adventures without having to do any organising themselves. They pick you up from your backpackers' hostel and drop you off when you've had enough. Companies like Explorer Tours have made a fortune and offer packages to suit all budgets. The concept has come a long way since the fledgling backpacker tour prototypes were trundling around in dishevelled minibuses when I was last here.

I'm ready to accept another night in Erldunda after a futile morning. A parked caravan thwarts our efforts at attracting cars by obscuring motorists' view.

A US-style diner with an adjoining saloon awaits us. In the saloon last night were people who would walk unnoticed into a Sergio Leone western film set. One wiry, lopsided guy wore a ten-gallon Stetson and cowboy boots with jangling spurs. He assumed control at the pool table. By the end of my third schooner, I was ready to put a few coins down for a game, but he glared at me territorially. Six other locals squinted at us. Cockroaches crawled around the tiny outdoor swimming pool and then hopped down the corridor to our cheap "backpacker standard" motel room.

Behind the caravan, at a roadside picnic bench, is a woman staring up at a gum tree while drinking from a red mug. I wonder if she's looking over at us too. Chucking the dregs of her drink into the earth, the woman suddenly yells, "Oi! Do you two want a lift?"

We don't hesitate. The Explorer Tours customers stare as we jog over to her car.

"Just squeeze all your stuff in the back somewhere and we'll find a place for you to sit," the woman says. "I've actually brought a flask with me. Can you believe that?"

She laughs as though we should be surprised that she has a flask, as though we would know she's not the flask-owning type. The boot is crammed full of cardboard boxes containing food supplies, camping gear, candles and extra clothing. The woman sees me looking.

"Don't worry about it," she says. "I've got too much bloody food anyway." She squashes her carefully stacked supplies to one side to make room for us.

Before we get in the car, she looks back at the tree, at where she was staring before. "I don't suppose either of you know what that bird is, do you?" she asks. "It was fantastic. I've turned into a right birdwatcher. I can't believe it. Ha."

Katia and our ebullient host, Sonia, chat convivially as soon as the doors are closed. There is no conversational barrier. Sonia talks with an infectious liveliness, peppering every sentence with giggles and exclamations. An impish smile is permanently etched on her face. She must be in her early 30s, perhaps a shade younger. She wears three-quarter-length green combat trousers, red trainers and a baggy mauve cardigan. Her close-cropped blonde-highlighted hair looks uncombed, like she's really determined to not to give a damn while "out bush".

Sonia is from Melbourne, ornithology is her latest fad and she's working as a midwife in Alice Springs hospital. She's there to gain first-hand experience of working with central desert Aborigines. She has five days off. No one else from the hospital could accompany her so, before she called us over, she was going to Uluru alone. I presume Sonia is as glad to have us along as we are to be with her.

"**Y**ou should see the state of them after they cut their genitals," Sonia says.

I wince, but she carries on. She is free of the prudishness that prevents most people from talking about circumcision within an hour of meeting each other. Aussies are disarmingly frank.

Sonia is describing the coming-of-age ritual practised by Aboriginal tribes in central Australia. At puberty, most males are circumcised during their initiation. Often the urethra is incised, the body is striped with scars or a front tooth is knocked out. Sonia claims these painful rites –

euphemistically called "men's business" by Aborigines – take place in inaccessible parts of the Olgas.

She also tells us about ruthless payback punishments inflicted for breaches of tribal law. In some cases, the traditional sentence for causing someone's death by autosuggestion is spearing in the legs. At the hospital in Alice Springs, she says, men still come in with horrific spear and club wounds. The anecdote ends with a gory anatomical depiction of their wounds. This time both Katia and I wince.

"Ah yeah, blood absolutely everywhere, pouring down their legs," Sonia says. "Hey, anyway, we're going to see the Rock, I'm so excited." The title makes it definitive: Australia's – and the Earth's – greatest single-standing lump of stone in the middle of a desert. Explorer Ernest Giles, the first European to see Uluru, described it as "the remarkable pebble".

With each mile that passes, Sonia becomes more excitable. Her fervour is authentic because, like many Australians, she's seen little of her remarkable country before. She marvels at everything as we pass. It heightens the anticipation for Katia and tints the landscape with fresh magic for me.

"Where are you, Rock?" Sonia shouts out, as if addressing a long-lost friend.

At my feet, among various cassettes and discarded fast-food wrappers, is a weighty compendium: *Birds of Australia*. Sonia sees me looking at it.

"Right, you two can keep an eye out for any of the eagles in this book. Hey, can you tell what that one is?" She points to a glowering bird of prey far above. "Do you think it's a wedge-tailed eagle?"

"It could be," Katia says. "Do you 'ave any, what's zer word, binoculars?"

"Nah, you'll have to check the wings with the birds in the book."

This keeps us occupied. It takes me back to my childhood, when I was dragged to wildfowl reserves with my family.

Gazing westwards, the dark clouds that hovered ominously on the horizon last night are building up, in the exact direction we are heading, over the Rock. The ochre shades of the desert are taking on a rich claret hue as the gloom spreads. There are ominous rumblings of thunder. We might see Uluru on one of the exceedingly rare occasions when it actually rains out here.

Katia says, "I can't believe it. I thought it never rains over Ayers Rock."

But Sonia has an optimistic interpretation. "Hey, we'll be really lucky if we can see the Rock in the rain. People have told me the Rock's amazing when it's raining. There are waterfalls down the sides."

Over to the left is a hulking brown flat-topped mesa, incongruous on the flat spinifex prairie.

"Is that it?" Katia asks, with tangible disappointment in her voice.

"You must be joking, dear, that's Mount Connor," Sonia answers.

Mount Connor is Nature's ultimate *doppelganger* con trick. It baffles thousands of people by looking nothing like their mental image of Ayers Rock. Last time I was here, I marvelled at Mount Connor for a full ten minutes, underwhelmed by its muddy colour, until someone made the observation that it was in completely the wrong direction for Uluru.

In tourism terms, Mount Connor is Uluru's poorer cousin. Called Atila by local Aborigines, it is perfectly aligned with Uluru and the Olgas, so one can understand why such sacredness is ascribed to this region. How extraordinary to be suddenly confronted with so many gigantic horizon-grabbing phenomena in the centre of thousands of miles of featureless desert.

We're about to breeze past Mount Connor when Sonia decides to stop at Curtin Springs roadhouse.

While I'm in the authentic roadhouse "dunny", Katia and Sonia inspect a menagerie of emus, camels and kangaroos scowling behind a chicken-wire enclosure. When I leave the unlit cubicle, Sonia is engaging a sinewy cowboy wearing dungarees, a reincarnated Huckleberry Finn, in deep conversation. He tells us he's a cameleer, a hardy outback adventurer, the kind of guy who would know which part of a desiccated wombat is the best to eat. Sonia, apparently guided by a whim at all times, decides we should go for a camel ride, even though the sky is bruised overcoat grey.

I'm on a camel, trying to look like I'm enjoying myself. It doesn't convince Katia for a second. She mocks my hangdog expression whenever I turn over my shoulder to see her. Paul the cameleer is telling us about the baby camel he feeds in his bedroom adjoining the barn-like pub.

"Oh, how cute," yelps Sonia, winking to Katia as she does so. Perhaps she fancies herself as a cameleer's wife.

"Ah yeah," Paul adds casually, "you guys might be amazed to hear that I actually spent eight months trekking from one side of Australia to the other on these beautiful beasts. In fact, it's a little-known fact that there are currently four hundred thousand wild camels roaming the bush, which is more than any other country, more even than in North Africa and the Middle East. What d'ya reckon to that, ay?"

My theory that paid tour guides always assume one is a dumb drongo, to use an Australian phrase, is confirmed.

"Do you want to know the story of camels in Australia?" Paul asks.

"I'd love to," replies Sonia. I keep silent.

Camels have been in Australia since the mid-1800s, when English pastoralist John Ainsworth Horrocks set out from Adelaide on an animal he had had shipped over. His efforts were initially mocked by rivals, but then applauded. Horse trader George Landells later brought twenty camels back from India, funded by the Melbourne Philosophical Society Exploration Committee. It was these beasts that were used by explorers Burke and Wills – Stuart's hapless rivals – on their disastrous journey across Australia. Settlers quickly realised how advantageous camels were. They were procured to carry goods across the bush. Once they had served their purpose, they were set free to live in the wild. Today camel herds compete with kangaroos and dingoes for the desert's insubstantial resources.

Paul's patter is relentless, stuffed with nuggets of colourful Australiana that depend completely for their intrinsic value on whether you enjoy being condescended to. But the dungarees, the torn singlet and the dishevelled suede cabbage-tree hat look too much like props to me. Katia is far less cynical, more polite, and keeps listening.

Most anecdotes begin "Now you blokes probably wouldn't know this..." or "Of course, as any cameleer knows..." and he ends, "...and camel meat is bloody disgusting anyway. I know; I've tasted it."

I ask him where he lived before. "I'm actually from New South Wales, buddy," he replies.

"'Ow long 'ave you been 'ere in Curtin Springs?" Katia asks.

"Too long, too long to even begin to explain. We just haven't got time. Now you might have seen *Crocodile Dundee*. Do you remember the scene in the pub with the dead croc? Well, Curtin Springs is like that heaps of the time." He stares into the embers of the quickening sunset and adds, "Yep, I couldn't live anywhere else now. Most wouldn't like this life, but it's the only one I want."

My camel Satchmo – so called because he blows a lot, like Louis Armstrong whose nickname he has appropriated – stomps languidly through the spinifex dunes, into dips that are so sheltered they could be freshly raked golf-course bunkers, and back up to ridges blitzed by sandstorms in the rising breeze. Horse flies attack the camels' nostrils. The lone edifice of Mount Connor is toffee hued in the failing light.

"Of course, Mount Connor is a feature that the Aborigines are far less bothered about," Paul remarks. "You see, it's widely known that the Aborigines' claims to Ayers Rock are based on the fact that it's more attractive to yous tourists, a bigger mark-up, I guess. I mean, the tribesmen never wanted it before. In fact, I think a lot of the rock paintings have been done since the 1950s, just for you guys to look at. Yep, that's correct, folks."

Paul could never work in the National Park. His crackpot rewriting of history would get him the sack. In the roomy anything-goes real outback he's all right. His "facts" are apocryphal urban myths about Australian history that got jumbled in Chinese whispers up the Stuart Highway.

He asks us to be quiet as we approach the feeding ground of a dangerous camel. It could leap out to attack, he says. Nobody says a word. And there directly in front of us is a camel skeleton, laid out in the sand like a museum piece. Paul looks pleased with the punch line to his shaggy dog story. I picture him setting out on his favourite beast each morning to check the bones haven't blown away during the night.

When we get back to the roadhouse it starts to rain. Large drops splodge loudly on the impermeable bitumen road surface. The clatter on the roof is fierce. Sonia is the consummate host. She talks up the sombre violet-charcoal sky so much that I almost do feel privileged, even though the scene before us bears no resemblance to the shimmering cerulean and crimson vista in the brochures.

"Hey, do you two want to stop to try out some bush tucker?" Sonia asks. She pulls over before we can respond. I can just about see Curtin Springs in the rearview mirror.

"I think that's a bush cucumber plant," she informs us, indicating an ungainly mesh of fibrous plants, webbed shoddily over the red ground. "I've always wondered whether these things actually taste like crap, or if you could actually eat okay from bush tucker."

She talks in a breakneck, giddy rush, stifling vowels, like she's just arrived at a birthday party. A few ripe bush cucumbers hide under flimsy threads of green. Katia is amazed how closely they resemble the real thing she peels and serves with lemony vinaigrette in France. But she insists I taste first.

Sonia slices with a pocket knife. I bite into the vegetable's flesh, and my mouth is filled with the sourest flavour I've ever experienced. There is no compensating aftertaste. I retch, spit out the remains and gasp for water.

"Oh, you poor bastard," Sonia says affectionately, as only Australians can when using the word bastard.

At the sunset look-out point in a near-empty car park directly in front of the Rock we huddle in our raincoats. Torrents of water tumble down the vertical incisions cut into the side of the surprisingly crumbly red stone. These are the parallel grooves known as "luru" to the Loritdja tribe, which gave Uluru its name. The water leaves black soot stains on the saturated sheer face. From this close up, the Rock looks like part of a mountain range rather than a lone oddity, an inselberg.

The colour of this soggy marvel changes with the ferocity of the rain, from brown to mauve to auburn to grey-black and an indeterminate puce. I could be in Yorkshire, debating whether the slate-mine visitor centre might be worth a look. There is actually a chill in the air. My denim jacket is on for the first time in many weeks.

Sonia is jubilant to see the Rock in these conditions. She sets up a tripod to indulge in another one of her hobbies, photography. Meanwhile she busies us with a suitable task. "You'll find a cask of red wine and some plastic glasses in the back. Let's have a drink to celebrate."

Katia finds plastic wine glasses with detachable stems. After just a few hours with Sonia, she's no longer surprised. This is the kind of service I can imagine being advertised by a deluxe tour provider: "We offer a glass of complimentary champagne while you marvel at one of the world's greatest natural monuments." And unasked-for generosity, the kindness of a stranger, is always sweeter.

At the base of the Uluru climb route, with its rope railing, are disconsolate figures in sodden fluorescent jackets. They each walk up to the sign stating that climbing the sandstone dome is disapproved of by the local Anangu Aborigines, an offence to their spiritual ancestors. Above this is another temporary sign: "Climb closed today. Danger: wet surface." Some visitors turn away, baseball cap peaks facing down.

Explorer Tours catch us up too. The bus occupants are sat down, wiping condensation from the windows for a view. On the side of the bus Uluru is terracotta coloured, the background burnished orange. Nobody gets out. Sunset is a damp squib. Explorer Tours have a strict schedule to keep.

In the visitor centre people stroll listlessly past displays describing how closely the Aborigines guard their most sensitive traditions. In photographs, faces of the dead are blacked out because it is taboo to refer to someone deceased. A short film tells how Uluru is at the very fount of creation for the Anangu, an intrinsic part of the life cycle rather than a freak geological occurrence. The narrative is spliced with footage of the 1985 ceremony when

the Northern Territory government handed back ownership to the original inhabitants. It was then leased back to
the National Park for 99 years. There remains festering
resentment from the white authorities over this.

Recently, when the Rock was closed to tourists out of
respect for Anangu elder Tony Tjamiwa, the Northern
Territory's chief minister Denis Burke said, "This is a very
bad decision. It will send shockwaves right through the
tourism market. It needs to be overturned."

On the information desk is a plastic box containing little lumps chipped from the monolith by previous avari-
cious visitors. Attached to each brittle souvenir is a label
explaining which country it has been sent back from.
There are also notes from the senders. Each one, with the
utmost sincerity, explains that since stealing the rock, the
thief has been plagued by ill luck. Formerly dubious
Europeans, white Australians and Americans return
chunks of Uluru to break an ancient curse.

In the morning the sky is poster-paint blue. Sonia shouts
us awake before daybreak to see the sun filter over the
Rock.

"Are you ready for the sunrise?" she asks. "It's going to
be bloody gorgeous."

Her voice is just centimetres away. She slept in a green
swag with a V-shaped roof partially covering her head. A
swag is a traditional rolled-up outback bedroom. The
Aussie anthem *Waltzing Matilda* is about a swagman.
Modern versions contain a foam mattress covered in hard-
wearing canvas.

We reach the recommended sunrise viewing place where breakfast pigments – apricot, orange juice, tomato – are already daubed over the Rock. The renewed richness is amazing. Baggy-eyed spectators jostle for position next to the exact point recommended by a sign for the best light angle at dawn.

Afterwards Sonia cooks us bacon and eggs on a gas barbecue next to a car park. She scours the dishes using her hands and coarse red sand, saying, "This is what the old bush rangers used to do with their billycans." She means it.

From afar, the early hordes struggling up the climb route look like ants. You can see them stooped double, wheezing, attempting a feat they would never dream of back home; yet because there is such pressure to climb Uluru, to validate the "I climbed Ayers Rock" T-shirt, they nearly kill themselves to achieve it. In fact, people do die every year. The gradient is very severe at points and slipping is easy. Uluru is nearly 1,000 feet high and extends nearly one and a half miles into the ground. There might be practical as well as metaphysical reasons for the Aborigines' climbing ban. Still puffing from the hairy descent, the first group down do self-congratulating high-fives.

Sonia, Katia and I agree not to climb. Sonia and I find it morally objectionable; Katia just doesn't like the idea of more treacherous mountaineering. But we do see the Rock and the Olgas from every conceivable angle. My neck aches from staring upwards in wonderment.

With Sonia, it is as though we have been snatched off the road by a fairy godmother. She demands nothing except our company. Our unwritten contract is based on unsaid *karma*. Sonia gives us the opportunity to appreciate everything in the Uluru–Kata Tjuta National Park at our own pace, to tag along, like cheeky kids playing truant and taking a bus into the city.

"Hey, just do as you would if it was only the two of you," she repeats.

"But we don't want to impose on your plans," Katia replies.

Inevitably, Sonia ends the debate by saying, "Look, you two are too bloody polite."

Hiking around Uluru's circumference, we stumble on caves and hollows in which congregating tribal elders took shelter. Dreamtime stories of spears being thrown by mythical giant wallaby-men become more vivid because we have the time to pick out the actual scar in the rock that resembles the characters involved, or the holes their spears allegedly pierced. Eagle-eyed Katia spots incisions that look like human kidneys, perfectly proportioned. We are barely disturbed. The circuit walk is a minority choice.

The Valley of the Winds trail takes us deep inside the Olgas, the curious knobbly cousins of Uluru. I gaze up at the unscaleable walls of Olga Gorge. This valley was once called Bubia by the local tribesman and was a place so sacred that only the elders could enter its precincts. According to anthropologists, most of their ritual chants are now lost.

In front of us are militaristic columns of Japanese tourists lining up for group snaps on a conveniently positioned footbridge. They are on a "Rock and Reef" package deal. One man twirls around maniacally, doing his best to fit the stupendous landscape into the viewfinder of his state-of-the-art digital movie camera.

We only have to walk a short distance to get away from the whirr of camera shutters. As we scramble up a steep, winding natural path, we stumble on something truly cosmic. Wow! This is the kind of panorama that will imprint itself on my memory as a marker from which to measure all others. We emerge at a point between two of the bulbous Olga boulders. Katia gasps in spontaneous awe. Sonia has heard about this view from a friend, but even she is temporarily gob-smacked.

"This is the treat I've been telling you guys about," she shouts.

It is as though meteors have landed intact, or dreamtime dough has been left in balls across the desert. Fired-earth pods ripple over fertile grasslands into the arid beyond. We are in blackest shade, but streaks of golden light filigree the rock. The view is cosmic, like nothing one could ever imagine existing in this arid, fly-blown strip of planet.

"Isn't that just fantastically brilliant though?" Sonia says.

"Wowaaagh," Katia replies.

When we get back down, Sonia has us scanning the leaves of a coolibah tree for ring-necked parakeets while she fills our water bottles from a sheltered creek. We sit on lemon-scented irairia, or kangaroo grass as it is known colloquially. Only we freeloading hitchhikers, Sonia and a retired couple from New Zealand are around for the spinifex pigeons' evensong.

Back on the Lasseter Highway at dusk, Sonia pauses to photograph opportunistic nardoo plants on a dune of scarlet sand with the ruby grapefruit sun in the background. After the rain, the spinifex looks as though it's been touched up by someone with peppermint green aerosol paint. A velvety darkness cloaks the sky. The beam of the headlights makes it appear as though we're in a tunnel.

Yet there is no stillness. Right now, it is feeding time and we're racing along the drive-thru lane at the outback's all-you-can-eat non-stop buffet. Less than ten metres in front, a pack of kangaroos, led by a six-foot Big Red, hop athletically across the bitumen. Sonia skilfully swerves around the trailing legs of the smallest, probably not long out of its mother's pouch. No sooner has she said "Wow, that was close," than an owl swoops gracefully right over the windscreen, momentarily blocking her view. It doesn't stop her continuing our stargazing lesson, which began at the Yulara campground. "Hey, over here these stars are just awesome. The Milky Way is just fantastic, eh. Can you see the Southern Cross that I told you guys all about? Look!"

"Shouldn't we be worried about hitting a kangaroo?" I enquire.

"Nah. What the hell are we going to do about it anyway? They'll just ruin my little car. Who cares?"

Katia nods off in the back, stuck in the kind of sleep that no wild creature will disturb.

"Hey, shall we just carry on?" Sonia asks.

"I thought you were due back at work in the morning."

"Oh, well let's just be crazy. Shall we do that? Do you think Kat-ee-yah will be all right about it? Maybe she wants a proper bed."

That's probably true, I think. But at the same time, I think we've reached a milestone. Katia is as absorbed in the outback adventure as I am. Any chance to carry on this ride has got to be good. So I say yes without rousing my girlfriend, who is now curled up in a foetal position with her blue walking boots still on.

Two days later, foggy from Tooheys lager, Katia and I are in the back seat of a Toyota 4×4 that Sonia has commandeered from a colleague. She wants to take a peek at Palm Valley.

The Aboriginal and Australian national flags flutter in the slightest figment of a breeze on Alice Springs' high point, Anzac Hill. The buffs of the MacDonnell Range foothills that enclose the town shimmer, bathed in overhead midday heat. A russet glow emanates from carbuncled rock faces. On both sides of the road, pointed crests of overhanging cliff faces rise above us.

This is a town that was once named Stuart, in honour of our illustrious predecessor. He came through the MacDonnells for the first time on his fourth major expedition, again sponsored by Chambers. On this occasion he went with two men, Benjamin Head and William Kekwick. For the first time, Stuart's precise instructions were to cross the continent from south to north. The South Australian government was offering a reward of £2,000 to the first person to achieve that feat.

When we reach the dry, white sand bed of the Finke River, Sonia instructs us to collect driftwood for a fire. Our intention is to sleep in a campground in the Finke Gorge National Park, near to Palm Valley. I mention nightfall – worryingly soon – and the sketchy route on my map only hints at how far away the plots might be.

"Don't stress, mister, it'll be great. I'm completely wiped. You can drive."

Downstream, local Aborigines select branches in the blissful cool of evening. The Finke River was Stuart's saving grace too as he and his two companions started suffering severe thirst. As on so many other occasions in the European colonisation of the outback, it was the resources that Aborigines had long treasured that became a lifeline. Stuart called the watercourse a "beautiful creek" and named it after his other patron, William Finke. Pursuing the course of the Finke led his party to the sandstone Chambers Pillar, and then on to the MacDonnells around Alice Springs. These honoured the then South Australian governor Sir Richard MacDonnell. This was the first time white men had encountered the staggering geology of the Red Centre.

The track becomes treacherous soon after we pass the information panel indicating the National Park boundary. The wheels of our hardy 4×4 lose traction as the route shifts to silty white sand. This is what rally driving across Saharan dunes must be like. I endeavour to follow two-foot-deep rivulets cut by previous vehicles, but the chassis swings wildly from side to side. The steering wheel lurches uncontrollably in my hands.

Turning a 180-degree bend, we swoop over a huge boulder and land with a scraping metallic clunk in a deep fissure. Another boulder lies directly in front. I rev the engine. Rocks grind into the suspension. I can see sparks flying off the metal in the side mirror.

Sonia chuckles, "Come on. You can do it."

Inspired by her confidence, I somehow guide the vehicle over the boulder. In front of us is a twinkling nectarine outback sunset.

For several kilometres we drive in the Finke River itself, deep enough for water to rise over the top of the wheels. Only by sheer fluke do we pick up the track at the other end. I shuffle on at five kilometres an hour. With unanimous relief, we are stunned to see the lights of camper vans and, even more staggeringly this far out in the bush, a toilet block.

The location is breathtaking. I switch the engine off and the sounds of wild central Australia come teeming through the window. To one side of the campground are oblong crimson cliffs topped by lush green vegetation. On these promontories are howling dingoes, serenading the Finke along its torrid course. Between the river and our tent come rustlings of wallabies chomping on fresh vegetation. The dingoes' baying gets louder, as if they are closing in on us.

"They're not dangerous, are they?" Katia asks, not wanting an answer.

"Ah yeah, they can be bloody lethal," Sonia replies.

As the last smoky vestige of daylight dips below the horizon, the walls of the reddened gorges become eerie silhouettes, like outlines of sleeping dreamtime giants. Katia shines a torch on the ground and picks out tiny marsupial mice with long tails. At night they do circus tricks over the domed roof of our tent.

The scuttling mice noises are occasionally drowned out by two redneck blokes camping near us.

"I don't reckon we should rescue foreigners who put themselves in danger in this country," says one.

"Ah mate, come on," his buddy replies. "What about that French sheila that had to be rescued by the Coast Guard? She would have been eaten by the sharks, ay."

"Shit happens. I'm sorry mate, but if people from overseas come to Australia, we shouldn't have to pull them out. It costs heaps. That's a lot of bucks."

The first Europeans to chance upon Palm Valley were amazed at the lush vegetation. They had found a miraculous pocket of greenery. Cycad and red cabbage palms that one would expect to find in the tropical rainforests of Queensland rise out of a gully where only the faintest trickle of a creek flows for most of the year. Scientists believe the vegetation has been preserved since the time of dinosaurs, when central Australia was part of the Gondwanaland landmass. Somehow the valley has remained sealed off from desertification. It is the nearest one will get to a prehistoric lost world paradise.

Once more, our hike with Sonia is unforgettable. Each new angle brings fresh wonderment. At one point I hang precariously over a green lagoon, with my arms wrapped around a slippery buttress of rock. I look up to fossilised shells engrained into the rock, perhaps proof there was once an inland sea. Stuart was just several millennia too late.

We scale a cliff to return along a ridge overlooking the creek. Beyond, the enormity of the dead centre stretches out in uniform redness as far as the eye can see. We are precisely on the fringe of where the isolated forest of eucalypts and palms ends and the sterile bush takes over.

"*Je n'ai jamais vu plus beau que ça*," exclaims Katia. She apologises to Sonia for talking in French and translates her compliment – I've never seen anything so beautiful. "Thanks so much," she adds.

"Will you two stop saying 'thank you'?" Sonia retorts. "You'll do the same for me one day."

She take us to Gosse Bluff, supposedly created by a dreamtime ancestral mother who dropped her newborn child's cradle; Ormiston Gorge, a waterhole idyll where we take a refreshing swim; ochre pits where Aborigines used to come for their paints – too much to note down. Our ride with Sonia has lasted more than a week and taken in more of the spectacular scenery of "Centralia" than even Explorer Tours' most expensive package. I don't think I've ever had a better lift.

And there was me thinking we might have to skip some of the sights for the sake of hitchhiking.

6

Dead Heartache

Morning in Alice Springs: three Aboriginal men lie prostrate on the dewy grass at the bottom end of the Todd Street Mall. Alice's tourist information centre is just opposite. They groan, roll over and shift back under the rotating shade of a ghost gum tree.

In the dried-up, dusty bed of the Todd river, the scene is less reposeful. Here two women let loose anguished, blood-curdling screams. One shakes a cardboard white-wine carton, as though to check there's nothing left in it. There are groups squatted in the sand the whole way down the river. The Todd, which floods only once every ten years, is the favoured meeting place for many uprooted indigenous people at night.

The walls of Scotty's Bar are covered by pictures of Alice Springs' white founders and its table mats decorated by eulogies to the same men. A long queue winds around the block behind the mall's main drive-thru bottle shop. The black people queuing speak little. Some clutch social security cheques, others count change. They have at least another hour to wait before the first cartons of wine can be distributed from the hangar-like serving area. One guy strays off course into the adjoining supermarket, and is swiftly chased back outside by a security guard holding a truncheon. A police van with a wire cage on the back, known as a hell hole, cruises past.

A large Aboriginal woman, still cradling her bottle of spirits, kicks up a fuss in a fried chicken takeaway. The owner waves her companions off his doorway with a tea towel. When the police arrive, they make for the drunken woman straight away. I watch them hoist her up by the arms and legs, as she writhes in feeble protest. They almost throw her into the hell hole. As they scoop her friend off the pavement, she slurs, "We only wanted some bloody chicken, you bastards."

Outside a restaurant selling kangaroo steaks and damper bread for tourists, an elderly Aborigine so covered in dust he looks like he's just emerged from a quarry tries to sell us some of his dreaming paintings.

"This one called 'Bush Tucker'," he says.

"And zis one?" Katia enquires, pointing to another abstract oil work in his portfolio.

"This one the dingo dreaming."

The proprietor of an authenticated Aboriginal art establishment looks on from the other side of the street. Caucasian Alice Springs makes plentiful profits from the canvases of Aboriginal artists. The colourful dot designs have become an idiosyncratic symbol of Australia across the world. Factory spray-painted versions of this unique representative art adorn souvenir didgeridoos, mouse mats and tea towels. But the original paintings are complex metaphysical maps, showing the routes of the dreamtime beings. Different symbols represent animals or birds.

Concentric circles depict dreaming sites, or where the ancestors paused. These designs once formed the centre-pieces of dances and songs. Strict rules govern which dreamings an artist cannot draw; it is taboo to sketch out the dreaming of one's own paternal totem.

The town's most famous Aboriginal artist was actually a watercolour landscape painter named Albert Namatjira. Namatjira sold his first collection of paintings in 1937. He became accepted by white Australians and was even given the Coronation Medal by the Queen. But in Alice Springs he remained only an Abo. So much so that he was refused permission to build a house with his earnings. Even though he had remained a teetotaller for most of his life, he started to drink. This resulted in a night in jail, as it was then illegal for Aborigines to consume alcohol.

In 1957, following a campaign by his supporters in Sydney and Melbourne, Namatjira became the first Aborigine to be granted Australian citizenship. Among his entitlements was the right to purchase booze.

His downfall spiralled from a lethal cocktail of grog and his disabling influential position in Hermannsburg, his home community. In keeping with tradition, he shared his newfound wealth. Personal property was an entirely unheard-of concept to Aborigines. Thus in 1958, in a brawl in which a woman was killed by her husband, people believed Namatjira was responsible because it was through his citizenship that liquor had entered the community. He was charged with supplying alcohol and sentenced to six months' labour. He served two months in the government prison at Papunya. Shortly after his release in 1959, he died of a heart attack.

We enter the railway station for shade. After a few minutes an Aboriginal man wanders over, steady on his feet and smiling, and requests a light for his cigarette. He asks where we're going, how we like Alice Springs, where we come from; polite conversation people have on railway platforms the world over. The platform ticket inspector rushes over.

"Get out, go on. I bloody told you twice already. Move it."

He bundles the unassuming man out of the front door. The Aborigine makes no protest.

"I hope that coon wasn't bothering you fellas," he says to us. "You shouldn't let them talk to you."

Come nightfall, a doctor sprints out the front entrance of the hospital maternity unit hunting for a patient. Apparently this is an all-too-common predicament. She suffers from diabetes and anaemia and urgently needs tests for associated antenatal complications, but has just disappeared, gone walkabout. Luckily, she only reaches the car park.

"You'll never get well if you keep walking out in the middle of your treatment," the doctor upbraids her. "If you keep doing that you'll die. You're too young for that."

In front of the hospital an Aboriginal man clutches his newborn child, a gleam of pride in his reddened eyes. He shies away when Katia compliments him on his adorable baby.

On the Stuart Highway, nine people squat by their jack-knifed station wagon, still a hundred kilometres short of Alice. A cask of cheap wine is being shared around. The engine is mangled. Nearby, another car has been abandoned to rust at the place where it broke down, like old furniture tipped into a hedgerow. Decaying vehicles left where they conked out are a common sight outside Aboriginal communities. The dad waves frantically at oncoming traffic, but people only veer out of his way. He might as well find somewhere soft to sleep.

We walk to a spot more than five kilometres out of town by half past seven. The self-induced heat of exercise evaporates; it's still chilly. Alice Springs can have crisp nights. Dew drops splatter down the side of lancewood plants. The kangaroos that thrive out here must be shivering as they complete their nocturnal grazing. My shorts are inappropriate, very Englishman abroad. I do star jumps in anticipation of a benevolent sunrise.

Opposite us is a roadside rest stop where a trucker has parked. There is no sign of him in the cab, so I guess he's taking a smoko.

I would mark this place down as perfect if I were composing a hitchhiking textbook. Our vantage point is at the summit of a slow incline sloping up from the town fringes, affording us plenty of time to analyse oncoming vehicles. Another beneficial factor is the Stuart Highway's unerring straightness. Three cars come past, all full. It's foolish to wish for something: the opposite will invariably happen.

Katia says, "I'd like to go in a Jagwar." This is one of my favourite mispronunciations of hers, which I will never correct.

There are a substantial collection of suitable contenders who look at us as they would at lions in a safari park. Each time a vehicle approaches, Katia has time to assess it.

"Zis one is a shitty one," she says of a Volkswagen Kombi van trundling slowly up the rise. "I'm not going in zat bloody sing."

Inevitably, this same rattling camper, wheezing uphill at a marathon runner's pace, stops. I have a few seconds to peek at the elderly man and woman occupying the front seats. They are quite the oddest-looking pair I have seen in a camper van since my first visit to Glastonbury Festival in 1990, when all the New Age travellers still got in.

The man behind the wheel wears a pair of oversized black-rimmed spectacles. The dominant feature of his face is a substantial bristly beard, which he tweaks with a forefinger as he looks dead ahead at the road, oblivious to us. He has a substantial gut, cleverly hidden by a carpet-patterned cardigan and baggy brown corduroys.

Straining to see, I notice his female co-pilot has thick tresses of uncombed grey hair. She wears a silver fake fur coat. Her mouth is childishly daubed with pink lipstick. The old lady then steps out of the passenger door and walks right past us, not saying a word. Underneath her coat is a long, flowery summer dress. Her legs are covered by black tights. Over these are thick walking socks and white Adidas trainers.

"You kids can get in," the driver shouts to us without opening the window. "She's just going for a piss behind a bush."

Katia is hesitant, although she shrugs in the way she has learned to as a newly enthused hitchhiker. But when I slide open the rear door, her slight opprobrium turns to disgust. An overwhelming stench of body odour and unwashed animals almost bowls us over. Katia follows me in diffidently with her nose buried in the folds of her poncho.

No sooner have I found a place for my rucksack than two scrawny dogs pounce on us, straining at leads buried under a mound of dirty clothing on the back seat. With the driver's attention still elsewhere, I endeavour to man-handle them into the boot. I manage to push a window ajar too. In doing so I notice there is a third human occupant, a small Aboriginal boy cowering beneath a pile of blankets.

At first just his shaven head sticks over the top of his den. But furtively a pair of brown eyes emerges. His pupils bulge with trepidation. Katia says hello and attempts a few questions. As she does so the little boy retreats. From beneath the duvet shroud, we hear mutterings in an Aboriginal language, with odd English words thrown in. I open my mouth to ask the driver about this little boy, but I am too slow. He starts talking, in an authoritative yet completely manic manner.

This is a no-small-talk kind of ride, picking up on an imaginary dinner-party conversation. No polite pauses or familiarising questions. The driver's words are a formless diatribe, a stream-of-consciousness ramble without a target. He needs an audience – us.

"She has to take a leak quite often, you know," he says. "Ah yeah, we only stopped at the fast-food restaurant in Alice, but she needs to go again. The doc in Adelaide said she's got a bladder problem, but I don't reckon she's crook. That's Mrs Christopher by the way, and I'm Alan."

It has to be one of the craziest opening gambits I've ever heard from someone who's just invited me into their car. Even in no-hang-ups Australia, most people wait awhile before discussing their partner's urinary problems. Added to that is Alan Christopher's strange self-important manner, enunciating every word with the gravitas of a university lecturer. His accent is distinctly Australian, but bears all the hallmarks of someone who has never completely shrugged off the Old Country. From time to time it drifts back to its roots, maybe somewhere between South Yorkshire and the Midlands.

As the monologue on the lack of feasible toilet stops for an infirm wife reaches a natural pause, I jump in with a stock question. "So where do you hail from originally, Alan?"

"I'm from Derby," he replies, manufacturing a passable imitation of his undiluted boyhood accent. "I left there with my family when I was still a kid. One of my first memories is of the big, Wild West steam trains out by the dock as I peered through the quarantine building in Fremantle. That was a hell of a sight for a little boy of my exceptional imagination, I can tell you.

"I still follow Derby County," he continues. "Hopefully they'll manage to avoid relegation this year. It depends on Coventry and Manchester City as far as I can tell. My interest in football only came about as a way of connecting with my father. He was a normal, working-class bloke and I was a kid with an IQ of 140 who wanted to be different. That's how I started watching soccer, you see. I remember seeing Derby playing a team wearing red and white stripes at the Baseball Ground. Now that could be..."

There is another offputting ingredient in this unending soliloquy that makes this feel like a day out with a psychiatric ward – the interjections of Mrs Christopher. Every few seconds, as I'm trying to decipher her husband's latest tangent, she mumbles something utterly indistinct. She provides unscripted, off-stage asides to his patter. But he ignores her completely, doesn't seem even mildly rattled.

Frequently, in the midst of one of her strange slurs, Mrs Christopher just falls asleep, perhaps from narcolepsy. Her chin sags down towards her skinny chest and saliva dribbles out of her mouth like a baby. Without warning, her head shoots up abruptly and she picks up where she left off.

Alan's descriptions move into another subject area entirely – washing machines.

"The beauty of that particular machine we had when we were living in Gawler, South Australia, was that the man-u-fact-ur-ers keep every part for every model they produced," he informs us. "Now I reckon there's definitely something to be said for that in these days of disposable white goods."

When he says a polysyllabic word he's particularly proud of, he pronounces every syllable separately. The phonetic lecturing manner grates.

Katia gives up listening and is engaged in a tussle of peek-a-boo with the little boy, who is named Virgil. His top front teeth are missing.

My role is to say yes whenever Mrs Christopher falls asleep. Alan requires no other encouragement. So preoccupied is he with his one-man dialogue that the vehicle trundles along agonisingly slowly. The speedometer drops below sixty kilometres per hour.

"This is a bonzer vehicle in desert conditions so long as I don't push it too hard," Alan says, apropos of nothing I've asked. "In many ways it is an ideal vehicle for travel through the Australian bush."

I'm grateful when the impulsive demands of Mrs Christopher's bladder prompt a pause at Ti Tree, a tiny settlement composed of little more than a roadhouse, a pub and a series of heavily irrigated melon farms that border the highway. The original Tea Tree Station grew up on the back of the Overland Telegraph Line, after a profound well of sweet water was discovered in the area.

One by one, we totter from the van. Only now can we see that Virgil has been kitted out in far superior clothing to most Aboriginal children. He wears new trainers.

When we stumble inside the roadhouse, he becomes an excited little boy. Katia accompanies him to the gambling machines. He just stares without putting in a cent, mesmerised by the flashing lights.

Alan collars a man behind the cash register and starts talking about comings and goings in Ti Tree. I hear him say, "You might remember me." But there is no reply. He talks on regardless.

Two stockmen gobbling down steak sandwiches at a wobbly plastic table watch us with confused stares. I ask Alan if we can buy him something to eat. The roadhouse owner looks grateful for the interruption.

"Have we got the little fella?" Alan asks, as if he's just remembered him.

Virgil chooses a plate of chips, chocolate milk and a packet of bubble gum. As each item arrives at the table, he stares in wonderment. Katia has to open the drink for him. Neither Alan nor his wife does anything. Virgil looks lost. No sooner has he put the drink carton to his mouth than he spills the chocolate milk down the front of his T-shirt. The chips prove even more trying. He patiently saws each one into smaller morsels, like an expert carpenter.

Belatedly, this seems like a good time to ask, "By the way Alan, where are you travelling to with Virgil?"

"Virgil's from a place by the name of Ali Curang, a few hundred kilometres short of Tennant Creek itself," he tells me.

The explanation for their journey is complex. Nine-year-old Virgil is the latest in a long line of Ali Curang children to return to his ancestral homeland after sampling an education in Adelaide. Alan, a retired teacher, is a zealous vigilante who runs his own entirely unofficial scholarship scheme for Aboriginal children. Having previously worked at Aboriginal schools in Arnhem Land and Tennant Creek, he devotes himself to escorting promising youngsters down to Adelaide for a year's trial in one of the city's best schools, acting as guardian during their time there.

"I worked in Tennant Creek area for years," he explains. "I know a tree-mend-ous number of people in this vic-in-it-y. I was also a major figure in the, ah, ed-u-cay-shon of a lot of the more remote communities in Arnhem Land. This was after the Northern Territory education board asked me to stop teaching 13 years ago."

S hortly after Ti Tree we pass a mountain discovered by Stuart. Central Mount Stuart is the approximate geographical centre of Australia. When Stuart and his companion Kekwick ascended the highpoint, they named it Mount Sturt after his original mentor. But like so many other places along the Track, it's Stuart influence that endures. In his log, Stuart wrote, "Today I find from my observation of the 0 LL 111 degree 00′ 30″ that I am now camped in the centre of Australia." He never was one for gushing about his own achievements.

Stuart and Kekwick wrote a message on paper, placed it in a bottle and buried it within a cone of stones at the summit. To this day, the people of Ti Tree have struggled to find the cairn.

A plaque at the side of the Stuart Highway commemorates the first European sighting of the mountain. It reads: "John McDouall Stuart and William Kekwick ascended and named Mount Sturt on 23 April 1860. Later the name Mount Sturt was changed to Central Mount Stuart in honour of the explorer."

We turn down the corrugated dirt road to Ali Curang, which has no signpost. The back of the vehicle clatters against the bumps. Alan, regardless, maintains his highway speed. Before it was plodding, now it's spine shattering.

Virgil's face is elated for the first time. He gabbles and points to what must be significant landmarks. Perhaps for him the bloodwood tree dipping into a dried-up creek on our left has the poignancy of Big Ben for a Londoner.

A sign declares that Ali Curang is a grog-free reserve. Normally, we would need a state government permit to enter.

Talking over the vibrations, Alan rhapsodises about the Walpiri friends he knew in Tennant Creek. I hear only snippets.

"They're all dog dreaming," he says. "Dog dreaming starts around here and goes right up into Arnhem Land. That reminds me of when I was cut off up there during the

Wet. That's when I really learned about what is called the dreamtime..."

"So she said, 'I don't know whether we should go out at all.' And I told her, 'Well..."

"...now the cleverest blackfella I knew was a bloke by the name of Cheera. He would play the whitefellas at their own game when they wanted a piece of land of no value to the Walpiri. He would concoct a story about a patch of bush that the tribe didn't care about and made the government agencies pay heaps for it. Fair go, I reckon. One of the old girls told me how they got visited by an an-throp-ol-o-gist. They invented bullshit tales. Blackfellas don't tell us the really private stuff. But to keep the tucker coming, there's got to be stories."

What I presume is a thick grey heat haze smudges the horizon in front of us. The sun fizzles out. I realise we've properly arrived when Alan executes a screeching hand-brake stop. A cloud of red sand drifts across the land to announce our presence. And just in case the residents didn't hear us enter, Alan sounds the horn.

"Your boy's done good down there," Alan tells Virgil's dad.

Virgil's father bows his head sheepishly towards the litter-strewn earth. He looks uncomfortable with the whole village listening in. He wears a red baseball cap perched awkwardly on an afro of frizzy, shoulder-length hair. He is barefoot, with a shredded black singlet barely covering his beer-barrel chest.

The boy's mother ambles languidly from a decrepit iron-sheet shack – presumably her home since her seminomadic family were forcibly relocated by missionaries to government reserves many years ago. Her legs are matchstick-thin, covered in the symptomatic blotches of malnutrition and anaemia. Alan goes on regardless.

"Now this is a letter from the headmistress," he continues. "She says, 'Virgil is doing extremely well in the special needs department. He has been a model pupil and is well liked by both pupils and staff. We would like him to continue his education here in Adelaide, with your permission.' So what do you fellas reckon? You should be proud."

There is no answer from Virgil's parents. They have not seen their son for over a year. Apart from offering him a brief show of affection on our arrival there was no visible emotion. They only revealed fleeting joy when Virgil handed over a McDonald's Happy Meal, which he secreted under his blanket throughout the long drive from Alice Springs.

Ever since white pioneers first traversed the sandhills of the Tanami desert on Afghan camels, "welfare patrols" have escorted Virgil's descendants, the Walpiri, out of their clan territory. They were herded into missionary camps before the creation, in 1954, of Ali Curang, named after a billabong associated with dreamtime dingoes. Dependent on white man's food, weakened by alcohol and imported diseases like tuberculosis, the Walpiri were marooned, unhappily cohabiting with the Alyawarra, an entirely separate nation with its own language on whose traditional land the reserve is situated. The Walpiri's own sacred sites are days away.

Today the community is held up as a perfect example of self-sufficient land ownership. It is officially alcohol free. A local Aboriginal council administers its affairs. On paper, with a youth centre, domestic violence unit and independent night patrol, all is harmonious in Ali Curang. But the reality is starkly different.

At the entrance is a futile park that contains a bench with no seat. Clods of turf dry out, unplanted. The community is circular, arranged around a square of bone-dry scrub with a set of twisted goalposts at either end. Settees lie rotting under shrivelled trees. We can hear the bass thump of hip-hop music emanating from a wooden building across the community.

Still unable to elicit a response, Alan starts filling bin bags with rusty cans and discarded food packaging, chucked on the ground outside the prefabricated homes. There are bins, but they appear unused. People lounge in the shade of their creaking verandas. Some rise slowly and lurch like daylight zombies towards us.

The gathering consists mainly of barefoot women in badly fitting flower-print dresses. Katia tries to engage some of them in conversation. They put their hands over their mouths and mumble like nervous children. I ask a man in a black Adidas tracksuit top with a station hand's mullet haircut where the other men are.

"Most of our mob is out hunting during the day," he replies casually, eyes fixed to the ground.

"I suppose they'll be looking for kangaroos?" I respond, thinking of it like a recreational outing, like fox hunting in Britain.

"No mate," he replies with a hoarse whisper, "it's goannas they're after. They've gone out with spears on the back of a ute. That's why they're burning the spinifex: it makes the little bastards come out of the bush."

So the caustic, foggy pall that surrounds us is not due to the scorching heat, but to Walpiri people torching the tinder-dry bush.

Virgil runs off, clutching his blanket. He looks thrilled. Meanwhile Alan and his wife talk animatedly with the locals while distributing gifts of junk food. There is a lot of affectionate touching of arms. They lived here for nearly ten years.

"Ah yeah, well you blokes can make up your minds while I'm in Tennant," Alan instructs Virgil's parents, evidently not dismayed by their apathy. Bent double, he resignedly reiterates, "Virgil could do good for your mob. He could stay at the whitefellas' school."

But without answering, Virgil's mum and dad just amble back to their home to eat the Happy Meal.

Ali Curang has its own primary school, where Virgil's friends are. From there, a minority go on to the blacks-only Yirrara College in Alice Springs. The syllabus includes courses on "learning to live in a house" and "learning the European".

I ask the tracksuit man if he thinks Virgil will go back to Adelaide. "I don't reckon, mate," he says.

He tells me some families have left Ali Curang to establish a remote camp further into the bush, into Australia's dead heart. After two generations of involuntary white civilisation, some Walpiri are retreating. Virgil's father intends to join them, he says, probably before his son's ritual initiation corroboree.

Before we leave, Alan enquires after one of his former protégés. This woman, Esme, spent 10 years working for the civil service in Adelaide following the successful completion of a university degree under Alan's supervision – before inexplicably going walkabout.

"Do any of you blokes know where I might find old Esme when I get to Tennant?" he asks.

The man in the tracksuit top again acts as spokesman. "Most mornings you can find her in front of the VB bottle shop or in the gutter nearby."

Half an hour later, we're skidding around the perimeter track, behind the white man's house with its picket fence and flowerbeds. Alan points out the primary school.

The journey grinds even more agonisingly afterwards. Alan's scattergun stories crash into one another at a frenzied tempo. There is another toilet stop at Wycliffe Well roadhouse, which boasts the most UFO sightings in the southern hemisphere. Sci-fi buffs stay in the adjoining campground. The bar is decked out in luminous prints of aliens.

Soon after, the Devil's Marbles roll by in a blur on the right-hand side of the road. These are giant, spherical red granite boulders perched one on top of the other, jettisoned in a solitary valley. According to geologists, these formations were once part of the same rock 1,700 million years ago. They were split into pieces by wind and water erosion. The Aboriginal explanation is that the dreamtime rainbow serpent deposited them.

We are sidetracked by another Aboriginal settlement off the highway: McLaren Vale. Here Alan stops a teenage lad and, inexplicably, puts on a phoney Aboriginal voice.

"You remember me?" he asks. The kid shakes his head. "Who's your mob? This is a nice community you got here, very good. You got whitefella here, eh. No bumma."

Bumma, he explains, is an Aboriginal slang expression for alcohol.

Fumes of smouldering stubble still pervade the sky when we reach the outer limits of Tennant Creek, smudging the sunset through an auburn filter.

"Would you be able to drop us at the caravan park?" I ask Alan. I think he hears me, but he's talking about Goole, Humberside, for a reason I can't remember. "Now that has to be one of the dullest places in the UK, I guess. Do you know what I had to eat in Goole? Well..."

He lets us out, and when we turn to wave, after picking our bags off the floor, he is already hurtling off in search of Esme and a new kid to replace Virgil for the return journey to Adelaide.

Tennant Creek is abuzz. A man with wraparound shades and a black Harley Davidson T-shirt with the sleeves cut off stands before us at the caravan park reception. He sports a black baseball cap, out of which flows a bleach-streaked mane of hair.

"You're here for the weekend. Good on ya," the receptionist says to him.

When he turns around I see the legend "Tennant Creek Outback Car and Bike Show" written on his cap.

In town there are hundreds of clones of this same bloke, all with mullet haircuts and clutching mid-eighties rock-chick girlfriends.

We follow the ZZ Top lookalikes to a pub in which the festival's opening ceremony is taking place. The entertainments happen in a sectioned-off area of orange sand, optimistically referred to as the garden. Through gaps in a whitewashed fence we spot local Aborigines, who out-number Tennant Creek's white population three to one. Some dejectedly walk up to the burly, goatee-bearded bouncer.

"Sorry mate," he says to one. "Yous fellas can't come in. Yous'll have to get your grog some place else."

All the men serving stubbies from a makeshift bar in a caravan wear event T-shirts. I purchase an Outback Car and Bike Show stubby holder. We sit on plastic garden chairs. Occasionally the boundless twinkle of the night sky is broken by green and pink disco lighting. Little kids dance in dizzy circles.

The music is provided by a band, all of whose members have mullets, playing Jimmy Barnes cover versions. Jimmy Barnes has been one of Australia's most popular solo artists since 1984, but is little known in the rest of the world. He sings chest-thumping anthems so fervently that he is dubbed "Jimmy the Screamer" by fans. Between every song, the band reminds the audience of the upcoming wet T-shirt contest, which wins howls of approval from blokes and their sheilas.

In the morning an unceasing engine roar tolls like a church bell, drawing people into town. Outside the shady bower of our tent pitch, it's so hot I feel my skin might melt.

The go-kart race is already in its concluding laps when we arrive. Competitors have come from across the Northern Territory, the announcer reveals. They parade their customised, V8-engined vehicles around the grubby circuit. One of the barmaids from the pub last night presents the medals. Each long-haired victor attempts a quick grope, to hysterical whoops, on the podium. Looking around from our perch in the hastily constructed grandstand, Katia remarks there are more marshals than competitors.

A man next to us, clutching a huge hot dog and a Tooheys stubby, says, "These blokes are fucking legends, ay. They've come right up through the guts of the country on those bloody machines." He notices something untoward between mouthfuls. "Stone the crows, the whingeing blacks are here again."

A thirty-strong band of Hell's Angels ride past on Harley Davidsons in a show of intimidating machismo. One biker parks by the judges. The others switch off their engines. Seconds later, after a wave of the chequered flag, the biker puts his foot down on the accelerator pedal but doesn't turn the throttle. A choking pall of toxic exhaust fumes billows out behind his motionless Harley. This carries on for two minutes. When he stops, a generous ripple of applause goes around. Mullet men scratch their goatees in sincere appreciation of this display of polluting strength. Another biker comes forward to do the same thing.

On the snooker-table-green central reservation of Tennant Creek's proudly irrigated main street, ten local Aborigines are gathered in the shade of an acacia tree. Its benevolent foliage must be a magnet. They lie in various states of indolence, passing around cartons of blended white wine. Compared to the Angels, they look as threatening as a teddy bears' picnic.

7

Croc Monsieur

Stuart's expedition party made it well north of Tennant Creek after they built their cairn on Central Mount Stuart. They got to within 800 kilometres of the sought-after north coast, travelling for over two months before reaching a point from which they had to turn back. On 26 June 1860, Stuart, Kekwick and Head were attacked by local Warramunga men. Stuart's journal entry records, "Suddenly from behind some scrub which we had just entered, up started three tall powerful fellows fully armed, having a number of boomerangs, waddies and spears."

Stuart testified how he made "every sign of friendship", but this was greeted by defiance. Soon there were more than thirty men surrounding them, he wrote. When Stuart turned his horse around to show his willingness to back off, boomerangs were thrown and the grass was set on fire. "Having now approached within forty yards of us," he wrote, "they made another charge and threw their boomerangs which came whistling and whizzing past our ears, one of them striking my horse." This was sufficient provocation for Stuart to give the order to fire, which he had so far avoided doing. He neglects to mention whether this was with guns pointed in the air or at the Aborigines themselves.

Although no casualties were suffered in the ambush, the stand-off showed no signs of dissipating. The tribesmen were trying to cut the three men off from their horses. Stuart, who was always prudent in his planning, added, "I have most reluctantly come to the determination to abandon the attempt to make the Gulf of Carpenteria. Situated as I now am, it would be most imprudent. In the first place, my party is far too small to cope with such wily, determined natives as those we have just encountered."

Today there is a memorial to this clash at a place called Attack Creek. The memorial is not necessarily at the exact point where the attack happened, but it's in the general vicinity. Essentially, it's a road stop, a memorial layby. There are a few picnic tables and a plaque that comments on the events. The monument serves as a reminder that Australia never was the *terra nullis* – empty land – that the explorers' backers in Adelaide and Melbourne assumed and wanted it to be. Such encounters must have been commonplace, and most pioneers were probably far less circumspect in their treatment of the native population than Stuart. It also reminds us of the dangers he put himself up against to achieve his dream.

By contrast, our journey couldn't be going more smoothly, even though people around here insistently advise us against hitchhiking because of one recent infamous crime that has left a lingering stain. The alarm is prompted by a single incident that made headlines around the world: the disappearance, and assumed murder, of British backpacker Peter Falconio.

Like me, Falconio was a Pom travelling around Australia with his girlfriend. And he too was in the outback, too far from anything to call for help. The crucial difference was this: he wasn't even hitchhiking. Falconio and his girlfriend Joanne Lees sensibly bought a camper van for their journey. They were far less foolhardy. That's why people think we're just wilfully stupid. We passed through Barrow Creek, the nearest town to where it happened, several days ago.

Peter, 28, and Joanne, 27, were flagged down by a motorist on a remote part of the Stuart Highway. Detectives reported that he duped them into stopping by driving alongside and gesturing there was a problem with their exhaust.

When Peter stopped, he walked around the back of the camper van to talk with the stranger. Then, at her boyfriend's request, Joanne moved into the driver's seat to rev the engine. According to her account, Peter was shot in the head at point-blank range seconds later, almost immediately on returning to the rear of the van to examine the allegedly faulty exhaust. She heard the crack of the weapon from the front seat.

As Joanne cowered in the cab of their vehicle, the ute driver came round and pushed her back into the van's passenger seat. There was a violent struggle while he tied her hands behind her back with cables. He hit her on the right side of her head. Newspaper reports state that Joanne resisted until the moment the killer put a silver handgun to her face. He then forced a sack over her head and tied it.

As she was marched towards the attacker's four-wheel-drive ute, Joanne screamed, "What do you want? Is it the money? Are you going to rape me?"

"Shut up and you won't get shot," the gunman snarled. She was then bundled into the back of the truck.

The amazing part of the story is that Joanne, a former travel agent, managed to evade her captor by sliding out of the back of his van. She squeezed the door open and ran for cover in the prairie of acacia, mulga and mallee that cloaks the Territory. She also twisted free of the binds around her wrists. For hours, she shook in fear as her assailant hunted her down. Several times he passed within a few feet of her.

Having presumably convinced himself he would not find the girl, the man gave up his search and left the scene. Joanne eventually mustered the courage to struggle to the highway and attract an oncoming vehicle for help. She never saw Peter again. His body is yet to be found.

In December 2005 mechanic Bradley John Murdoch was convicted of the killing at a court in Darwin. Murdoch, 47, who was said to be a loner who ran truckloads of guns and drugs around the outback, was jailed for life.

After the first detailed accounts of the episode hit the newsstands, Katia asked me if we should still hitchhike. Peter and Joanne's route was similar to what I had in mind.

"Of course," I insisted, "this doesn't change anything. All it proves that people are just as vulnerable when they buy their own car as when they hitchhike."

"Hmm, I'm not too sure," she said.

"So what will we do?" I said.

"We'll see when we get zere."

Now, leaning back on the comfy back seat of a silver Holden saloon, I'm confident Katia has forgotten all about the incident. I haven't asked her. My memory was only jogged by the sign for Barrow Creek that we passed in Alan's camper van. There is plentiful leg room and the welcome hiss of air conditioning in our current ride, which extinguishes all nagging doubts.

From time to time the driver's foot slips off the pedals. He has a lit cigarette in his mouth, glued to his lower lip. His clothes are tiny blue shorts, the kind a long-distance runner wears, and a sullied white T-shirt that has seen better days.

"Sorry if it's a mess," the driver Steve says. "We got up in the middle of the night to look at the Devil's Marbles out in the desert. We've driven from Barkly Homestead already today, which is heaps of kays." A kilometre is often abbreviated to the single letter *k* by Aussies.

"Don't mind if we're quiet, we're just bloody tired," he continues. "I guess we'll stop for some tucker later if that's okay with you blokes?"

His girlfriend Christine is upset after leaving her valuables at the Barkly Homestead motel that morning. Steve puts his foot to the floor. The speedometer never dips afterwards. He clicks on the stereo and, just before turning the volume up high, asks, "Do you like Neil Diamond?"

During Side One, we traverse one of Australia's natural blurred borders. Khaki green replaces burnished red as the dominant scenic colour. We cross the frontier line that demarcates subtropical and arid desert on maps. Land here shows signs of the recent wet season: sporadic dense thickets of fresh eucalypt saplings, knee-high native grass trees and distant brimming billabongs. Plucky tributaries from the Gulf of Carpenteria might forge a fruitless route down here, through the Barkly Tablelands. The horizon closes in. Side Two of the cassette starts up, beginning with *Song Sung Blue*.

"We bought this when we started our trip, ay," Steve says. "I didn't know Neil Diamond before, but I reckon he's awesome."

Steve and Christine intend to start a new life in Western Australia, somewhere near Broome. Their trip is open-ended. They might be back where they started – Noosa, near Brisbane – in a few weeks. So far, they've stopped in outback stations and fruit farms where 34-year-old Steve used to work.

Christine has never left the east coast before. She is wearing full make-up. She spends a lot of time staring out of the window, saying, "There's just nothing out there."

At Elliott, named after the Second World War captain who established a camp here, we all pile out. We sit around a Formica table looking at the roadhouse menu written on a plastic board above the bar. Most selections consist of fried meat.

"I'll have a double steak sandwich," Steve commands, "with extra bacon and no bloody beetroot."

Katia asks Steve what he used to do.

"I was working as a photocopier technician in Noosa," he says, momentarily downcast as if making an admission, "but that job was too much like hard yakka, ay."

Katia nods, having had "yakka" defined as work.

"One day I quit and thought I'd try running a back-packers' hostel. A mate told me it was quick bucks for doing nothing. No dramas, I thought. First few months, I was just cleaning for food and a bed. Next thing I know, I'm driving the bus and earning three hundred bucks a week."

The steak sandwiches arrive, thick rump fillets for a couple of dollars each.

Between mouthfuls, Steve explains that after discovering the rich pickings of the backpacking business he started his own hostel. He convinced a Noosa motel owner he could fill a room at least three nights a week with eight cheap beds instead of two empty ones.

"First the motel bloke just gave me the one room, but they just kept coming, ay. Then he let me take over the whole place," Steve boasts, wiping the smear of grease on his lips with the back of his hand rather than a paper serviette.

"Christine couldn't believe how easy it was, could you, darling?" he asks her rhetorically. "When I left her place in the morning in my shorts and T-shirt, she asked me, 'Aren't you getting changed for work?' I said, 'This is my uniform.' I reckon she thought I was a dingbat until then, ay!"

In the parking bay outside, passengers alight from a McCaffertys Alice Springs to Darwin bus. Some do leg stretches for their contorted muscles.

"I used to put sixty bucks in my pocket every time I sold a tour," Steve adds. "No tax. They came to the reception and I'd tell them I bet I knew where they were going. I was right every time."

"We'd always get backpackers to do the cleaning for accommodation," Christine interjects. "Every Sunday we arranged a hostel barbie. I think we charged five bucks for heaps of salad and a couple of snags. We were running amok, ay."

Long after leaving Elliott, Steve realises he's left his expensive tinted shades on a petrol pump at the road-house.

"Where's my bloody sunnies?" he cries. "Oh, you're shitting me. I fucking left them. Those were my best sunnies."

He threatens to chuck a U-ey – do a U-turn – but Christine dissuades him. His loss is instantly forgotten as he talks again about his passion for remote Australia. "I spent a lot of time in Western Australia and the Territory. These places just have their own pace. I used to say WA stands for Wait Awhile and NT stands for Not Today. I reckon we'll have some of that over in Broome."

The bush bordering the highway is thicker. Brown three-metre-high termite mounds spike through clearings between gums as far as the eye can see. We're entering the part of Australia where the termite mounds are often higher than trees, a symbol of the soil's fertility. Termite mounds are like icebergs; most of their mass is hidden below the ground. They are magnetic because their tips point towards the north to limit direct sun exposure.

As we cross the rarely full tributaries of Newcastle Creek, I notice a few hardy cycad palms. We pass two men on sit-down mowers heading south, trimming the vegetation to prevent it obstructing the road. Belching grey smoke on both sides of us indicates deliberate land-management bushfires. Under Aborigines' careful control, acres of stubble return to full fecundity after being set aside for a year. Flames lick right up to the side of the highway.

Newcastle Waters was another watermark in Stuart's explorations. Having made it back relatively safely from

Attack Creek – albeit with advanced scurvy that turned his legs black – his achievements were lauded as being equivalent to the discovery of the Nile. In rival Melbourne, however, critics dared to suggest Stuart had actually faked his expedition. The Royal Society's assistant secretary Robert Dickson wrote to Stuart's rival Burke, "His whole trip is still enveloped in impenetrable mystery." Stuart took no heed of this nonsense. Inspired by his previous success, the South Australian Parliament voted to give him £2,500 to lead a far larger and better equipped expedition than ever before.

This time, on 11 January 1861, he left Chambers Creek with twelve men and forty-nine horses. The preparation had been meticulous. He had chosen each man himself. He gave every one a copy of the expedition rules to ensure the venture would run smoothly, without complaints in the ranks. Stuart wrote, "No one is to leave the line of march without my knowledge or that of the officer in charge. No one is to set fire on the natives without orders unless in self-defence. No swearing or improper language shall be allowed." The strictness was such that the Sabbath was always observed even when no shelter was available.

By setting off from the Flinders Ranges at the height of summer, Stuart's party suffered the worst of the drought and heat. The expedition dog Toby died early on. But by May, they had passed the previous northernmost point of Attack Creek. From there on, it was the scrub vegetation that provided the worst obstacle. Men and horses were torn by lancewood and bullwaddie plants. Stuart was about ready to concede defeat when they came upon the chain of waterholes at Newcastle Waters.

But the salvation was only temporary. Travelling from there, the bush became hostile again. The physical exertion required of the party leader in the daily search for water contributed to an even worse deterioration in his already fragile health. With no viable route through, Stuart had to return to Adelaide, unfulfilled once more.

Thanks to Steve's lively speed, we cover 550 kilometres in less than five hours, that's with the steak sandwich stop. At the turning for Mataranka thermal springs Steve decides we should all go for a swim. He espouses his philosophy again. "Mate, it's no dramas. If we don't find work, then shit happens. The way I see it, money's just for spending. Like when we set out on this trip, I treated Christine to three nights on Hamilton Island in a bloody five-star hotel. The night after, we spread our swags out and slept on the beach."

Mataranka Springs is a natural treat, a thermal pool of fizzy, healing warm water in the rainforest. When you've been burning up the Stuart Highway for hours, nothing could be more dreamily enticing. Most people stop here for a night or two. Soon after lowering ourselves into the 30 °C, mildly sulphurous water, we decide to stay.

We bid goodbye to Steve and Christine after buying a round of Victoria Bitter; "the Old Green Death" Steve calls it because of the green bottle labels.

Sun streams through the glistening palm fronds that encroach on the springs. The springs are actually a tiny clearing in the rainforest, a heated waterhole from a tributary of the Roper river. They've built steps opposite, like a proper swimming pool. A green tree frog hops across the stones in front of us, closely pursued by a dawdling goanna.

Floating on her back in the cyan water, Katia enjoys the rare lull in my ruthless hitchhiking agenda. I think this is more what she had in mind when she thought of Australia.

We get talking to a matronly grandmother from Perth, who warns about the dangers of hitchhiking. She heard about Falconio on the news.

"Now why would a pair of lovely kids like you want to put yourselves at risk?" she admonishes. "There are heaps of ratbags and freaks out there."

"But everyone's been really nice," Katia says. "I like Australian people. I would never 'ave thought of 'itchiking before, but zis one made me do it."

Katia winks at me, and the woman shrugs her shoulders, disappointed.

Men with overhanging bellies sit on a terraced stone island in the water and congratulate each other on being Australian.

"Oh I tell you what, mate," one says. "This is a great country. When you go to little places like Barrow Creek, you can just feel the history. That pub was 140 years old."

"Ah yeah, that's the go," his companion replies.

Mataranka Springs is near Elsey Station, a pilgrimage location for Australians. In the nineteenth century it was the furthest outpost for cattle drovers. It was immortalised in the book *We of the Never Never* by Jeannie Gunn. As I mentioned before, never never stems from the equivocal feelings of outback inhabitants towards the tough environment in which they lived. They've built a replica of the original Elsey homestead here. It was constructed for the film adaptation of Gunn's book in 1981. In the bar, the movie is on constant replay.

At night a husband and wife country and western duo play hackneyed ballads in the Mataranka Homestead resort bar. They sing about the good ole life at their local sheep station, and how the bush gets lonely for a wandering swagman. Outback Australians have absorbed wholesome cowboy-boot-wearing crooners as if they were their own. Our bluegrass-by-numbers entertainers even holler with Texan vowels.

We stride into a cauldron of sticky tropical heat immediately on leaving the shade of the campsite. A procession of caravans and rented Britz campervans go past. Britz vehicles are even more common now we've entered the Top End.

Katia insists we stop for a break in the limited shade of a wilting paperbark tree.

"Zis is just too much walking for me," she says.

"Sorry, I didn't plan this, honest."

"I know," she says, "but zat doesn't stop me saying it."

"Look, we'll get a lift soon," I claim, not even believing it myself.

Both of us become aware of a rotten stink coming from nearby. I look up to see hawks circling impatiently. Crossing the road to where a coffee-coloured termite mound has collapsed into a pile of dust, I pick out three kangaroo carcasses. On one there is still some flesh. The heads, with those lustrous ebony eyes, remain intact.

The only car that does slow down belongs to a Dutch Christian evangelist who was camping next to us in Mataranka. Last night he made pancakes on the best fold-up gas stove I've ever seen. We listened to white gospel singers on a radio station he managed to pick up. His favourite personal parable concerned a visit to the American Midwest for a church conference, where the Lord gave him a sign. "I will go back to the Netherlands and the Lord will decide what he wants me to do," he said.

So when he stops, I assume room will be made in the spirit of Christian goodness. But there is not enough space, he tells us. I inspect the car. He's lying. Perhaps the Holy Ghost is in the back seat.

It takes us two hours to reach the Stuart Highway. No one pulls over, not even the barramundi fishermen returning from a trip to the Roper river with their rods strapped to the roof. All of us are going in the same direction. It's only seven kilometres. Why the hell can't they let us in for even that short journey? I'll never understand it.

We lay our rucksacks on a sward of downy grass and droop to the floor. There is not a wisp of cloud in the sky. Katia looks at me with eyes that say (for the umpteenth time) never again. This is no time for conversation.

Within half an hour we get a ride. The vehicle is a camper van, but significantly not a hired one. Inside are an Irish couple, Gregory and Marie.

"We only left Sydney two weeks ago," Gregory says. "We have about another six weeks to do the loop all the way back."

"And what were you doing in Sydney?" I ask.

"We both got jobs there and we really liked it," he replies. "There were quite a few of our friends over here, so we managed to find a flat in Bondi. To be honest, we didn't really want to leave, but we thought we'd better have a look around."

Marie chips in, "There are just so many Irish and British people in Sydney. And the nightlife is great. When we weren't working, we were down on the beach sleeping off our hangovers. We were in Sydney for, like, ten months altogether. It was like being at home."

They make their camper van journey sound like a tagged-on chore. The distances between places in Australia came as a shock to them. Gregory drops us outside the Coles supermarket in Katherine. Except for a brief toilet stop and petrol refill, they waste no time in hurrying onwards to Darwin. "Apparently the hostels there are buzzing," Marie says.

At the turning for Katherine Gorge, another of the Territory's wonders, we march past a swelling estate of weatherboard bungalows made from plastic slats in a factory. You often see these being moved from one part of Australia to another on the back of massive trucks. They are called dongas.

For half an hour we are entertained by a station hand, apparently blind drunk, who manages to steer an agricultural truck into a ditch. His mates come to dig him out.

A man in a heavily cushioned four-wheel-drive jeep stops. Inside it's like the Antarctic. He's on his way back to Victoria after staying on a cattle station owned by a buddy of his. They fought in the Vietnam War together, he tells us.

It's easy to forget about the scars Vietnam left on Australia in the 1960s and 1970s. In all, 47,000 Aussies served near Saigon. Anzac soldiers were famed for their jungle stealth tactics. Critics say then Prime Minister Robert Menzies exaggerated the threat of communism emerging from South East Asia so he could strengthen the bond with the US. Australia was never asked for assistance, they contend, the war was pointless. Whatever the case, Australia had battle-scarred conscripts, antiwar protests and Agent Orange casualties like the US. But here the war wasn't made into movies.

The driver isn't keen on remembering Vietnam. He only says, "We all went through a terrible thing." His favoured topic is the "darkies".

"Hey, there's a lot of dark people up here in the Northern Territory," he says. "I just couldn't believe it. You hardly ever see any where I am down in Victoria."

He deposits us outside a caravan park and country club. Katia reminds me that we forgot to refill the water bottles as we both try to squeeze into the slither of shade provided by a palm with four leaves.

Eventually, miracle of miracles, a Britz motor home stops. The occupants are from Birmingham, a few miles from where I grew up.

Sian and Rob talk at us in Jerry Springer show staccato. They have been in Australia less than a week – and they know everything. They have everything they need in this little unit, including an unwieldy photographic compendium of Australian wildlife that they brought over from England in their suitcases. They are going to see every single tourist attraction on the list and every animal in the book.

Leaning over to point to particular pages, Sian says, "We've seen most of the animals in this book, but it just doesn't have them all in."

"Wow, you've discovered a new species?"

"Well, we saw some wombats when we went on our first tour, and I'm sure they weren't the same ones as in the book," Rob replies.

Sian's job is to put a tick next to each creature they see. The book is ridden with red pen marks. Amazingly, they've already seen some fauna confined to the temperate forests of Victoria here in the humid north.

Katia asks them what they plan to do after ticking off Katherine Gorge. She's refreshed enough to take the piss; few English people realise when a French woman is undermining them.

"Well, roight," Rob replies in broad Brummy, "we can't decide whether to buy one of these camper van things in one of the backpackers' magazines or whether to get one of those bus tickets with 12,000 kilometres on it."

"I mean," Sian adds, "there's a lot of stops on the bus pass, you know where you can get off it, like, but I just don't know if you'll see absolutely everything, you see."

Both Rob and Sian take it upon themselves to offer us advice on what we should do with our remaining time in Australia. I spy a crate of beers above their little fridge.

"You'll have to do a tour in Kakadu National Park like we did," Sian informs me. "We were worried there might not be many English people on it, but we were lucky because, actually, there were six of us. Oh, it was just such a laugh, weren't it Rob?"

Rob can't resist. "It was really great. The best thing about it was this French bloke who sang stuff like Robbie Williams and Queen every time we reached a lookout point. You could hear him right over the rainforest. It was absolutely hilarious."

Come evening, wallabies gather around our tent. Flying foxes glide between the river gum trees above. The fierce Katherine Gorge rapids gurgle and slosh. Katia stirs dinner on the camping stove, guided by a beam of light from her miner's lamp. It remains blissfully warm – heaven. Then I hear them; Rob and Sian the know-all couple have found us.

"Do you want some bread to give to the wallabies?" Rob asks on his approach. "It's great for photographs. We've already done loads."

He pretends not to see the wooden sign instructing campers not to feed wild animals.

The last time I was in Katherine Gorge National Park, I did a drunken night hike with a bunch of strangers. The gorge is one of those outback places permanently stamped on my mind. Thankfully, it remains a revelation even without unseemly litres of wine. The river dissects an immense high plateau of reddish-grey rock. From the water level, one gets dizzy staring up at the steep walls. Birds of prey hover from precarious eyries and swoop over all-consuming rainforest.

This broad fissure carves through the sandstone for hundreds of kilometres. The part we're in, known as Nitmiluk to the Jawoyn native owners, is where the sheer sides of the ravine are most awe inspiring. Each section of gorge is separated by swirling rapids that run over giant boulders like dam sluice gates.

Most people choose to see Katherine Gorge by scenic flight, guided boat cruise or canoe. The park authorities cater for all, from the money-is-no-object tourist to the shoestring-budget backpacker. You pay less for a sore neck and backache. We go for the latter option; half-day rather than two-day canoe hire obviously. I mean, spending money on transport goes against the grain.

I overhear a tour party leader saying, "All right, you blokes listen carefully. You rarely see crocodiles this far down the river but you've gotta be careful. These are fresh-water crocs – the cuddly ones – but they could still bite your leg off. Some guy saw some yesterday near the start of the second gorge."

We hire a cumbersome plastic two-man canoe from the river bank boathouse. I sit at the front. Our toy-like yellow craft bobs about after we are shoved off a gently shelving beach. We wear red life jackets. Looking around at the other canoeists, it's as if some brightly coloured, badly trained amphibious army is preparing to invade.

Both of us are soaked within minutes of setting off. Our inept paddle strokes are thrashing and out of sequence. It's half an hour before we get any kind of rhythm. The gorge walls sparkle with a strawberry blond tint in the morning sun. Sometimes, we drift into semi-blackness beneath overhanging rock. Water trickles where torrents flow at the height of "the wet" (the local term for the mon-soon season).

At the end of the first gorge, everyone has to get out of their canoe to climb over jagged rocks that lead into the second ravine. Without shoes, the walk is an ordeal. It takes up half an hour of our precious waterborne time.

"Zis isn't fair. Zer people on the boat only 'ave a short walk over sand," Katia points out. "I'll say somesing when we get back."

"There's no point, babe."

"Yes zere is. If you don't speak up..."

An Aussie guy eavesdropping on us says, "Good on ya, darling."

By the time we reach the end of the second gorge, it's time to head back. If we go over four hours, we have to pay double. So when we reach the rapids that separate the first and second gorges, the long walk over rocks is an unappealing prospect.

"The river doesn't look that bad," I say. "We could try canoeing down that."

"If you say so."

"You're not sure."

"If you say it's safe, I'll try it."

At the first set of rapids, which barely break the gloss of the river, we manage to get jammed against a rock. Afterwards, a still pool gives me time to reflect.

"*Tu es sûr que c'est bon?*" Katia asks, gesturing towards the next, more ruffled rapids, querying if it's genuinely safe in French for extra assurance. The water is frothy white, but the descent is hardly steep. A Japanese pairing paddle past, giggling. They sail effortlessly into the next gorge.

"Look, if they can do it, we'll be fine," I conclude.

I tell Katia I will steer from the back, too confidently. After two paddle strokes, we become entwined in the current. I've got no control. We nosedive. The canoe turns around, so our backs are facing the obstacle. I can barely see through the spray.

"Don't worry..." I shout. But before I reach the end of my pathetic reassurance, we capsize. The boat tilts on its side. Katia slides into the water first, I think, then I tumble in.

Everything is very blurred. I've got no idea what's going on. I drift and then panic grips. Where's my girlfriend? Where am I? Where's our stuff? The words of the guide come back to me. "Shit, there are crocodiles here," I realise.

I desperately tread water, straining to scan across the water. Where is she? My arms are flailing. I'm terrified. My shouts turn to fearful gasps. "Oh my God, oh my God, oh my God..."

"*Ici, ici.*"

I spin around. Katia is behind me, latched on to the upside-down canoe. We swim to the opposite bank. I grab a branch and cling on to it, stubbing my toe on a rock in the process.

For a few minutes all I can do is breathe heavily, exhausted with panic. Katia manages to clamber onto the muddy bank. Both of us are speechless. Then she remembers something. "*Aie, merde*, shit."

"What?"

"Where are our sings?"

"Oh shit."

In my relief at reaching the shore – with Katia and without crocs – I forgot completely about the plastic cylinder containing our valuables. Where the hell is it? I scan the water and there is nothing on the surface. We're screwed.

"What are we going to do?" Katia screams. "We're stuck."

I keep searching. When things like this happen I tend to repeat the same idiotic instinctive reaction over and over till I'm satisfied it's fruitless.

Luckily for me, Katia is more logical. She has the good sense to look under the canoe – where the plastic cylinder, our shoes and a bottle of water have all miraculously remained wedged tight.

*S*itting on a flat stone on the precipice above the gorge at dusk, the smouldering forest perspires from evening humidity and stretches far into the northern horizon. Crimson finches flit near us. Far below, the Katherine River sneaks through sandy orange valley walls. At this distance, it looks as calm as a boating lake. The vantage point belies its hazardous ebbing currents. I can hardly believe it nearly killed us today.

As Stuart noticed many times, Australia's beauty is deceptive. The outback hides its cruelty under a seductive disguise. Whatever locals justifiably say to us, I'll feel safer once we're back on the road – hitchhiking lifts with total strangers.

8

Going Troppo

Ivy, the proprietor of the best hostel in Australia so far, drives us to the highway. This is the first time I have seen her courtesy minibus leave its garage. With the exception of two Japanese guests, we were the only people taking advantage of Ivy's clean, fully functioning facilities last night. Through a window near the swimming pool barbecue, we could see her and her husband watching television in their living room, feet up; the antithesis of the get-up-and-go types who usually manage hostels. Most backpackers were crammed in a "lodge" down the road that is mentioned in guidebooks.

Our side of the road is in direct sunlight. Ivy chucks a U-ey and waits in the layby on the opposite side of the road to check we don't get mown down. Her homespun care isn't an act for our dollars. Thankfully, we get a lift within five minutes.

John Burrows is a School of the Air tutor based in Katherine. His most distinctive feature is his ginger beard. This is complemented by a combover attempt at covering his glowing bald patch. His first words when we sit down in the car are, "I can't stand the air conditioning in this car, so I think I'll switch the fan on."

Tiny wisps of air gasp through the air ducts. Katia makes a move to lower her window in the rear, but John says, "No, don't do that. We'll get flies in the car."

Within minutes it's suffocating. I look in the mirror to see Katia clutching her spare cardigan (she always has one at the ready, just in case) to her nose. She can probably smell John's body odour. Prior to this trip, she was always armed with a mini dispensary of perfumes to ward off foul odours in train carriages.

John switches topics. "Where are you hitching to today?" he asks.

"We might head towards Kakadu if we can get a ride that way."

"Yeah, yeah, ahmm, I get it. Tell me this: do you guys speak English or French when you're together? It must be hard work, ay."

"We try to use a bit of both really. Often we swap midsentence."

"Right, yeah, yeah, I see. Okay."

Katia asks about the School of the Air. John fidgets, scratching his arms. "Where are the children that you teach?" she persists.

"Yeah, that's quite interesting for you guys, I guess. Australia was the first country in the world to use the School of the Air for kids who live in places that are so isolated they could never get to a normal school. That's fascinating, isn't it? Right, well, the kids I teach are scattered on cattle stations right across the Territory. I have a classroom that's probably bigger than France, ha, ha, yeah."

John loses focus within a minute. He tells us, however, that he works at the Katherine branch of the School of the

Air, one of twelve nationwide. The School of the Air caters for several thousand outback youngsters in Australia's most remote locations. It has grown from just a handful of children brought into the educational system via the airwaves in 1951, when the first radio broadcast was made. Alice Springs School of the Air alone caters for 140 children living on properties covering over one million square kilometres of central Australia. This was the idea of teacher Adelaide Miethke, himself inspired by the Reverend John Flynn's Royal Flying Doctor Service. Nowadays, much of the curriculum is covered by mailed correspondence.

"Yeah, I just thought I'd hang out in Darwin for a few days, you know," John says. "Sometimes you can feel like you're completely cut off in Katherine. I get very lonely."

I notice that beneath the sunburn he's blushing. He's the first person I've seen today who isn't wearing sunglasses. As though embarrassed by his confession, John turns to the pressing issue of Australia's domestic air network, a bland generality. Thankfully, I spot the turning for Kakadu National Park at Pine Creek.

"And I'll tell you guys another thing…"

When he stops, John rummages in the glove compartment for paper.

"Well, yeah, it would be good to keep in touch with you guys. You never know, I might be coming over to Europe some time, yeah, yeah. Maybe we can exchange email addresses. That's the best way to keep in contact."

Katia files the address in her back pocket, a black hole of deliberately misplaced contacts.

The humidity is unbearable. Equally niggling is my itchy back, savaged by mosquitoes a few days ago. I didn't realise until yesterday morning when Katia called out, "Urgh, what 'appened?" My back is wattled, the texture of a ribbed rubber bath mat. Red spots run from my neck to midway down my spine. I can't scratch it; despite Katia's thorough packing we didn't bring a scrubbing brush.

This morning we had a row. I stare into the window of the Pine Creek general store desperately trying to remember what it was about, and I can't. It must be the sticky air.

According to local accounts, most people up here in the Top End – a colloquial name that doesn't need explanation – get more irritable about November. They refer to that seasonal period as the build-up, when the humidity increases drastically prior to the wet. Tempers are frayed, brows perpetually sodden. Behaviour is affected by continual discomfort. The condition is called "going troppo". An alternative description is the suicide season. We're here out of "the wet", so theoretically it shouldn't be too bad. The ideal time to visit is during "the dry", from June to October.

The Top End is the most geographically estranged settled part of Australia. It has more in common with Indonesia than Melbourne or Sydney. The Northern Territory capital Darwin, named after the *Origin of the Species* author by the commander of the British ship the *Beagle* in 1839, is an isolated place. Its population is a cosmopolitan mix of South East Asian, Aboriginal and sunburnt white. Traditionally, Darwin is also Australia's favourite get-off point for on-the-run criminals and all manner of quirky eccentrics.

"I promise we won't spend all day sitting by the road."

"It's not a problem," Katia replies. "Just leave me for a minute. Stop going on and on."

"But I'm not going on and on."

"You see zere you are, repeating yourself again. Stop, please."

"But I never even started..."

Eventually, I bite my tongue and search for insect bite relief cream.

Pine Creek, fifty miles north of Katherine, is the site of the Northern Territory's first gold rush. In the 1880s a huge nugget was discovered by accident. Hundreds of prospectors made their way up from Victoria and New South Wales. Many got rich quick on the reef of precious metal. But the boomtown was torn apart as quickly as it was built. When the wet came, people at the sodden tropical camp began dying from dysentery and malaria. Pine Creek was a rusting wreck of abandoned mining gear by the twentieth century. Today the community is another place with brown heritage signs where you can try fossicking, like Coober Pedy. It is also the junction for the Kakadu Highway.

A battered camper van pulls over. After the lift with Alan Christopher, Katia studies it warily. A little man is hunched up over the wheel. He doesn't say anything.

"'Ello, can I ask where you're going, please?" Katia enquires.

"Flaming hell, I won't bite, darling. Get in or I'm off."

He's actually a lot nicer once we're inside. He claims to be a retired water buffalo shooter. Water buffalo were introduced to Australia from Indonesia in the 1830s to pull carts. After being set free they thrived in the Top End swamps. The government tried to control feral water buffalo, but, in spite of this guy, they're still around.

"You'd see buffs over there, you see that marsh. They're bastards to move when you've shot one. The bloody critters weigh over a thousand kilos."

He opens up the dashboard to reveal a bag of grass as big as a rugby ball.

"Either of you want to smoke some mull with me. I'll be smoking a cone anyways."

We stop at a lookout with stunning views across the marshy wetlands for which this area is internationally renowned. Freshwater mangroves and paperbark trees poke through waterlily-covered floodplain. Wildfowl swoop across in flocks. After the monsoons the whole region is a swamp, the boundaries of the rivers impossible to distinguish. Cataracts cascading over sheer escarpment drops must be viewed from the air, as roads are impassable.

In a matter of weeks, when the dry takes hold, this whole tract of land turns from damp bog to a brittle tinder box. Nowhere in Australia gets the extremes of weather like Kakadu. There are two climates – monsoon and unrelenting scorching sunshine.

By the time we get to the driver's turn-off I can't make up my mind whether he's deranged or not. The combination of marijuana and tropical heat has fuddled his reason. But my doubts about the buffalo hunter story are ended by looking in the rear-view mirror. I spot a shotgun on a shelf. He skids off into the bush, down a bulrush-lined dirt track just before Jim Jim Billabong, proudly claiming he's lived in the same rotting wooden shack between crocodile-infested lagoons for over twenty years.

"No bugger bothers me out there," is his mantra.

He leaves us with a story. "When my brother was stationed in Mount Isa, I went out on a fishing trip with him and his cop buddies," he says. "Mate, those blokes can drink, ay. They're worse than normal blokes. I reckon there must have been forty-five bloody cartons of piss in the back. I was driving and they kept bringing me these XXXX Gold stubbies. Some of them were telling me to put my foot down while they climbed out of the window to grab a beer around the back. Bloody oath, I had to keep stopping to pick police officers out of the sand."

While we stand listlessly at the roadside pondering our next move, a gangly Aboriginal guy, perhaps of the local Oenpelli or Gagadju tribes, emerges from the long grass on the other side of the Kakadu Highway. His strides are as long as a hurdler's. Without stopping, he says a friendly "g'day".

Giddy from the last lift, I call out, "Hello mate, where are you going?"

"Edith Falls," he replies.

That's about half a day's drive away. As he paces away from us, I can see the sinew ripple on his calf muscles. He barely sweats.

Katia and I both lethargically drop down to the ground. The air moisture saps my energy. My T-shirt clings. I can no longer see the Aboriginal guy, who's vanished into the undergrowth. Going troppo must be a European affliction.

Stuart embarked on his fourth and final expedition to the north coast towards the end of 1861. The plan was to follow the previous route as far as Newcastle Waters. Afterwards, the group was to continue directly northwards, instead of attempting to reach the Victoria river to the west as previously. Again, the South Australian government provided funding, and again those pulling the strings insisted on a large support party. This included Frederick George Waterhouse, a naturalist of little practical assistance.

It took three months to reach Stuart's former camp at Newcastle Waters. Records suggest that they found the exact same camping spot, which is an incredible feat when one sees the landmark-free desert they traversed.

Having reached this psychological and physical barrier, Stuart was slowly edging towards despondency. In his diary he wrote, "I feel this heavy work much more than I did the journey of last year, and feel my capability of endurance giving way."

They attained the Roper river – which we passed at Mataranka – on 25 June 1862, more than six months after setting out. Stuart pursued its course into the swampy territory we're in now, through the floodplains of the broad rivers where water rises halfway up the trunks of tall stringybarks. At long last there was dampness everywhere, umbrageous shade, and plentiful animals to hunt, not to mention crocodiles to be eaten by. But Stuart could barely sit in his saddle. The mosquitoes quelled any sense of excitement.

Two damp hours pass by tortuously as though locked in a room with a dripping tap. Even though we're surrounded by stagnant swamp, our own water bottle is empty. This clammy spot is just short of Cooinda, which is the first campground complex on this highway. It's the worst kind of place to be dropped off because most people in cars are tourists admiring the scenery. National Park rangers shrug when they pass. Flies pester us from the speargrass.

Even though the worst heat has passed, putting the tent up in the clinging climate is an ordeal. I take a shower, but the freshness is gone within minutes. An attempted stroll in the marshy mangrove forest at the edge of Yellow Waters billabong is thwarted by the National Park authorities, who have blocked the trail because of flooding. Dusk falls quickly. We cook pasta beside ineffective mosquito coils. Thousands of large moths zip around the dim light of our torches. Then the batteries go.

"*Ça m'énerve, ça m'énerve,*" Katia decides – this is really annoying.

When I get more mosquito repellent, two feral horses run right by me. Behind them come a pack of dingoes, or mongrel cross-breeds. No one else notices. I wonder if I'm hallucinating.

Later, inside the tent, I spot a huge spider glowering from between the main canvas shell and the flysheet. Katia spends all night looking at it. She barely sleeps. I lie on top of my sleeping bag, feeling like I've drifted off in a Mexican restaurant kitchen. My back itches. Everything in the tent smells mildewed.

In the morning we enter the resort complex. Fresh coffee aromas and piles of fresh croissants taunt us. People staying in the hotel wander over from their chalets, fragrant from washing in their temperate bathrooms. Yet again, Katia curses me and demands breakfast. I can't really blame her after last night, which was definitely a non-negotiable limit to what she'll put up with.

I fear a symbolic compromise coming on; we might have to take that long-postponed tour bus. Kakadu National Park is just too vast for hitchhikers. Last time I was here, I ended up pitching my tent by a crocodile-infested billabong where I had been deposited. I stupidly ignored ferocious carnivore warning signs at the water's edge. Most of the tracks here are dead ends to waterfalls or scenic viewpoints, and asking for a return ticket isn't viable when you're hitchhiking. Like a chess player, you've always got to be plotting your next move.

But, as always in Australia, the next stroke of good fortune is imminent.

The people sitting at the table next to us smile as Katia makes her feelings clear to me. They don't seem embarrassed to be eavesdropping. As Katia goes for orange juice from the buffet table, the man says to me, "Don't vorry, mate. My vife used to spit ze dummy ven ve vent camping in the bush."

I laugh and thank him.

"Zer Top End is a tough place to take a sheila. Zey like to be spoilt on holiday. Ver are yous going today?"

I explain that we're supposed to be hitchhiking.

He looks at his wife, questioning her with a shrug of the shoulders and raised eyebrows. She agrees to his unsaid request with a turn of the head to the side, like someone saying, "Fine, whatever."

"Vy don't yous kids come vith us today? Ve can take you to see some of zer places in Kakadu. Ve are going on a tour of an Aboriginal community this morning, but zis afternoon, ve are taking zer car to Ubirr Rock."

Normally Katia would be too well brought-up to accept an offer like that, but today she has no qualms. I explain what's on offer when she gets back to the table. She doesn't even say, "Are you sure that's all right?"

German-born Dieter and his Australian wife Anne are on a week-long trip around Kakadu after flying to Darwin from their home in Perth yesterday. Dieter, who has just retired, has the most curious German-Australian accent, an unintended mixture of influences. The harshness with which Germans pronounce English is smoothed over with the Aussie twang.

Prior to settling down, he and a mate hitched all over the place. This was back in the 1960s, shortly after he arrived on a passage from Europe. In post-Second World War Australia, thousands of displaced people were admitted by the then Labour government. By 1950, 150,000 people a year were arriving. Most were from Germany, the impoverished Baltic countries, Greece, Italy and Yugoslavia. Dieter must have been a young teenager as he stepped off the ship. He had a whole continent to roam.

"I did plenty of roughing it ven I vas a young guy, like you kids do today. Only, in zose days, zere ver no backpacker hostels, no Greyhound buses and no bloody sealed bitumen roads up in zer Top End!"

"It must have been amazing to see all of this before the roads."

"Vel yes, but there vas absolutely nothing but bush, you know. Me and my mate got stuck out in the back o' Bourke in Queensland ven we ver at a mine. I reckon it vas an oxide mine. Sorry, do you know zis phrase back o' Bourke. It's what ve Australians say for the middle of bloody nowhere."

Looking wistfully out of the window across lowland plains of stringybark, ironwood and woollybutt, Hans says Australia has "lost its innocence". His lucky generation of new arrivals were the last to experience Australia as an antipodean paradise where they could detach from the horrors and depression of Europe, he explains. "Mate, I'd like to go valkabout again, but zer missus likes a little comfort now ve're turning into old buggers."

He and Anne look across at each other affectionately. They live in a comfortable house in suburbia. Every few years, they jet back around the world, retracing, from thirty thousand feet, the route Dieter thought he would never make again.

"Zis is ver you backpackers have got to vatch out for zer crocs," he jokes. "Zey are particularly fond of French people, you know!"

Katia laughs. "Of course, everybody knows zat French people taste betteur."

I can tell she has already charmed Dieter and Anne. They are knocked over by her quirky turn of phrase and French accent, her beaming smile and bubbly confidence, her garrulous explanations of the simplest story with reams of superfluous background detail and, most of all, her readiness to admit that she hasn't got a clue what they are talking about.

In the afternoon, Dieter duly picks us up. He pauses first at Cahill's Crossing, a ford where the only road into Aboriginal-owned Arnhem Land crosses the East Alligator river. Fishermen tease barramundi from the rocky, sun-drenched shoreline. An old man with wispy white hair below his shoulders wades across the river with a rod in one hand and a stubby in the other. An Aboriginal fisher-man catches a giant barramundi, which he throws back in the water, saying it is too small to be bothered with. Bar-ramundi – abbreviated to "barra" by Aussies – are consid-ered northern Australia's premier freshwater fish. They commonly grow to 1.2 metres in length. With their salmon-like ability to leap out of the way of anglers, barra-mundi are Australia's ultimate catch.

One of the paintings at Ubirr Rock, which would have been virtually impossible for us to get to without Dieter and Anne, is on a steep overhanging cliff. According to mythology, this is the work of dreamtime Mimi spirits that came out of cracks in the rocks, pulled the ceiling down, painted the yellow and red sorcery image, and then pushed the rock back into place. One of the images is of a thylacine, a Tasmanian tiger, which has been extinct on the Australian mainland for over two thousand years. Another must be a recent addition because it depicts a man carry-ing a gun. Aboriginal hunters sheltered here until recently, but it's difficult to imagine now.

From the summit of the rock, the vista is tantalising, full of mystery in the way that only real wilderness can be. It sucks me in, just as it did years ago. On one side there is lush green savannah broken by marshes and palms. The broader panorama is the distant Arnhem Land escarp-ment. A splintered-off section is lime green after the wet. We European visitors can have no idea what lives down in those unreachable valleys, I decide. Standing on this pinnacle – not far from a uranium mine – comforts me with the thought that so much of this country is still unexplored. I stand in selfish, trance-like silence.

Beside me, on this dynamic promontory, Katia and her new friend Anne talk about teaching. At least Katia is being polite. I hope Dieter and Anne are glad to have surrogate children gatecrashing their holiday.

T wo days after, following a voyeuristic tour of the crocodile-shaped hotel in the sterile Kakadu township of Jabiru, Dieter drives us nearly all the way back to Darwin. He leaves us outside the Bark Tree Inn, where water buffalo heads hang above the bar and stockmen sit on stools made from foot-thick ironwood planks.

"Look at zis old place. Zis is ze old outback, I reckon. Zese blokes are proper larrikins."

They promise to check the road tonight in case we're still here. There is little traffic. Two minutes later, a newly married Spanish couple on their two-week honeymoon stop, disproving all my preconceptions. We cram our dusty rucksacks in beside their matching suitcases and suit carriers. They wear gold rings that shimmer as the relentless heat fizzles through the car windows. The man works out that their two-week luxury touring holiday is costing more than our six-month jaunt. He laughs about it.

They ask if we want to come with them on a wetlands cruise on the Mary River. I look at the map; it's just down the road and as close as we're going to get to Point Stuart, the place where our hero John McDouall first paddled in the Indian Ocean and a fitting climax to the north-south leg of our journey.

The waist-deep mud and tangle of mangroves that give Kakadu its unique place in the natural world conspired to frustrate Stuart continually as he neared his lifelong goal. Sloshing through the final three hundred kilometres took over a month. But as the coast neared, Stuart found an extra gear. He went out on scouting trips, buoyed by a hunch that the sea was near. Such was his fastidious nature that he didn't tell his men about the imminent triumph until it was virtually upon them.

On 24 July 1862 – a historic date in the Australian calendar – Stuart realised that his time had come. With typical understatement, he wrote, "I advanced a few yards to the beach, and was gratified and delighted to behold the water of the Indian Ocean in Van Diemen's Gulf."

Afterwards, when they realised where they were, the men cheered and jumped into the sea in wild jubilation. Stuart only dipped his toes in the salt water and washed his hands. A Union Jack, embroidered with Stuart's name by James Chambers' daughter, was raised on the beach. But that was it for celebration. Pragmatic Stuart denied his underlings an extra cup of tea out of fear the rations might not last the gruelling 3,400-kilometre journey back. One of the party, William Patrick Auld, later recalled that Stuart seemed to collapse after reaching the sea and said, "I have tried all my life to do this and now have succeeded."

We find seats at the rear of the small cruise boat, near Germans primed with state-of-the-art video cameras. The guide has an encyclopaedic grasp of the Top End environment. He patrols the floodplains as though raised in a reed bed.

The boat churns past pandanus and marsh grass, where the guide points out egrets, magpie geese and night herons. A white-bellied sea eagle surveys from his perch high above. As the throttle quietens down, a jabiru – the bird that's become an icon of this part of Australia – descends right in front of us. Kingfishers and humming-birds dart across the bow as we cross a paperbark swamp.

In gungy, stagnant water, we see our first saltwater crocodile up close. First there are the eyes just above the water level and then the slithery body – all three metres of it – unfurls in front. Everyone gasps, a collective intake of nervous breath. There are five more crocodiles further down, all fearsome specimens. This is nature at its most potent and most cruel.

On the return to the easily biteable wooden jetty, the sun descends, leaving a mauve glaze across waterlily paddy fields. Caws and splashes echo around us, sounding like nature that has lain undisturbed for millennia.

I can't even begin to imagine how Stuart mastered this terrain. Being here confirms his indefatigable courage. When you read about his struggles with the wet, it seems as though the Top End is a deliberate final high hurdle before the north coast. After the waterless desert, the swamps of Kakadu are a vindictive trick.

Hot on Stuart's heels came one of the key achievements in the colonisation of Australia, the Overland Telegraph Line, the thin metal wire that first connected the country to the rest of the world. The Overland Telegraph was conceived by Charles Todd, a Greenwich Observatoryeducated scientist and astronomer. His arrival in Adelaide with wife Alice – after whom Alice Springs is named – coincided with Stuart's first major forays.

The pair met after Stuart's return from his successful expedition. Todd quizzed Stuart about specific details of how to reach the Top End. Although Stuart's maps were eventually to prove of little practical use, it was his trail-blazing that enabled the grand telegraph scheme to go ahead. Todd convinced American cable agent Francis Gisborne that the overland route from Adelaide to Darwin, loosely following Stuart, was the best bet, fending off the rival colony of Queensland in the process. Morse signals from an underwater cable laid out on the seabed from Java could be picked up in Australia's northern port and pulsed down to the south. The five-month time lag with Britain would be cut to seven hours.

Todd spent years meticulously planning for his epoch-making scheme, calculating the exact number of poles needed to cross the continent. In October 1870, the southern team of the country's most ambitious engineering project planted their initial twenty-foot sapling pole close to Stirling North. On top of it was a glass insulator, which would prevent Morse code messages tapped back in London and Manchester from vanishing off the cable into the desert. For every mile they covered, the team would have to plant twenty poles, even in areas where no trees grew. They dug a thin furrow the whole length of the line. Along the route, permanently manned repeater stations were constructed so the received message could be tapped out again.

Of course, it was the final section of the line, starting in Darwin and running down to the Roper river, which nearly unstitched the whole enterprise. As Stuart had found out, the Top End conspires against the best-laid plans. The first pole-laying team was besieged by mosquitoes while the wet drenched them non-stop for months on end. Behind them came the supply team, who decided to offset the rigours of the hostile climate by drinking all the rum stock.

Todd eventually boarded a ship from Adelaide to Darwin to take personal charge of the last stretch. When he got there, he found half the men living on boggy islands on the Roper, having been caught out by the rising waters.

We sit in Bicentennial Park looking out over Lameroo Beach and the Arafura Sea, the bit of Indian Ocean between Australia and the Indonesian archipelago. Personally, I feel deflated. I've reached a melancholy threshold. I was so eager to see the outback again that now we've crossed the central desert, Darwin – a buzzing, compact city – is a letdown. I remember a favourite dumb cliché: it's not where you go, it's how you get there. Even though it's great to have the trappings of civilisation again, my thirst for "the great bugger all" isn't quenched. With a whole continent's worth of sand and charred spinifex behind me, I yearn to go back.

To be frank, I don't have that much appetite for the east coast; it seems too busy, too popular. But there are Katia's koalas to see and a lot of desert to cross before we get there anyway.

I start to tell Katia how proud I am that we've hitched all the way from Adelaide, without a single bus ticket, when a piercing sting pain shoots up my arm, making me scream out loud. A hornet-like insect zips off into a shrub. My forearm turns red and begins to swell. It feels dead-weight heavy.

"You see, you can't even sit in a park 'ere wizout getting beaten by somesing weird. Zat could only 'appen to you."

A doctor gives me some cream and says he's no idea what attacked me. "This is the Top End, mate," he says. "It could be anything."

In a pub down the street, we order schooners of home-made lager. Around us customers down glasses of the misty blond brew like it's the elixir of life. Tables are full of empties.

Katia scowls after her first dainty sip. "Yuck, *c'est vraiment pas bon*." She needs French to describe the revolting attack on her palate.

I slug my beer back Aussie style and nearly retch. The beer is sour and, worse still, has an aftertaste of olives.

"Mate, we wouldn't be drinking this if we hadn't gone troppo," says an amused bloke in regulation vest and tight shorts along the bar from us. He must have been watching.

Suddenly a wolverine howl erupts from the back of the pub.

"Gosh, what's zat?" Katia asks the friendly barfly.

"That's the bloody stripper, darling. New one tonight, I reckon."

From the frenzied, mostly male throng emerges a middle-aged bottle blonde tottering on high heels. Flab cascades over her purely theatrical G-string. She juggles with her sagging breasts as she takes to the stage, having lost her bra in the *mêlée*.

Her act is without suspense. The one remaining gar-
ment is gone by the time I turn to Katia, who has taken a
sudden interest in her beer glass, not because she's even
slightly prudish but because it's just a nasty sight. The
blokes roar for more as the stripper turns her drooping
backside to the crowd. Two men rush the stage. One pulls
down his shorts. "Oh Jesus," I say out loud. I struggle to
hold down my olive-tinted lager.

No one else seems to mind the live sex show except for
us and the skimpily dressed barmaids, who turn away
embarrassed. "Bloody perves," one says to her topless colleague, "that's full-on gross."

The night before leaving Darwin, we meet an old dropout, aged 50, with a groggy, world-weary voice. He doesn't
look 50 until sundown, when the deep crevices on his
brow are unmasked in the shadow.

We go to Mindil Beach sunset market, a melting pot of
Asian, Aboriginal and bohemian influences. You can get
henna tattoos done, have your hair braided, taste Territory
honey, watch an impromptu corroboree performance on
the beach, listen to folk singers and stroll, arms linked, the
way happy couples do through markets the world over. All
of which would be nice enough if it wasn't for the insuf-
ferable humidity. Where's the sea breeze?

As I look up I see the hippy swimming in the sea and
hear him singing drunkenly. The waters in front of the
beach are a known haunt of crocodiles and deadly box
jellyfish. Savaged bits of limbs have washed ashore around
here. But it's so dank and humid that a midnight skinny
dip is just too tempting. I can see why he'd do it. I understand what they mean by "going troppo".

9

Burke's Great Bugger All

Like most outback communities we've been to so far, the existence of Threeways Roadhouse can be traced back directly to Stuart's south-to-north route blueprint. Henceforth, fresh pioneering paths would branch off his route, off the tiny communities that sprang up along the Overland Telegraph Line.

From here, however, we are thumbing towards the region that lost out as Australia's principal trade link to Asia and the world beyond. The empty swathe of land below the Gulf of Carpenteria might look very different today if Robert O'Hara Burke and William Wills – Stuart's unlucky and disorganised rivals – had been victorious, or at least made it home. The main route from the populous south to the wild north would have gone from Melbourne, where they started, to somewhere near the border of Queensland and the Northern Territory instead.

So thanks to Stuart, Threeways is a pivotal T-junction. That's all there is to it, signposts to three points of the compass. Hence the prosaic name. Thankfully for the Territorian dignitaries who named Threeways, there is never likely to be a fourth way. The settlement is a roadhouse stop that is too close to Tennant Creek to merit much of a population. It hasn't altered a jot since I camped in the sand behind the pub eight years ago, I'm glad to notice.

We aim to thumb east along the Barkly Highway as far as Cloncurry and then we'll review the situation. In order to keep the nice loop shape we'll have to go north from there, but the number of people making that journey to Norman-ton on the Gulf is likely to be in single figures. Already, we've been warned that Threeways is a notorious nightmare for hitchhikers, who get stuck waiting for a hypothetical vehicle.

"What is 'ere?" Katia asks me, pointing at an empty space on my precious map.

"Not much."

"So why... oh, it doesn't matteur. So long as we don't get stuck out 'ere."

Fair point, I think, looking at the space. I don't honestly fancy our chances.

Getting here from Darwin was easy. We were wedged at the back of a minibus containing half an Aussie Rules football team and their sheilas. They shared out a carton of Tooheys and ignored us. The couple beside us leafed through a peculiar Aussie weekly, half softcore porn for the men and half trashy real-life features for the women.

Two vehicles arrive in rapid succession and the second pulls over. Just goes to show, you should always treat hitch-hiking folklore with a pinch of salt.

Now this is the ultimate ute. The commodious front cabin has a padded back seat, wide enough to lie down on. The wheels are about the same width as two of me, but considerably more solid. There are fibreglass-protected aerials on the bonnet of the dust-stained white 4×4.

The driver is on the telephone when we get in. That explains the satellite aerials. "Jump in," he says to us. Then he returns to his telephone conversation.

"Mate, I have to be at two stations today to make a drop, and after that I reckon I'm going to need another two or three days before I can get to Townsville."

I make a mental note: this lift could take us right across to the East Coast.

The business link-up ends, with a rugged Australian, "Yeah, she'll be right. Catch ya later."

The driver actually apologises to us for not introducing himself. I want to say, "Hold on, we're the ones who've just invaded your lovely space."

"My name's Mark McIntosh. How's it going?"

I reply with the now customary optimistic "good".

"You Australian, mate?" he asks.

"No, I'm a Pom," I say, realising that maybe I'm starting to pick up the contagious Australian accent like I did the first time I was here. The outback drawl, known as "strine", must have evolved from the surroundings, and perhaps also from the Cockney accents of the first shipped-over convicts. Shrill, uptight British speech sounds out of place in Hicksville bush towns like Threeways; you sound "up your own arse" as Aussies would say.

"And what about you?" Mark asks Katia.

"Oh, I'm from France." There's no mistaking Katia's accent. It would take years for her to pick up an Aussie twang.

Mark is a muscular, broad-shouldered guy. He's 32, with a wife and child. Their photographs are tacked to the dashboard. He wears a blue denim shirt tucked into beige chinos, over six-hole walking boots. Mark looks weather-beaten, healthily moulded by the elements. I ask him what he does for a living, having understood nothing of his business conversation.

"I work for an agricultural company called Bestmix Nutritionals," he tells us. "I'm sales representative for the Northern Territory, the top half of Western Australia and northern Queensland. We make the mineral feed supplements for cattle, you know, phosphorus, iron and calcium. Most of my work is going out to stations to show the cattle managers what our latest products are. These guys have several hundred head of cattle and only spinifex growing out of the desert. You can't rear beef stock on that. Sometimes there's not even spinifex. They need artificial sources of nutrients."

Mark's sales patch is about the size of western Europe. This is the return leg of one of his thrice-yearly trips right across the outback, from his east-coast home, near Townsville, to the furthest reaches of the Kimberleys.

He is consistent in waving to oncoming drivers, a commonplace practice in the outback, where motorists are so few and far between. The proper Aussie wave is an almost indiscernible raise of the right hand, or just a single finger over the top of the steering wheel. It acts as an acknowledgement of the other's presence. It is also a way of telling who the locals are.

"Do you stay on the cattle stations?"

"Some times they let me; otherwise I just roll out my swag by the side of the road and crash under the stars, ay."

"Don't you get scared?" Katia asks.

"No way," Mark rebuts. "I'm a lucky bloke. I'm out here working, but I'm travelling across the outback too. It's a pretty dinkum deal, I reckon."

"What about the dingoes?" Katia asks. Wild dogs remain her biggest bush phobia.

Mark laughs. "Dingoes will never attack a fully grown bloke. It's the snakes you want to worry about."

His working life is uniquely Australian. Being a travelling salesman becomes romantic when your clients are country-sized cattle stations. It's like taking a three-week break to collect your thoughts and reassert your independence every few months. I'd love it.

"What are the cattle stations like?"

"A lot of these places are like little towns. They've got heaps of facilities for the station hands. There's one owned by a Yank in the area we call Little Florida, up in the Top End near Darwin. It's awesome this joint. There's a bloody nightclub, a swimming pool and air-conditioned flats for all the workers. Kerry Packer owns heaps of stations in the Kimberleys and they're nearly as good, I guess."

Kerry Packer is Australia's richest man. He built his fortune in the media, owning 60 per cent of all magazines sold in Australia as well as the Channel Nine television network. He has a penchant for polo tournaments in the British Home Counties with the Royals and Arab sheikhs. His investment in outback cattle stations proves how profitable they are.

"There's heaps of money in beef cattle as long as there's no drought," Mark explains. "That's what made Queensland rich. It was the drovers that made the money before the gold rushes."

The first place we stop at is Gladstone Downs cattle station, about one hundred kilometres on from Threeways. Mark has to deposit samples and mineral supplements. They also need to discuss the health of the cattle.

We approach along a thin dirt track, through desert oaks and mulga bushes. The station is a mini outback village. I spot the worn outline of a cricket pitch. There are swings and a climbing frame for kids. Around a central roundabout are workers' whitewashed chalets, each with their own front yard and rainwater tank. Amazingly for a property with no permanent waters, the main farmhouse is enclosed by shrubs and flowers. I spot a jackeroo and a jillaroo (male and female station hands respectively) mending machinery in a metal shed. Twenty people live here, tending to 18,000 cattle on the 500,000-hectare property.

We sit in the vehicle while Mark negotiates. Dark clouds bestride the Barkly Tablelands plateau.

In August 1860, as Stuart crawled back to Adelaide from Attack Creek, former policeman Robert O'Hara Burke led a team of sixteen men out of Melbourne. As with Stuart's expedition, the purpose of this pioneering venture was to forge a route for the telegraph line to Europe. In contrast to Stuart's muted opening forays, Burke left Melbourne amid scenes of raucous fanfare. He was already revelling in folk hero status. The extensive team left with 21 tonnes of supplies – including two years' worth of food – loaded on to 26 camels, 23 horses and several wagons. Breaking camp took so long that they only travelled to the edge of Melbourne on the first day.

According to accounts of the time, Burke had no idea who was doing what.

Just under three months after the top-heavy party left Melbourne, a base camp was set up at Cooper Creek in southern Queensland. This was after some of the men, and much of the cumbersome load, had already been dumped further south at a rearguard camp in Menindee on the Darling river. Originally Burke had said that this support crew would follow later with the additional supplies. Burke and William Wills, the expedition's studious 26-year-old official surveyor, should have waited for them before heading north, but irascible Burke wouldn't hang around. Having received word of Stuart's great leap forwards, he was terrified of being beaten to his place in history. So, having slimmed down the group to four, he ordered immediate departure. They would worry about replenishing provisions on their return. This was to prove the costliest of many errors of judgement.

Mark gets back in, having bid goodbye to Gladstone Downs for six months.

"Where is everyone? It looks quiet."

"They're out on the first muster of the year, for about two months. They have a cook with them."

Mustering is done on motorbikes and horseback, he explains. Some stations use helicopters.

"They must be pretty tough guys."

"Bloody oath," Mark replies. This is his favourite affirmation. "They're a bonzer bunch. We sit around the fire eating from our billycans. You can't beat it."

"Have you always liked ze bush?" Katia asks.

"I was born on a cattle station," Mark responds. He is delighted to tell stories about his family property near

Toowomba, southern Queensland. One day, his dad jumped on a "brumbie", a feral horse normally used as a bucking bronco, in a bid to convince his men the animal could be tamed. Mark chuckles as he describes Mr McIntosh senior being thrown head first over the paddock fence.

"Have you ever seen feral pigs?" Mark enquires. "Jeez mate, those are really wild creatures. When we were growing up they used to have a competition for the kids at the country race meetings. Some of the blokes at the pub would cover this pig in grease and us kids had to catch the bastard. It was good entertainment for the adults, I reckon – flaming dags. Usually the slippery bugger would get away."

From feral pigs we get on to hunters who used to scatter poison-laced food around outback towns to lure dingoes. They would earn fifteen bucks per pelt.

"Those blokes were making a living," he says. "Wild dogs' numbers need to be controlled. But now they're starting to drop too much."

Dingoes were thought to be introduced by Aborigines who came over from Indonesia about 3,500 years ago, or perhaps Asian seafarers who traded with the indigenous population. There are roughly 35,000 pure breeds in existence now. Conservationists fear that so many have bred with feral species that the pure dingo could soon disappear.

"What did you think of those dingoes being culled on Fraser Island?" I ask.

"Mate, don't get me started on that. It's a bloody disgrace."

Dingoes have been all over the news bulletins in recent times. A nine-year-old boy, Clinton Gage, was savagely mauled to death at the Waddy Point campsite on the popular sand island, off Queensland's east coast. The attack happened when he and his brother took an early morning walk without their parents. The boys were stalked by the wild dogs, which lurk around campsites for food.

For Australia it has been a sensational story. It comes more than twenty years after the conviction of Lindy Chamberlain for murdering her baby daughter near Uluru. At the time, no one believed her claim that Azaria was killed by a dingo.

The authorities have responded to the little boy's death by ordering a cull on Fraser Island, which possesses Australia's purest dingo population. Local Aboriginal leader John Dalungadalee Jones appealed against the decision in court, saying, "This is our brother, the dingo. How would you feel if 30 of your brothers were knocked off?" He lost.

Mark shakes his head as if personally involved in the whole sorry saga. "Dingoes are wild creatures," he adds. "If these tourists come along and feed them, the dingoes will keep coming back for more. It's just stupid bloody politics. John Howard's just trying to win a few points, you know, headlines in the newspapers, because that kid died."

Like many of the Australians who've given us rides, Mark possesses an intuitive outback characteristic – a built-in bullshit detector.

Australian historians have written that the sparsely populated inland, the outback, is what formed the Aussie character most. The egalitarian notion of "mateship" – doing whatever you can to help out a bloke in need without making a big emotional deal out of it – comes from the bush. During the nineteenth century, squatter settlers, labourers and cattle drovers faced an incessant battle with the harsh environment, so everyone had to be mates. Old World social hierarchies were abandoned. Alongside common-sense democracy is the idea that everyone gets a fair go in the outback.

Mark shakes his head as a few gutsy drops of rain splatter on the front windscreen. They trickle down to the bonnet and promptly dry up in the searing heat. In every direction, there is a carpet of smooth, tomato-soup-coloured sand. Yet because of this minimal rainfall, the desert could flower by tomorrow. In Australia's most arid areas, seeds lie dormant for years. The patient plants survive by deep root systems and small leaves that limit evaporation.

During a stop at Barkly Homestead roadhouse, we see a group of malnourished Aboriginal women gathered under a petrified gum tree. They are waiting for somebody, seemingly without anxiety, at the northbound Tablelands Highway junction.

"When I was driving up this way from Dungowan station near Top Springs, I passed these three Murries sat down in the shade of this wreck of a station wagon," Mark says. "This thing looked like it hadn't moved for years. Turns out, these guys had been waiting for three days. They were just hoping someone might come along."

"Did you take them with you?"

"No, they didn't want to come with me. But I did tell the head of the next station I came to about them, so he could pick them up. Murries are notorious for lighting a fire wherever they end up."

Murries is the generic name given to the indigenous people of Queensland. Although the dividing line is obviously blurred between modern-day states, they are regarded as racially separate from the Koories of South Eastern Australia and the Nungas from South Australia.

"I grew up with blackfellas," Mark continues. "Some of them are top blokes. Some of them aren't like us whites. A lot of them are good stockmen."

This is the best accolade for black people I've heard since we left Port Wakefield.

Mark sums up his views on Australia's indigenous problem. "It's really sad to see. They're a beaten race. But the government just throws money at them. And we've got a Prime Minister who won't even say sorry."

Mark's stories come one after the other, each as insightful as the last. As we drive past proudly restored colonial bungalows at the edge of Camooweal, propped on timber stilts in the traditional Queenslander style, I realise we need at least another five hours to cover everything he has to offer.

But he drops us off at Mount Isa, the first big place in Queensland. He's going to stay at the Mercure Inn. We make some vague arrangement about meeting in the evening for a drink, but already Mark has mentally retreated back into his ute, a professional on his way home after a tiring business trip. In any case, breaking the transitory empathy of the ride would be a betrayal of one of the cardinal rules of hitchhiking. Without the role play of driver and guest, we would be intruding on this man, who probably keeps his opinions buttoned up during his normal day-to-day talk of mineral supplements and cattle health. Quick-flowering hitchhiking friendships lose their petals once you no longer have the bond of the road. They are brief snippets of human warmth.

Mount Isa is an industrial oasis in one of the most arid regions of Queensland. Its fuming chimneys are as surprising as the neon-lit spectacle of Las Vegas in Nevada. The 265-metre-tall mining winch dominates the skyline of this sprawling city and the saltbush scrub around. Marginally shorter is the lead smelter stack.

Mount Isa owes its existence entirely to mining, to the extraction of silver-lead, zinc and copper. And it makes a lot of its one dubious claim to fame, being the largest city in the world by area. The town council has a total administrative reach of 42,904 square kilometres. Camooweal, which we passed about two hours ago just over the border into Queensland, is technically a suburb. In fact, the permanent population of Mount Isa is 20,000, which wouldn't even constitute a town in more densely packed parts of the world.

We spend late afternoon at Lake Moondarra, an artificial reservoir north of Mount Isa that is large enough for waterskiing and canoeing. There are gas barbies, a brilliant Aussie invention that you'll find at every outdoor eating area across the land. The shade is too plentiful to consider leaving, which makes me wonder why the hell everyone else isn't here.

Mount Isa itself is a weird place to rest from hitchhiking. The caravan park people are bewildered by us. They only usually get busy during the rodeo – Australia's biggest. The city has a mall, a decorative fountain, a large swimming pool, but everywhere you look there is some kind of extraction or processing plant. Standing at the Hilary Street lookout at sunset, the metropolis teases with street lights. Peek beyond, and the desert furnace looks ready to incinerate what it rightfully owns, once the last silver and zinc are gone.

We spot a train hissing out of the station, bound for Townsville on the east coast.

"Zat could be 'andy if we don't get a lift," Katia says.

But the station attendant says the next departure is in three days. So we find ourselves a shady thumbing spot in the 35-degree heat. If we can at least get to Cloncurry, it's a move in the right direction. We might have to make concessions to convention after that.

I curse a camper van that goes past. "Oh come on, you must have room in there." I've actually developed a personal dislike of these inanimate objects. Then, as if to make me swallow my words, the vehicle stops and reverses gingerly down the highway.

As I slide open the side door and offer my gratitude, the woman in the driving seat immediately explains the hesitation. "Sorry, I didn't stop because I thought you might be criminals, but my little girl Charlotte thought you looked nice."

This assumption is a worryingly frequent one, we've found. That's why I made the effort to shave this morning. Rarely, however, do you meet people who change their minds.

The mother's name is Becky. Her daughter, Charlotte, is five. The little girl peers at us over the parapet of the front seat, but remains suspicious for just a matter of minutes. Becky, 32, wastes no time in telling us their tale.

"We've been travelling for about three months," Becky says, "but only a few weeks in Australia. I decided we should do something crazy after I got dumped by my boyfriend in Melbourne. The first thing I did after kicking him out was to have these breast implants. You probably can't see now, but I'll show you later. I think they're fantastic. After that I just saved up all the money I could and bought me and Charlotte round-the-world tickets. We checked out New Zealand first, didn't we honey?"

Charlotte doesn't answer. Her shyness has been replaced by an eagerness to make use of two new friends. She's glad of extra company. Mum has picked us up purely to keep her daughter distracted.

"Are you cosy?" Charlotte asks, bubbling over with amusing fussiness. "I'll bring you extra pillows."

Katia asks her about the soft toys littered about.

"This is my favourite," Charlotte replies. "His name is Frederick. Do you want to play my new game? You can be the shopper and I'll be the shop assistant."

The game consists of buying clothes for the fridge magnet man and woman. "How much are the trousers?" Katia has to ask.

"That's three dollars," Charlotte responds. "Would you like to buy them?"

Katia plays along for a few minutes and then swaps roles. Charlotte is quickly bored.

In the meantime, Becky smokes a joint, one she rolled before, and hums along to the techno anthems compilation in the tape deck. We're in a mobile nightclub.

When Katia asks Charlotte if she can take a break from playing shop assistant, she gets pinched.

"You have to play with my teddies too," Charlotte dictates. "This one is Pedro, and the other one is Growler."

"How have your travels been so far?" I ask Becky by way of diversion.

"Well, we haven't really done much since we got back to Australia," she says. "I met this bloke called Jason at the airport in Darwin, where we landed. We moved in with him for quite a long time. Show them the pictures, Charlotte."

Charlotte produces a whole album of happy snaps of them with Jason, looking like the perfect domestic unit.

"Will Jason be joining you later on?" I ask.

"No, the bastard chucked me when he realised what a pair Charlotte and me are. Didn't he, baby?"

Charlotte doesn't answer. She hands me the fridge magnets. She is so insistent we give her our undivided attention that I almost miss the blood-bronze rocky ranges on both sides of the road. Sheer cliffs rise out of the parched landscape.

"Show them the pictures of all the men we met in Darwin, darling," Becky asks her.

The now becalmed daughter gets out another album, full of mummy posing with various blokes; sometimes just one, sometimes the full group.

"That's us surfing with a bunch of guys," Becky says, craning her neck to see. "You liked them, didn't you, baby?"

Charlotte nods.

"One of them had this amazing tent that he let us stay in," Becky continues, "but I had to keep asking Charlotte to stay with the others. Wasn't he that Israeli guy?"

She winks conspiratorially into the rearview mirror. The no-holds-barred photo narrative incorporates men the way others might focus on architectural monuments. Every place Becky refers to is recollected by a smooch or a shag. Scenery is the background set for countless one-night stands. She confides more excruciating details, unravelling rows that took place in the living room of her Melbourne apartment. Snippets of physical abuse are tossed casually into the fray as though we're old friends meeting up and discussing life developments. Having hitchhikers in the van gives Becky verbal diarrhoea.

"I thought, 'What the fuck?' If he's going to keep hitting me, I'll sell the fucking house. Why should I accept that shit, you know? So when he went out bingeing with his grog buddies, I did just that. Mate, my life was just on the bloody ropes. We left that dump overnight."

"What about Charlotte?" Katia asks. "Does she like life on the road?"

"Charlotte's so cool," she replies. "She makes friends with anyone."

"Doesn't she need some friends of her own age?"

"No way, she's happier with adults." She looks into the mirror again and grins at her daughter. "Aren't you, darling?"

I turn around to see Katia frowning at the thought of being pinched again. Becky's master plan is to find El Dorado – a golden city paved with readily available hunks and 24-hour childcare facilities. Currently, she thinks it somewhere on the east coast, possibly Cairns. But if she can't locate it on the drive down to Sydney, she's prepared to search in California, Fiji and across Europe.

Burke and Wills endured an arduous journey to the Gulf of Carpenteria. While camped on Cooper Creek, they were plagued by rats that ate through their gear. For many gruelling days they clawed across sandhills in scorching heat, for twelve hours without pause. The jagged Selwyn Ranges were a maze to navigate. Yet they had some luck, chancing upon the Diamantina river system and being left alone by the war-like Kalkadoon tribe, probably because of their fearful camels. By January 1861 the terrain flattened out and they reached where we are now. Cloncurry is named after Burke's cousin, Lady Cloncurry. They should have turned back, having used up more than half the food in half the scheduled 90 days.

Cloncurry doesn't satisfy Becky and Charlotte's wandering attention for long. Becky waffles on about her woolly film-script ideas while we stand outside the roadhouse. Neither of them give a damn that it is the birthplace of the Royal Flying Doctor Service, after a single-engine aircraft with a doctor on board took off in 1927. That suits me fine. With no obvious seduction motive – unless I've missed something – Becky agrees to head north with us up the Matilda Highway to Normanton. This makes me more anxious than glad, as she doesn't appear to have a map or any idea where I mean.

Alongside blokes, smoking weed and writing scripts, her main distraction is taking photographs of trees. Becky is completely obsessed with certain drooping trees that pepper the spinifex strip by the road. She finds lanky, bushy-haired brigalow trees particularly fascinating. A stunted white gum tree next to the slothful Corella river that Burke and Wills supposedly followed north really does it for her. At one point she insists we reverse to a tree she liked.

"Hey, that was a great tree, wasn't it? Did you see it?" We shake our heads, because there are gnarled trees everywhere.

"Sorry folks, but I have to take a picture of it," she says. "I'm going back down the highway." She reverses slowly, pausing to indicate a copse.

"I don't think that's it, is it?" she asks.

We manage to convince Becky that the tree we are looking at is the right one. She asks us to get out and pose. I imagine our portrait being filed at the back of the next album. There are no possible love-interest anecdotes to accompany it in the spoken caption. Perhaps there's a whole separate album of tree photographs that we haven't seen.

Further along, we turn off down a dirt track for a break. Carcasses of famished cattle, undone by drought and far from their station, lie by the roadside. The tall spinifex is yellowing. Termite mounds outnumber trees. As we stand in front of a dead trunk, I remember my ambition to find places in the outback where no one else has stood before. I'm sure it has already happened numerous times on this trip, but this boggy ochre sand is so virginal I'm absolutely positive we're first on it. Not even nomad hunters would have come here. There are no food options.

Right then, Charlotte picks up a hollow log and a four-inch thick brown snake slides out of the other end. Tucker! That could be a venomous Common Death Snake, I think, remembering the boring couple's wildlife guide in Katherine. Charlotte screams, her mum screams louder and Katia loudest of all. I scream internally, being the token fella, but run nevertheless.

"Screw that," Becky says.

Halfway up the track to Normanton is the Burke and Wills Roadhouse. Following the Flinders River to its estuary on the Gulf, the explorers passed near here. They noticed that the vegetation was closing in and the water was too brackish to be drinkable. They were close to their destination. But, typically, the ill-fated duo had to turn back before they could see the sea. Twenty kilometres from the coastline, the mangrove swamp was impassable. Burke wrote, "It would be well to say that we reached the sea, but we could not obtain a view of the open ocean." The emaciated explorers had to trudge back through deep monsoon mud. Wills' notebook records how supplies dwindled so low that they had to cook a python, prompting a bout of dysentery. One of the two helpers, Charley Gray, died from malnutrition and dysentery, as did several animals.

For us, the roadhouse is a life saver. The petrol tank is virtually empty as we pull into the garage forecourt. The sun is a juicy crimson orb cascading final flecks of orange onto swampy box tree scrub.

Later, the presence of new faces at the caravan park in Normanton puts paid to our hitchhiking friendship. There are lively local lads everywhere, easily fascinated by Becky's silicone implants. All are attentive to tales we've already heard. As soon we've helped Becky put up her tent, she decides we can offer no more. Her flirtatiousness has a new direction we cannot satisfy. Charlotte follows her mum. The new game is to make refreshments with a toy tea set. Photograph albums appear shortly after.

Katia and I cook a short distance away. I don't mind that we have fallen down the pecking order. Normally we wave people off until their car becomes a speck in the distance, whereas now we are neighbouring tents in the caravan park. We have outlasted our natural alliance.

In the morning, however, Becky drives us 150 kilometres east to Croydon, an even more torpid relic of a place, so far "beyond the Black Stump" that the stump is no longer visible. All that remain of this former boomtown's gold-rush days are the squat nineteenth-century Club Hotel pub and the general store. They really milk the historic precinct. If you stand still for too long, you get heritage listed. Croydon is the epicentre of the Gulf Savannah cattle country; most of the blokes from surrounding stations are out on the muster.

Needless to say, Becky finds a man. Unsurprisingly, she gets the pick of Croydon's male population. Katia writes a thank-you note and we slip away unnoticed.

The cruellest mishap in Burke and Wills' ill-fated expedition is part of Australian folklore. After hanging around watching supplies dwindle for the agreed period of three months, William Brahe, who had been left in charge of the Cooper Creek base, finally packed up and left. He buried minimal supplies under a tree beside the creek after carving the word "DIG" into it. This was the day before the exhausted Burke and Wills got back.

After their first meal for weeks, Burke and Wills' predicament became clear: they were trapped still 600 kilometres from the main depot at Menindee with barely any food to sustain them. Stupidly, they departed without leaving any sign of having been at the camp. When Brahe returned for one last check, having bumped into a similarly weakened group marching up from Menindee, he assumed Burke and Wills had still not arrived and commenced his own retreat.

Burke was forced to accept that escape south was impossible in the intense heat. The expedition team was stranded. Once the camels had all been killed and eaten, they tried to copy local Aborigines by making flour from nardoo plants, but this didn't help. Wills was the first to die, left alone in a native gunyah shelter further down the Cooper. Burke passed away under a coolibah tree close by. The only survivor was John King, who lived with the Yandruwandha Aborigines until he was found by a rescue party sent up from Melbourne. When he got back, he was greeted by scenes of wild excitement. The expedition's fate had gripped the public imagination.

Today, the "dig tree" at Coopers Creek is a treasured national monument. More people I've spoken to in Australia are aware of the tragic tale of Burke and Wills than of Stuart's expeditions.

At night, in the flickering strip light at the side of the Club Hotel, cane toads splodge across the ground. They are out in their hundreds, an absolutely disgusting spectacle. Two blokes emerge from the lounge bar.

"Right, are ya gonna go out shooting tonight?"

"I've drunk too much piss, mate."

"Fair go, mate. I'm off to shoot some fucking cane toads."

He's not joking. Later on, we hear the crack of a shotgun severing the outback silence. Cane toads are Australia's most despised pest, a poisonous nuisance. They were actually introduced from Hawaii in 1935 to control scarab beetle pests on sugar-cane plantations. No one considered that Australia would be their perfect breeding ground.

Such are their numbers that killing them has become an outback sport. Apart from shooting the warty, six-inch-long, obese brown and yellow toads, a favoured method is thwacking them with a cricket bat. There was a report about the cane toad issue on the television news a few nights ago: the RSPCA advocates killing the feral irritants by putting them in a freezer.

A bizarre fact about cane toads is that their toxic secretion has hallucinogenic properties. You can get high by licking them. It strikes me that someone desperate enough to actually discover that would have to live way out bush, in "the great bugger all", in somewhere like Croydon.

10

How Mount Sorrow Got Its Name

Lake Eacham Van Park is a cool, peaceful spot high on the Atherton Tablelands plateau west of Cairns. The campsite is on downy grassland, thick with dew. Crimson rosellas and rainbow lorikeets make a kaleidoscopic dash into the forest.

A large goanna slides from the pond in front. Even Katia has got used to seeing scaly, sinewy goannas, hardly a threat compared to the giant beast we were confronted by last night. Driving back from the pub at Yungaburra, where the local darts team were training in matching T-shirts, we noticed something lying across the road, surrounded on both sides by dense jungle. The man we were with, Bob, put his headlights on full.

"Must be a branch, I reckon. Let's move it," he said.

Bob and I got out of his Winnebago. We got to within about five yards of the "branch", which I could now see was at least a foot thick, when it started to move. I grabbed the torch from my pocket and shone it on the object – a snake, longer than the width of the road. At a conservative estimate, it must have been six metres long. Its rump was podgier than a small child. We all got out as it slithered inch by inch into the rainforest, coiling half its brown-black-gold form around a tree's buttress roots. The snake was in no hurry. No one said a word. How many grotesque monsters like that are lurking in the darkness?

Katia has visions of this beast forcing its way into the tent or wrapping itself around the flysheet, constricting us both to death. I thought that when we reached the east coast Australia would be less threatening. But here in tropical north Queensland, where Captain James Cook landed in 1770 on the *Endeavour*, there are a whole reference manual full of new hazards. That's before you even paddle in the sea, where the sharks and stinger jellyfish hang out.

Bob is from Bundaberg, much further south in Queensland. He is travelling around Australia with his wife and their three children, two boys and a girl. They have a palatial mobile home, like those you see in American RV parks. The three angelic, blond kids sit with mum under the awning every afternoon to do School of the Air homework for their satisfyingly remote teacher.

Bob wanders over. "G'day. So what have yous two been up to today?"

"We were going to hitch a ride to Cairns, but it didn't work," Katia says.

"Fair dinkum," Bob replies. "But why the hell would you blokes want to go there? This is where you want to be. I reckon this is really God's country, near the water."

He says the word "water" with a long vowel sound – waarter.

"Is zis nice or is zis nice?" Katia has been saying. It's her latest catchphrase, fitting now we've left the ravages of the Gulf Savannah behind.

"I tell yous, when I told my boss in Bundaberg that I was packing the whole bloody thing in, he thought I was crazy, ay," Bob says, thoughtfully rubbing his ample Victoria Bitter belly with his spare hand. "But I reckon this is the best thing I can give my kids."

Bob, who is in his early 40s, still lives the spontaneous existence that most people in Britain lose sight of some time after they stop buying cheap booze and shortly before they try to understand what remortgaging means. He doesn't find it unusual to be upping sticks at an age when it is customary to be consolidating private pension funds and attending school parents' evenings.

Come evening, Katia and I struggle to concoct a meal from tins. Bob wanders over as I heat pasta on the Camping Gaz stove in a tin shed.

"Would yous like some barramundi? We caught it over in Kununurra and it's been properly filleted. This is the best bloody fish you can get in the world. You'll never taste better. My wife grilled it on the electric barbie. Come on over."

He returns to their table and asks us to sit down. "Get these two some drinks, sweetheart," he calls to his wife inside.

Bob and his wife Marnie are charming. They ask all kinds of questions as we hungrily gobble down forkfuls of grilled, firm-grained white meat. In restaurants, this meal would cost a small fortune.

"Yep, it took me a few hours to catch these beauties, ay. Heaps of blokes down there where the creek gets rough. You've got to have a strong grip on the rod to hook one, I tell yous."

He tells us an amazing fact about barramundi: they change sex. Barramundi are actually hermaphrodites, starting life as males, reaching maturity at around four and then abruptly changing gender. Because of their sex swap, there are strict rules about catching females.

Marnie serves the meal with an Australian snack staple, potato skins.

"So do yous have the School of the Air in Europe?" she asks Katia, who, being French, is initially mystified by them serving the part of the potato she would chuck away.

"Oh no," she replies, "evrysing is too small. This country is just massive. I couldn't believe when we first started 'itchiking. You could fit England and France into Australia many times."

Bob likes that. "Yep, I read that Lake Argyle in Western Australia is bigger than Scotland. What d'ya reckon to that?"

Exaggeration of already extraordinary statistics is a common trait I've noticed in outback Australians boasting about their country. They know their homeland is bigger, sunnier, cleaner and freer than anywhere else. Why bother to check the size of Scotland? Bob wants us to be totally overawed by Australia, of which he is rightly proud.

"We met this lovely couple from Holland at the last place," Marnie says. "That's near England isn't it?"

"That's right; it's only across the English Channel. And Holland's tiny. Holland would probably fit into Kakadu."

"Fair dinkum," Bob sighs wistfully. That's a new half-truth for him to trawl out when he gets back to Bundaberg.

As if to reward us for praising Australia's size, he asks, "Do yous two fancy coming with us to see the waterfalls tomorrow? We're going to have a look around the Atherton Tablelands. We'll take the camping chairs, the Esky and some grog." The Esky is an essential accessory, a cooler.

Katia nods to me, which is unnecessary. After all this hitching she's come to accept virtually any change of plan.

"Right kids," Bob shouts. "Forget school tomorrow."

*C*lear water cascades over abrasion-sculpted rocks in an idyllic glade roofed with foxtail palms and straggly knot vine. The Babinda Boulders have such a sheen they look almost artificial. The atmosphere is fresh in the muggy jungle.

Down the road are shabby Queenslander bungalows on stilts. They belong to farmers growing sugar cane, mangoes and pineapples. The next stop is Josephine Falls, just off the trail to Bellenden Ker, the state's second highest mountain. Frothy streams tumble over a series of sheer rock faces to collect in effervescent pools. Filtered sun rays dance across the forest blanket.

We have a picnic – provided by Marnie – at Mungalli Falls, which are in winding farming country and surrounded by manicured lawns. Bob and Marnie buy us cream teas in a quaint eatery, so English I can't believe we're still in tropical north Queensland. Then comes Millaa Millaa falls, where we all go for a swim in the little pool, diving underneath a pummeling deluge of water spray; the famous curtain fig tree, a curious rainforest curtain caused by an epiphyte that strangles its host with roots hanging fifteen metres down; and finally eighty-metre-deep

Mount Hypipamee crater, caused by the explosion of a volcanic vent.

Bob and Marnie's Atherton Tablelands tour is so comprehensive, I've probably missed something out. I'll never again see so many waterfalls in a single day as long as I live.

The following morning, they deposit us in Mareeba.

"Watch out for these Abo hoons," Bob says as he looks for a place to park.

"That's all right," Katia says, reacting diplomatically to this outrageous statement.

Bob's words are prompted by the now common sight of Aborigines gathered in the shade of a large tree. This one is a native Leichhardt, I think.

"Oh mate, I'm bloody ashamed," he adds.

Before I can confirm it's not a problem, his son butts in, "Look at the blackfellas, mum. They're all pissed."

Marnie, so courteous towards us, doesn't upbraid her child. Instead she adds her voice to the chorus of disapproval. "Ah yeah, I wish yous two Poms didn't have to see that. I feel embarrassed too."

Dad wants the last damning word. "Keep a look out that those blackfellas don't dent my bloody car."

Later, as we pass a sign advertising Bundaberg Rum outside a bottle shop, Bob simpers with pride.

"See whitefellas managed to set up their own distilleries too, no worries," he says. "Blackfellas never managed that before we got here."

A week passes quickly in the temperate bolthole idyll of Palm Cove. The guy in the caravan opposite us has been here for fourteen years, and is only now thinking of a move. "Even paradise gets too much sometimes," he says.

Whisper it quietly – because it's a secret worth keeping – the Palm Cove Caravan Park is the stuff of dreams for a weary hitchhiker: shady, well watered, about ten metres from the palm-fringed beach and close to seafront bars. The owners don't advertise anywhere; word of mouth is their only publicity. Five-star hotel guests pay hundreds of dollars to stay in neoclassical-style resorts just down the road, with lesser views. The only downside – and that's marginal – is the communal changing room. Oh, and the showers go freezing cold every time someone switches another one on. But still, you can't have everything for five dollars a night.

A white ute pulls up while Katia is brushing her teeth in a freshwater stream by the highway. Inside is a mixed-race couple. They live in a place called Yorkey's Knob; only an amusing name to Poms, I discover. The lift lasts fifteen minutes. Today looks like it will be a hitchhiking sprint relay. They let us out at Hartley's Creek, outside a famous crocodile farm where blokes in tight shorts chuck hunks of meat at saltwater crocs so they jump in the air like dolphins.

The Captain Cook Highway curves majestically beside coveted crescents of coral beach on one side, with the burgeoning rainforest leaning down heavily on the other. Traffic is slow, retirement-age, off-season speed. Sometimes the road hugs the coast so tightly I can see sheer drops into the placid sapphire ocean from my window.

We arrive in Mossman far too quickly, with a Torres Strait Islander who works in a domestic violence unit. He hugs the tight bends of the jungle-piercing highway with a Grand Prix driver's nerve. This good-looking man, also a talented dancer he says, lets us out in front of the Mossman Hotel, adjacent to the town's hardware store.

A man in a green cooking apron emerges from the rival Imperial Hotel nearby and asks if we want a cheap room. His "hotel" is a typically cavernous rotting pub with a wooden-boarded balcony terrace and an industrial-sized bottle shop attached.

Our new host is keen to please. "We don't often get you fellas stopping off here," he says. I can well believe it. Most backpackers – that's "us fellas" – bypass Mossman town *en route* for picturesque Mossman Gorge after leaving Port Douglas or Daintree National Park. The town has few obvious photo opportunities.

He shows us to a room. It smells of cat urine. The sheets and scrawny towels are stained. Although the hotel is virtually empty, the landlord has given us the worst room. We ask if we can change on the pretext that the television doesn't work. He knows we are lying. We are given a different room facing the road that smells equally bad. A single bare light bulb illuminates peeling white paint on wood slats. The bedcovers are of early 1970s design.

"It will do," Katia sighs stoically.

By night, Mossman dies a little more. The grill is turned off in the town's takeaway. There is skeleton custom in the Imperial Hotel. We are the only non-regulars. A blackboard advertises topless waitresses on Thursday and Friday. It is Saturday, so the blokes have to content themselves with watching the big rugby league game on the television in the corner: Melbourne Storm versus Brisbane Broncos. Mysteriously, the landlord's set works.

Our fully clothed waitress brings over two burgers with "the works". A proper works burger – and this is a terrific example – is a veritable Scooby snack with a huge slab of prime steak, topped with fried egg, bacon, tomato, beetroot, a pineapple ring, and whatever else they feel like chucking in, like ordering a meal sufficient for the next two days.

Cape Tribulation is a symbolic headland in the European colonisation of Australia. On its maiden voyage to Australia, after setting ashore in Botany Bay, the *Endeavour* continued up the east coast under Cook's command. As the ship sailed north Cook drew accurate charts of the coastline, a vital reference for the future colony he had been ordered to claim for the Crown. But unbeknown to captain and crew, they were sailing between the coast and the 1,250-mile-long Great Barrier Reef. Not until you get up into northern Queensland does the protective coral barrier close in. Cook realised this and said it was "the most dangerous Navigation that perhaps ever ship was in".

The *Endeavour* struck the reef not far out to sea from where we are now. It lay stuck precariously on the coral for a day. Eventually, to float the ship off to a safe haven for repairs, Cook ordered all superfluous objects to be thrown overboard. The crew made it to a river near Cooktown, north of here, which the explorer also named the Endeavour. They spent six weeks patching the ship up, time that was used to take samples of the singular Cape York flora and fauna and to mingle, in a friendly way, with the local Aborigines. It was during these meetings that the word kangaroo was first heard. Cook managed to ignore the locals, however, when he claimed the eastern part of Australia for Britain, calling it New South Wales.

Cook named Cape Tribulation such because, as he wrote in his diary, "here began all our troubles". Of course, the strife that his party endured back then is easy to forget about. Cape Tribulation is a gorgeous, serene setting. Most people visit North Queensland – at luxury hotels in Port Douglas, for example – for a laid-back break, to be pampered in a heavenly virgin paradise.

But I get bored perspiring under dried-palm beach cabanas. I want to get under the skin of this sun-gilded beach nirvana.

PK's Jungle Village caters for tenants in Gulag-style bunk cabins sealed beneath the majestic canopy of the Daintree rainforest. At night it turns into a holiday camp, with a three-hour happy hour providing everyone with a chance to sink jugs of beer before dusk. Hordes of guests revive briefly forgotten football songs. Some like it so much they do several hours cleaning a day for a bed.

I manage to persuade Katia to embark on a walk, which is no mean feat after our previous efforts. "How's about Mount Sorrow?" I ask. The name should be a giveaway (think of Captain Cook, you idiot), but I fail to make the connection.

The marked track is hidden away, just off the main road. As soon as it starts, we are in thick, dark forest. We scramble through dense foliage, over a tangle of thick hardwood tree trunks that have tumbled onto the barely visible path. Occasionally, scraps of flagging tape reassure us we're going the right way. Spiky palms, ferns and fig trees serrate our skin as we brush against them. Parasitic creepers, which we use as handholds, wind about giant melaleuca trees. A continual chatter of birds and the scramble of other creatures – possibly snakes or giant lizards – emanates from all around, but we see nothing. Added to all of these not particularly pleasurable distractions is the gradient – between very steep and almost vertical.

As I pull Katia with both hands up a sandy clearing in the forest, she glares at me. *"Plus jamais, jamais avec toi,"* she says. I've heard it before in English – never again.

Two hours into this bad idea, Katia is weeping and muttering French swear words I've never heard before. I insist we go back, this isn't worth it. But she keeps her head bowed to the forest floor, so she can prove what an unrealistic idiot I am when we get back. If we get back at all, that is. I haven't read the instructions about carrying enough water till now.

We eventually arrive at a ridge, where a tiny path winds through the jungle at the top of Mount Sorrow. I peer over the edge and see a sheer drop down on either side. We clamber onto a bald rock that marks the summit, scared to move too much for fear of slipping over the edge. There's little manoeuvring room. But the 360-degree view is revitalising, making the walk worthwhile. At least that's what I think.

We can see the reef clearly in the deep blue ocean, the pristine creamy beach, and behind that the sparkling emerald jungle. Not that it makes any difference to Katia. The fractious tension doesn't ease. She wants to get down.

The descent is so steep it practically snaps my calf muscles in two. I slip over about five times, Katia probably even more. She doesn't let me help her up. We get back to the Jungle Village seven hours after our departure, which could hardly be called a recreational stroll.

On the beach at night, beside the embers of someone else's fire, I pick up a leaflet describing local landmarks. Cook named Mount Sorrow. He sent two men ashore to take bearings from the high point while the *Endeavour* remained stuck fast to the coral reef. Both men died during the climb, apparently finding it too treacherous to ascend. The name Mount Sorrow was probably designed to serve as a warning to future generations, like Cape Tribulation and Weary Bay. If only I'd read that first.

We leave Cape Tribulation two days later with a barman called Sel who is crossing the Daintree river to buy some new lures for his fishing rod, and possibly a crossbow to shoot feral pigs in Lakeland National Park. Those are just two of his weekend hobbies. He skips from distraction to fleeting distraction. On the car ferry he inspects the current, checking for the best fishing holes. The river is like a beam of optimistic light, a thoroughfare out of the sinister jungle. Today the scene is shrouded in thick mist, making it extra haunting.

We check in at a backpackers' place in Cairns. Guests lie by the pool listening to personal CD players. Cairns is a tourist honey trap, yet from my memory of the place there's not really much to it. Along the Esplanade, every building is a backpackers' hostel, a dive school or a Barrier Reef cruise outlet. People sunbathe on the prickly grass strip behind the unappealing muddy beach. No one warns visitors of the lack of sand in Cairns. It takes many by surprise. People stay here for weeks instead of going to somewhere better like Palm Cove. They must be filling in time between scuba-diving trips.

At night, two common neologisms draw people out like moths to a light bulb: all-you-can-eat and all-you-can-drink. We go to Jonno's Blues Bar, a legendary cheap booze haunt in Cairns. They serve massive jugs of beer for five dollars, which is enough to keep the punters happy. The entertainment is the same every night. I remember it from eight years ago. Jonno, a shambling, stooped musician, appears on stage with his band. He wears a Mexican poncho and floppy bush hat. When he judges the collective level of drunkenness to be about right, he sets up a limbo contest on stage, with a booze prize for the winner. Our neighbours know the routine so well they correctly guess all of the songs in sequence. Jonno sings some self-penned numbers, including one blues tune called *Cape Tribulation*.

For no other reason than because we're here, we book an excursion to the Great Barrier Reef. I feel I'm betraying our original quest, which is strictly on dry land.

On the way to the boat, we pass through Cairns' biggest Australiana trinket emporium, the Pier Marketplace, next to the boat moorings on Trinity Wharf. I buy a waterproof camera and, ridiculously, try to find a bush hat like the one I bought last time I was here.

Our boat is called *Noah's Ark Too*. The name sets the tone. The captain, a portly heavy-metal rocker with a pig-tail, gives a sarcastic introductory speech. The gist of it is this: in an emergency jump overboard.

The journey to our allotted lump of coral reef takes an hour and a half. When we drop anchor it still appears that we are in deep waters. We can't get to one of the reefs that can be easily swum to at leisure from a sloping beach until later. There are strict controls about how many people can go to different parts of the reef at one time, since it's a protected Marine Park. You get what you pay for.

Without confidence, I put on my snorkel face mask and flippers and belly-flop off the side of the boat. I've never been good at snorkelling even in still waters, but here there is a strong current, carrying me away from the motor boat. I find myself swallowing huge gulps of sea and spluttering as I panic for air. I climb back on board to regain my breath, without having seen a single coral polyp or fish.

In the meantime, Katia swims gracefully, pausing every so often to shout at me, "I saw some fish, pink and green ones."

After lunch, I finally get to see some of the reef at Michaelmas Cay, where the drift is less and the white sand-bank close enough for safety. In some parts the water is shallow enough to stand in, but the seabed is composed of brittle, calcified coral. Even then I end up holding Katia's hand to breathe properly; I'm so pathetic. The mini world of the atoll below is absorbing. We see giant turtles, red and purple fish darting between wafting green coral, yellow and blue butterfly fish and winding bivalve clams. Just as I'm getting to terms with snorkelling again, we're off, back to dry land.

"Hold on, you guys, it might get pretty choppy on the way back," the captain says as the engine cranks up.

We crash directly into the waves. He sets a straight course for Cairns, no messing about. Water tumbles over the side of the boat as we pound into the swell. The weather has taken a turn for the worse since this morning. There is no respite.

Now it's Katia's turn to be inadequate. She becomes so nauseous she's unable to speak. I can't even get a gesture response to my questions. She sits stock still, looking down at the deck in the hope it will stop shaking about. Then the instruction, "Get me a plastic bag. *Vite*."

Katia is the only passenger to throw up during the voyage. The captain finds it funny. Most of the people who come on these trips must have sea legs. One American guy, a scuba diver, drinks five beers during the time Katia wrestles with her plastic bag. By the time we reach Cairns harbour she can't move. With the help of a dive instructor I get her to a bench, where we remain seated for an hour. For the whole evening Katia is bedridden and feverish.

That's another adventure activity crossed off the list, just behind white-water canoeing and bushwalking. Why do we bother doing that stuff? Hitchhiking is so much safer.

I don't know whether I'm overcome with seasickness or nauseous from last night's beer, but something in me cracks this morning. Katia is still too ill to eat after the

Great Barrier Reef boat ride. She can't face the hassle of catching local buses out of Cairns to find a thumbing spot. We're too late to hitchhike today. So I stand in a queue at the Greyhound bus terminal. I hand over nearly one hundred dollars for our fare to Townsville. Our bags disappear down an airport-style luggage carousel. Ouch, that hurts.

We sit on metal seats in the corner of the drab waiting room, leafing distractedly through books. Fellow passengers look bored. An announcement blares from a speaker in the corner of the room: "All aboard please."

What have I done, I think. This is what I swore we'd never do.

Once we've been packed like sardines into the modern, slickly operated, temperature-controlled bus, I look out of the window. Now I've made this absurd mistake – choosing, without outside pressure, not to hitchhike – we might as well take the opportunity to gaze at the scenery. We can do like bus passengers the world over: ignore the people around us.

But the driver has other ideas. No sooner have we hissed south onto the Esplanade than the commentary begins. Being unaccustomed to the layout of these buses, we've managed to select seats directly below the speakers.

"G'day to all of you backpackers who joined us at Cairns. This is the Greyhound bus to Brisbane. If you're staying on all the way to Brissy you've got two drivers. I'll be taking you to Mackay, and then we'll be changing over."

So far, so functional, that's all we need to know. But this driver has a microphone and he desperately wants to use it.

"So once we get out of Cairns, there will be quite a change in the scenery. What you'll see now is lots of sugar cane and rainforest. Okay, no worries. This area is where most of the sugar cane in Australia is grown..."

Until today, I thought that long-distance buses just got you from place to place as quickly as possible. I didn't know the drivers double up as tour guides. I'm not sure if I can stand it. The driver tells us that, as backpackers, we'll all want to get out at Mission Beach, a resort about 140 kilometres south of Cairns. And indeed, as we cruise down the approach road to Mission Beach, more than half the passengers do alight. Some clutch Lonely Planet guide-books to their chests.

On the approach to Cardwell, opposite the mountain-ous hulk of Hinchinbrook Island, the condescension reaches a new low: we are told how to find the toilets.

"When we get to Cardwell for our comfort stop, the beaut little roadhouse that we always use will be on your right. Okay, so that's no worries. For those of you with some litter, drinks cans or whatever, there will be a rub-bish bin on your left-hand side as you get out of the bus. You'll see the toilets on the right as you enter the road-house. Now, the people that make the food there are very good. I'll just run through some of the dishes you might like. Okay, no worries."

As we alight, Katia says to the driver, "Is it possible to have some quiet for a while, I would like to sleep?"

He looks at her in utter disbelief. "We have to keep pas-sengers informed, madam. It's what people want."

So the teeth-grindingly patronising announcements con-tinue for the remainder of the five-hour journey down the Bruce Highway. Our speed is desperately slow and the journey is constantly interrupted. We grab our bags at

Townsville, relieved. The hitchhiking pact is reinforced; Katia's had enough of buses too.

Backpackers temping as minibus couriers for the town's hostels bombard us with gratuities to entice us to their accommodation. One at a time they come over and repeat the same sales pitch – a cheap bed and free breakfast. I feel like factory farm fodder, ready to be fed through the mincing machine. There are ten minibuses parked before us.

Katia and I go back to doing what we do best: walking through Townsville's suburbs looking for a caravan park with good hitching access for when we move off again.

11

Roadtrain Rage

Two vehicles typify Australia to me – the ute and the roadtrain. I've seen utes all over the world since I was last in Australia, but here a ute really means something. If you're serious about living in the outback, you've got to have a ute. So many of our rides have come from Aussies driving utes with their life's possessions stashed underneath a tarpaulin in the back. To be totally overblown about it – and as this is my book I might as well be – the ute is to the Australian Dream what the Harley Davidson is to the American Dream.

As I spout this romantic claptrap, I'm staring at a ute parked next to a permanent trailer at the Strand Caravan Park in Townsville. Its owner, Glenn, is one of the very Aussie ute-driving blokes I'm talking about. He's found his karmic balance here, but his vehicle is always parked pointing towards the road and has a caravan tow hook at the back. At any point he can fold up his awning, which doubles as a garage and workshop, and drive off to the opposite end of Australia in search of a fortune. The ute is the modern Australian equivalent of Dick Whittington's knapsack.

People like Glenn make up a substantial portion of the Australian population. They are unseen, subculture fringe dwellers. Having the ability to move at the drop of an Akubra hat is far more important to them than property ownership. In this country, being an itinerant drifter is a viable lifestyle choice.

This is our third night in the company of Glenn and the neighbour he calls his "special lady friend". Glenn's especially smashed tonight. He holds his pet python, Cecil, which he told us earlier is commonly known as a "children's python". Apparently it's harmless, but I'm content to keep a good distance. Katia is terrified of it. When Glenn gets drunk, he starts to fondle Cecil like a baby. What's truly unnerving is when he almost sucks its face, forked tongue and all, as if to give it a kiss.

That disgusting habit apart, Glenn is great company in the evening.

Excitedly Katia tells him her big news, the magic moment of our trip to Australia so far – we saw wild koalas today, eating eucalyptus leaves on a bush trail on Magnetic Island. We were walking on a path beside Second World War lookout ruins, built to prevent a Japanese invasion. Suddenly, peering up at a gum tree for no particular reason, I spotted a cute, grey, furry koala looking directly at us with an air of irritation, like our paces had interrupted its afternoon nap. It was clutching the tree trunk, sleepy. More than ever before in Australia, Katia was spellbound.

"*Je ne crois pas, c'est un koala enfin,*" she said, expressing disbelief at seeing a koala at last. Then she added that he was "so bootiful".

We stayed at the base of the tree for half an hour, during which time we saw another koala munching pensively on the leaves. Both koalas stretched themselves before clambering off to find a comfier perch. Katia was so happy that she hasn't stopped singing since. I'm not exaggerating. She is as overcome as when she sees a really chubby baby in a pram while we stand in a supermarket queue.

"Of course, koalas are actually vicious little bastards. They've got claws that could rip through your skin, no worries," Glenn reminds Katia.

"Yes, maybe, but zey look so lovely."

"I was going to poach a koala as a pet. The chicks would love it." Glenn nods towards his special lady friend. "Imagine telling a sheila that she can cuddle your koala if she comes back to your place, ay."

"Good idea," Katia says.

"Too right! But I've got Clive instead. He brings 'em in. Don't ya mate?"

His other pet is a crested cockatoo, Clive. When Glenn's not kissing Cecil the snake, he brings Clive out to perch on his shoulder. Glenn works sometimes, and spends the rest of his time here at the caravan park, entertaining new arrivals like us. "I've got new neighbours every week," he says. "You can't beat it, I reckon."

Glenn is a veritable encyclopaedia of Australian history. "Either of you blokes know why Magnetic Island's called Magnetic Island?" he asks.

Katia shakes her head. She does know, she read it on the ferry back to Townsville this evening, but she was still buzzing from the koalas.

"Well, I can tell yous. Captain Cook named it Magnetic Island because the dumb Pom thought that the island was a magnetic field. It sent all his ship's compasses way out of whack. They were lost, buddy. The bloke actually believed granite rock was altering his compasses. Of course it wasn't magnetic, was it?"

"What was it then that made the compass go strange?"

The wine cask is empty, the Bruce Springsteen album has finished, and Glenn's wandering mind is elsewhere.

"Hey, Cecil, how do you fancy chatting to a French sheila?" he asks, lurching forward with his pet. He almost stumbles into Katia, holding the snake out with one fumbling hand.

And there ends the history lesson for the evening. As both of us are petrified of the sociable reptile, we make our excuses and leave for our tent.

Roadtrains are the fifty-metre long beasts of the Australian road network, eating up vehicles in their path. Roadtrain trucks surge violently round the country, with containers careering wildly across the carriageway behind the driver's cab. Nervous motorists swerve onto the gravel as a roadtrain closes in on them, its loud horn blaring as it approaches. Roadtrain drivers only brake when stopping for a break.

These vehicles, with their snake-like cargo flailing, are a uniquely Australian means of transporting goods. The term train is used because of their extra length, like nothing else to be seen on the world's highways. But we've yet to get a single lift in one. As I mentioned to Katia when we left Port Wakefield, drivers are forbidden to pick up hitch-hikers for insurance reasons. They would be fined for carrying passengers who don't wear a seat belt.

Nevertheless, a lift in a roadtrain is her new ambition, now we've seen a koala in the wild. As a convert to the hitchhiking life, Katia views a ride in a roadtrain as the ultimate. I hardly dare mention to her what happened to me the last time I hopped in with an Aussie trucker. That was probably the only ride in my life that left me mentally scarred, the only one to make me pause briefly and question the wisdom of what I was doing.

It happened in the middle of the night, at Glendambo Roadhouse, slap bang in the middle of nowhere. The driver, butch and full of laddish bravado until that point, propositioned me. He wanted us to retire into his poky sleeping quarters in the rear of his cab. "Mate, I've tried everything," he boasted.

For what seemed like hours he rebutted my refusals and I was properly trapped. I feared violence. If he'd grabbed me, I could have done absolutely nothing about it. We were parked. He was the stronger.

But eventually he rolled asleep. I remained wide awake, frozen to the spot. Two hours later he was back with a volley of heterosexual male banter. Our impasse was forgotten. Come morning, the driver made me peel off the remains of a hawk that collided with his machine's roo bars. Globules of flesh had cemented the stiff feathers to the paintwork. This chore was the only cost of the whole trip, a full eight hours of road. He bought me breakfast afterwards.

"*Allez, arrêtez vous*," Katia cries at a roadtrain as it pounds across the bridge south of Rockhampton – come on, stop for us. Crossing the bridge is dangerous as it is just wide enough for two trucks coming in opposite directions, without pedestrians squeezed on the side. This is a hitchhiking danger we've rarely come across in Australia, the outback roads being so broad and little used. In Europe accidents are more likely as you walk up a road to find a thumbing spot. In 1999, a young woman hitchhiker was mown down by a drink driver as she tried to thumb a lift in Scotland. The man was found and jailed for five years. He believed he had hit a deer and continued on his wobbly journey.

Pointing at the roadtrain I confidently pronounce, "He'll never stop."

But as the truck goes past we hear a hissing sound, the release of the air brakes. It's a three-truck roadtrain, caked in red outback dust. Eventually, the vehicle comes to a rest. I assume the driver is having a smoko, after crossing the Rockhampton city limits. But a short figure leaps out from the passenger side and gestures for us to approach. I point at myself as if to say, "Do you mean us?" He carries on beckoning, so we walk up.

We waddle penguin like towards him with our too-heavy packs.

"Hi," I pant idiotically. "Did you stop for us? We weren't sure."

"Course. No dramas. I wouldn't be stopping this bloody great rig otherwise, would I? Throw your gear in."

"Right. Great. Thanks. Where are you going?"

"Don't worry about it, mate. South."

I do my best to look strong enough to pull Katia's weighty rucksack with me as I climb the little stepladder up the side of the cab. Sadly, I can't manage it. The driver looks on amused. Katia has to prop the bags up as I struggle, like an upturned beetle, to get them in the little hold. We squeeze ourselves onto the one passenger seat.

Rick, the roadtrain driver, waits until his pick-up at a salt-purification plant before unveiling his pouch of white methyl amphetamine powder hidden under the dashboard. The stash is concealed in the inner pocket of a black leather Filofax. He eats the crystalline white speed with a plastic spoon, like sugar.

"Snorting's bad for your health," he says. His hands shake so much he almost spills the precious stimulant. They are encrusted with deep sores. Across both palms are thin scar strips, like rope burns. His fingers are engrained with black oil and soot, like he is about to give prints for the police.

I guess somewhere in his frazzled mind he realises this is the perfect moment to explain his boasts about driving for four days non-stop. After all, we are at the end of an isolated one-way dirt track and can't escape. Rick has put my bag in the back of the third truck because we were too cramped. So we're up a gum tree if we want to do a runner. From the moment he pulled over for us on the Bruce Highway, he has seemed extraordinarily agitated. Now I know why. Speed makes people fret, shift needlessly from side to side, bite their bottom lip, chew on thin air, and forget about daily habits like personal hygiene.

"I've been taking this shit for years," Rick explains. "Lots of young blokes can't do it. I knew one critter that had to go to bloody hospital. He had a complete meltdown in his cab, heart palpitations, ay. I fucking laughed."

Katia covertly checks our whereabouts out of the window. We're somewhere towards the coast south of Rockhampton, that's all I know. By a salt marsh, I suppose. There's another, more sensible-looking trucker behind us in the loading bay. Perhaps he can bail us out?

"But I can't drive chemical free," Ricks adds. "It didn't bloody work. So my boss buys it for me now. I told him I needed gear or I couldn't drive."

Rick tells us that roadtrain drivers' speed consumption is the government's fault: it insists on rapid transportation of goods across the unwieldy continent, yet removed prescribed uppers like ephedrine from the market. He has a point, of sorts. State police carry out checks on truck drivers every year, and each time a considerable number are found in possession of illegal drugs. In one recent clampdown, four drivers were found with amphetamines over a two-week period on just one stretch of road in Victoria. The police message to truckers is, "If you're tired, pull over and sleep." But the commercial reality is different: if they don't make a delivery in time, their firm loses a contract. And being on time is no easy task when you're covering thousands of miles across the outback.

I ask Rick if he has had any sleep recently.

"I don't need sleep, mate," he growls. "I spent a few hours in my cab at the truck park in Townsville waiting for my eyes to close, but it didn't fucking happen, ay. Sometimes you just reach meltdown, and you just have to sit in the cab with the air conditioning on and put a fucking wet cloth over your face."

He started in New South Wales two days ago, made a changeover in Brisbane, carried on to Townsville and, after the salt is loaded, will continue back to Brisbane without stopping. Once that is complete, he has to drive back to Rockhampton, pick up another load and hurtle south to Brisbane again. In total, that makes over 5,000 kilometres.

Katia looks increasingly worried. I'm sure she's had her fill of roadtrain travel already. By my reckoning, Miriam Vale is the next substantial place on the highway and it is probably a few hours away. Rick is so shaky he doesn't look able to make it that far.

Rick must have noticed Katia is ill at ease, because he makes this reassuring speech. "When I split up with my sheila in Brisbane, the bitch accused me of deliberately running her over. She went to the bloody police. I mean, I did run her over, but it wasn't deliberate. She's a crazy bitch anyways. That gate-rider copper knew there was nothing he could do. I went in with my solicitor, but the bastards had to let me go."

"Oh right, I see," Katia says.

"Yep, I told them the dumb sheila was standing behind me on the driveway, and it was dark. The critters couldn't pin anything on me."

Rick has another half spoonful of speed while a forked-lift truck loads bales of sea salt on the back. As the drug takes hold, his rasping drawl becomes more indecipherable. Katia nudges me, silently mouthing *"Quoi?"* each time Rick speaks. He coughs constantly as he chain-smokes. And there is a whole new vocabulary to learn. Everyone he refers to is a "critter" or a "gate rider".

Rick is the scrawniest truck driver I've ever seen, with matchstick legs and sinewy Popeye-like biceps. He has a mane of unkempt hair trailing down his back. He wears black work boots, a red polo-neck T-shirt covered in oil stains and tight blue denim shorts. There are no snacks on the dashboard. His only distraction on the road is talking to other drivers on his CB radio or listening to music.

"Right mate," he says to me, "you better help put the tarp on." I have no idea how to assist. It takes me five minutes, long enough for Rick to smoke two cigarettes, to realise he means the tarpaulin.

A stiff wind blows through the sparse blue-gum-lined plains. My attempts at tying down the canvas, by yanking the rope through metal eyelets and trying to remember Boy Scout knots, prove useless. I avoid Rick. Whenever I catch sight of him at the opposite corner of the road train, he is scratching his head, redoing my knots. The elderly trucker behind, who arrived after us, is finished in half the time.

Finally, three hours after we leapt gratefully aboard at Rockhampton, we are off again.

Rick seems rattled, and I assume it's because of my knots, but he blames the tarp. "Flaming drongos, I've got a fucking 45-foot tarp for a 43-foot truck. They don't get it. They give me the wrong tarp. How can I do my job properly if I don't have the right back-up?"

I can see the tarp on the rear container flapping in the breeze as Rick crunches through the lower gears.

The coast-clutching bends of the Bruce Highway near Rodds Bay offer a perfect chance for Rick to demonstrate his driving prowess. "Mate, I never drive with two hands on the wheel, ay. I do ninety hours a week, I reckon. I'm a workaholic like my old man. My last girlfriend finished with me because she said I didn't take her out enough. I said, 'I work all the bloody time so what do you expect?' So I'm bloody good. It's the old bastards driving slow in the caravans that cause the accidents."

He points to a dent in a sugar-cane field inland where one of his colleagues met his end. With the speed kicking in, he is totally absorbed in describing the accident, no hands on the wheel. Katia cowers, her hand on the door handle in readiness to leap. A split second after the narration ends, Rick brutally manhandles the wheel to turn sharply around a trundling mobile home.

"Jesus, you racking road hog," he fumes, honking his horn.

The Queensland sugar-cane plantations originally relied on slaves forcibly transported from South Pacific islands for the crop to be harvested. Some 60,000 Polynesians were shipped to Queensland before the Australian Federation was formed in 1901. That racist taint, alongside the alleged abuse of Aborigines rehomed in places like Palm Island, has been difficult for Queensland particularly to shrug off.

For the next two hours, we brush aside every vehicle in our path. We have a year's worth of near collisions. Rick is right about the amphetamine, it certainly makes him a confident driver, if not a safe one. Maybe we need some.

Our ride with him reaches its nadir during a pause at the roadhouse cafeteria in Miriam Vale.

Although he confesses to not being hungry – a major side effect of taking speed – Rick orders a rump steak.

"I'll have a steak, chips and salad, without the chips and salad," he tells the waitress.

The steak is larger than his plate, thicker than a hard-back novel. While he chews, he peruses hardcore porn magazines bequeathed to him by a haulage buddy, in full view of the other customers. He burps, and then picks out bits of gristle stuck between his teeth with a serrated knife.

Katia has reached the stage where she no longer cares, appreciating the peculiarities of our outback encounters as much as I do. "At least we'll get there," she says.

Before touching the steering wheel, Rick holds his head in his hands for a full minute, inhaling deeply through his nose and then blowing out slowly. I take that as a good sign, that he's psyching himself up.

I don't know whether it's the speed or the steak, but as we pass through the tranquil town of Childers, he loses his composure. "I've got two more bloody pick-ups by tomorrow night!" he screams.

Childers, a sugar-cane and fruit-farming town, has gained notoriety since fifteen foreign backpackers, seven of them British, died in an arson attack on a hostel. Their murderer, Robert Long, is Australia's worst single convicted mass killer. Long – described in the press as a "homeless loner", a "fruitpicker" and a "drifter" – developed a seething hatred of backpackers, which he vented by pouring petrol into a bin in the hostel's television lounge. He had already threatened to burn Childers' main hostel down once.

Our route is paved with the crimes committed against our travelling predecessors since I was last here.

A driver from a rival Brisbane firm (with better vehicles) has the audacity to overtake us ascending an incline.

For fifty kilometres we are locked in an impossible duel, terrorising sunset-snapping tourists, double-overtaking on twilit bends.

I relax by eavesdropping on Rick's CB radio conversations. They all follow a similar pattern. More often than not, the inadequacies of the tarpaulin are a major source of rancour.

"G'day Rick. Where are ya?"

"Miriam."

"Ah right."

"Yep, gave me the wrong fucking tarp. It's crook."

"Ah yeah."

"Yep."

"Who were ya rooting last night?"

"Same sheila as last time."

"Fucking oath."

"Yeah, she was full on."

"Fair dinkum."

"There's cops down past Maryborough, I heard. Two of them. Don't let the gate riders touch ya."

"Thanks buddy."

"Yep, see ya later."

"Catch ya later."

We are neck and neck with our enemy on the single-carriage highway. Someone has to submit. Rick grinds his brown teeth and glares across. The other driver smiles.

"Okay, mate, you've shown him," I say, seeing the far-off glare of oncoming headlights.

"You reckon, ay," Rick replies. "Fair dinkum. That showed the critter." And he brakes. I can see my interference has rattled him. He's obviously not one to come second in a race. He asks me to get a Jimmy Barnes tape from the box.

Without warning, Rick pulls over at a truck stop north of Gympie. "I've gotta stop here, all right," he said. "You blokes can walk the rest."

We are still a long way from Gympie, with little chance of another lift tonight, yet even Katia is glad to be stuck in the middle of nowhere. With much relief, we start walking down the highway in the pitch dark. Gympie is shut for the night and no one takes pity on us. But the unhurried walk is just what was required after our frenetic day with Rick.

"I bet you've never had a lift like that," Katia says.

I think back through hitchhiking journeys at home in Britain, in Australia and across Europe, and I can't remember anything that resembles it. As we stride towards Gympie, another once-booming gold-rush town, I recount some of my most hair-raising lifts, white-knuckle rides that I've brought up in other company as shoulder-shrugging anecdotes, but deliberately never mentioned before we came to Australia.

The worst was a ride in the north of England, from somewhere on the M62 in West Yorkshire to Bishop Auckland in Teeside. It was an absolutely freezing February day, which I mention because it perhaps explains the absolutely idiotic risk I took. After a long, shivering wait a small box van pulled over. I noticed there were three large blokes in the cab. The two passengers were colossal, with drooping beer bellies, and were clearly very pissed. But the guy behind the wheel appeared just about composed, so I got in.

They jeered, burped and farted the whole way. I couldn't get a word in edgeways. I was pushed right on the edge of the seat, by the door, with my hand pressed against the window. There was no point asking for more room. The fat guy next to me momentarily passed out and pushed me away from him in his drunken stupor. About half an hour in, I realised the door wasn't shut properly. I tightened my grip on the dashboard and tried, in vain, to close the door with the other.

As the journey went on, it became clear that the driver was as out of his skull as his companions. They were on a bender, he yelled. He refused to budge from the outside lane. A Mercedes was right behind us and its driver flashed his lights for us to move over. That was like a red rag to a bull. My driver suddenly swung back into the middle lane, without checking his rear-view mirror. As the Mercedes came virtually parallel to us, he veered back into the outside lane, prompting a screech of brakes and furious horn. The car almost crashed into the central reservation barrier. I heard the scrape of metal on metal. The lads thought it was hilarious.

Moments later, the door I was leaning on flapped open. I was halfway out, while we kept up a ridiculous speed down the motorway. But the maniac refused to slow down so I could close the door; instead he deliberately slalomed to make my precarious sitting position as parlous as possible. For a while, I actually believed he wanted me to fall out. As we got near to Bishop Auckland, it began snowing heavily. I thought I was going to die. Only when we had to stop at a junction on the edge of their town could I leap out to safety. They hardly noticed my going.

"You never told me about zat," Katia says. "I don't need to ask why."

Sod's law: the delightful family who pick us up in the morning are the most charming, polite and sensitive people one could ever hope to meet. They go out of their way to tell us the nicest things to do in their region.

They are a mother and her three daughters, on their way to the annual family appointment at the dentist. The daughters wear flowery dresses. Their front teeth are glistening pearly white. They want to know everything about us, about where we come from, why we're here. We stop at a little café in Tewantin where they buy us tea and biscuits.

"You guys are such a lovely couple," the oldest Heidi-blonde daughter says to us after a final floss in the café toilets. "I really hope you enjoy this part of Australia. Make sure you see the coloured sands at Teewah if you can, guys. They're just so lovely to look at."

They are the perfect antidote to Rick. By lunchtime, as we watch pelicans dive across the everglades at Noosa harbour, he's just a blur, a living personification of the road-trains that make the bitumen tremble up and down the highways of Australia.

12

Pacific Highway Paradise

Souths of Brisbane – the bustling, balmy, bountiful Queensland state capital that has seduced us for the last two weeks – the high-rise hotel developments of the Gold Coast start in earnest. Real estate and time-share holiday apartment renting are the biggest businesses in Southport. The architecture is boring. Nothing distinguishes the shift from one resort town to another. Japanese tour groups, all with baseball caps peaked down against the cancerous sunlight, stand in huddles outside Movie World. At Surfers Paradise, that most glamorous of names, you can just glimpse the red-and-yellow bathing caps of perma-tanned beach lifeguards between skyscrapers.

The Gold Coast is Australia's Florida, playing host to more holidaymakers than anywhere else in the country. It is a sprawling 75-kilometre-long ribbon development, slowly swallowing up the belt of green land that keeps it separate from Brisbane. Hotels, casinos and nightclubs back on to the famous strip of beach that originally lured developers to the area.

Not until Burleigh Heads, one of the southernmost outposts of the hedonistic strip, does nature intervene again.

Coves that haven't yet been cleared for development are lined with pine and bottlebrush trees. Soon after, Coolangatta and Tweed Heads fuse into the more restrained, octogenarian pastures of the conurbation. Golf and bowls clubs abound.

Tweed Heads is the first place that we can seriously consider hitching from. Stuck on the butt end of the Gold Coast, it thrives like everywhere else around here, mainly thanks to the packed amusement arcades behind its surf beach. At the southern tip of the town is a little peninsula on which a memorial monument to Captain Cook stands proudly, apparently. We glimpse a sign for it through the local bus window.

Cook sailed right up the Gold Coast. He was nearly shipwrecked on the Cudgen Headland near here. As with Mount Sorrow, the names Cook gave local landmarks tell the tale: Mount Warning and Point Danger. He must have felt jittery about the whole coastline. The 18-metre memorial itself is in the form of a capstan, and was moulded from cast-iron ballast jettisoned off the *Endeavour* and recovered in the 1960s.

Duranbah Beach is packed with families here for the weekend. We dump our rucksacks on the sand and lay out our towels. Somehow sunbathing isn't as mind-numbingly satisfying when you know that you've got to rub the sand off to thumb a lift later in the afternoon. But sleeping bags make great head rests.

"*On est bien ici, hein?*" Katia asks, translating "zis is nice" back into French.

"I know it's comfy, but..."

"I know, I know, I know. We 'ave to get a lift. I don't

mind, honest. Yuck, look at zer weird swimming costume zis woman is wearing."

This epitomises the progress in our travelling relationship: Katia is enjoying her favourite beach hobby of spotting weird-looking people, and the impending move isn't affecting her in the least.

"You'll need another bus to get out to the highway," a Greek sandwich-shop proprietor tells us when we reluctantly leave the sand behind.

For the first time since this trip started, we are confronted with the same difficulties one has while hitchhiking out of large cities in Europe. Just when you think you've reached the edge, another outlying housing estate gets in the way of the open road.

The bus driver actually drops us off on the very thin relief lane of a three-lane freeway before turning down a side road. I decide that he's never had hitchhikers on his bus before, otherwise he wouldn't have selected such an abysmal position. Lorries almost chop off my thumb as we walk tentatively along the side of the road looking for somewhere less exposed. Drivers wouldn't be able to stop even if they wanted to. Outside-lane motorists, the most likely lift givers, can probably not even see us.

The road goes over a river and there's a slip road up the other side. The only chance we have of getting a ride is to cross the river below and rejoin further up. In a car the viaduct crossing probably takes ten seconds; it takes us more than half an hour of slog through a convoluted jumble of subways and filter junctions. Fishermen crowd a jetty on the Tweed River, which heads inland to Mount Warning, an extinct volcano that last erupted twenty million years ago. There is a tempting caravan park right next to the water.

At the new spot our unmapped presence nearly prompts countless smashes as careful "grey nomads" roll their steering wheels. Perhaps they think they're about to be unwilling participants in our double suicide pact. But, as I predicted, a selfless lunatic speeding down the fast lane risks his safety by zapping right across the highway to halt a few hundred metres in front of us.

He's a civil engineer from New Zealand, rotund and dark haired, with a library full of fantasy fiction on the back seat of his car. At one point, I do a mental double-take as I hear Katia talking with him about concrete. He is happy to drive us to Byron Bay, a healthy sixty kilometres out of the Gold Coast urban jungle and well into New South Wales.

The scenery changes drastically at the state border, as though the boundary is naturally delineated. Verdant meadows and spongy coppices cloak wide, frothy rivers as the road winds sharply through undulating hills. The ocean breeze streaming through the gaps in the vehicle windows is fresher, making the occasionally fetid subtropical air breathable. Sometimes the view is so green, so vibrant that it looks artificial, like the backdrop to a children's cartoon. I think of Ireland, not Australia, as I gaze out, happily letting Katia discuss construction work with our host.

Byron Bay marks Australia's easternmost point. Cook sailed past in May 1770 as the *Endeavour* tacked its way north up the coast. He wrote, "I named Cape Byron... a tolerable high point of land. It may be known by a remarkable high peaked mountain lying inland north-west."

What a buzz that would have been, lying in your hammock with your telescope pointed towards land and going through your address book until you find a decent name for a headland or mountain. "I haven't seen Steve for a while; I'll name it Steve's Promontory." Imagine your friends' reaction when you get home and show them the new map!

As elsewhere in the colonisation of Australia, the local Aborigines, the Banjalang people, weren't spotted. Names they had for the places Cook espied were conveniently ignored. In this case, the Byron after whom the town is named is actually Vice-Admiral John Byron, the Romantic poet's grandfather. Byron was one of Cook's peers, a renowned British navigator.

Today Byron Bay is well known for other reasons, as Australia coolest hippy hangout. Since the 1970s, it has been a countercultural meeting point where virtually anything goes. Sadly, the New Zealander tells us, Byron is a shadow of its former rebellious self. Like in all the world's coolest spots, its best properties have been bought up by the rich and famous. On the global profits of the corny lines in *Crocodile Dundee*, actor Paul Hogan built himself a Spanish-style mansion in the Byron hinterland.

But at a caravan park overlooking the sweeping bay and across to the Cape Byron headland, there is little evidence of this gentrification. The path down to Belongil Beach is lined with people getting high in time for sundown. The earthy herb smell of strong marijuana wafts across the sandy cliff edge. A hippy couple in purple dungarees curse, blaming each other for leaving their cigarette papers in the camper van. Two blokes leaning on a fence smile inanely at their shoes, muffling giggles. I pick out one bunch of bongo players leaning against a rock, but the sound isn't coming from them, there are conga-beating groups right across the beach. They coordinate their disparate rhythms as the dying sun makes strips of cloud glow amber and turns the wave crests blood red.

By my reckoning, more than one band of amateur percussionists in a small town authenticates its hippy status. Byron Bay easily passes the test.

We wander to the main beach where surfers, barely wearied by the day's action, light fires. The Cape Byron lighthouse sweeps across the rocky outcrops like a night-club strobe. In the streets behind, boutiques sell incense, crystals and stained-glass curios. Vegetarian cafés are packed. Dreadlocked cyclists convene on street corners to discuss the night ahead.

Meanwhile, proper money-spending holidaymakers chat noisily at bustling beachside bars. You can pick out the trendy kids up for a few weeks from the seasoned, patchouli-scented hippies. Yet Byron Bay remains a proper community despite the influx of affluent Australians with holiday homes. Public pressure has prevented Club Med and McDonald's from infiltrating the town. The local council is dominated by green politicians, who banned drive-in takeaway fast-food joints from the town centre.

We find a pub doing cheap meals. It is a cavernous old place, with tables sparsely dotted around like a flea-pit cabaret club. For our first two large beers, a big screen shows a documentary film of California surfers who travelled the world looking for the ultimate wave. For the meal and the two beers after it, we endure a stage show entitled "Australia's Best Freakshow". These aren't freaks in the Victorian circus sense, but uprooted drama-school students with a desperate desire to perform their hazy free-verse poetry and acrobatics in front of an audience.

The moment we walk out of the front door into a darkened street, an Aboriginal guy approaches us. He's decked out in shabby hip-hop sportswear. He says, "G'day, my name's Rivers, like a stream, you know."

He waits for a response.

"Nice one," I say, weakly.

"Do you want to see my little mate Ginger juggle with fire?"

From behind a tree emerges Ginger, a skinny, freckled white kid. Ginger throws one unlit juggling baton into the air and drops it. He retreats, and looks dumbly at the pavement.

"Anyway, like I was saying," Rivers goes on, "do yous two want a smoke?"

I shrug vaguely. Rivers bends down to a nearby flower-pot and rummages about in the soil. He comes back with a clump of sticky grass wrapped in newspaper. It looks a lot, but it's difficult to tell as it hasn't been properly dried. Rivers asks if we want to join him and his buddies later for a jam session around a camp fire. Katia and I nod.

But later, as I listen to the surge, crash and fizz of waves outside the tent, the suggestion is instantly forgotten. Katia curls into a ball beside me, unable to speak.

In the morning, a man standing in front of the lurid psychedelic frontage of the Byron Bay community centre tells us he can help us go where we want to.

"Well, we're heading south, but not for a few days," I reply.

He wanders off without a single word of advice. Hippies' advice is rarely literal, usually obscure.

"What's the best way to get to Nimbin?" I shout after him.

"Bring your own spaceship, buddy," he calls back, "but if you haven't got one come with me."

He drives an ageing VW classic camper to Nimbin. Scrawled on it, in bold, childish lettering, are slogans like "Think global, act local" and "Grow your own". He calls himself Chance. His explanation for the odd title is suitably kooky. "My name's Chance, like, you know, 'hey, take a chance'. I spell it c-h-a-p-e-l though."

Chance tells us he's originally from Victoria, but he enunciates his words with a stoned Californian twang. He looks like a cross between David Crosby of Crosby, Stills and Nash and a mad scientist, without the white coat. He is tubby, with bouncy shoulder-length hair and a thick moustache.

Katia immediately regrets mentioning she is French. The mangled floodgates of Chance's fuzzy existence open.

"I like Italian, actually," he tells us, "because I need to learn it as I'm wanted by the Vatican, you know, the Catholic Church. What do I do? You know mathematics and archaeology. I do a lot with numbers, like *A* is a *V* upside-down, and a *B* is two *D*s. You understand. I'm waiting for *W* to come along. Okay, I'll tell you guys, I know all this because I've died seven times."

All of this is said straight-faced. Stirred in with the madness are occasional statements that are just too detailed to be fictional. Chance mentions his children, all by different mothers. He talks about the guy he used to buy pot from while homeless in Sydney's red-light district, King's Cross.

The journey to Nimbin passes in a blur. Rocky pinnacles draped in green palms, pines and firs spike the undulating scenery, but there's hardly time to focus. I register the fact that the region is as unmistakably idyllic as anywhere I've seen on the east coast, but get drawn back into the conversation.

Chance parks in front of the garishly painted Nimbin Bakery on the main street. I haven't seen Katia move as fast since we got out of the roadtrain last week. The road layout is like any other small Australian bush town, except that all the establishments have rainbow-coloured signs, Middle Earth wizardry murals on their walls and dread-locked "dole bludgers" sitting on upturned fruit cartons underneath the awnings. At the end of this goofy street is subtropical rainforest.

Nimbin was once a sleepy dairy village, hidden in lush, fertile hills, hardly altered since the first European settlers arrived in the 1840s. In 1973, it was struck by the human equivalent of a seismic shock, in the same way that sleepy Woodstock was in 1969. Thousands of commune dwellers, alternative-technology advocates and students made tiny Nimbin the venue for the experimental Aquarius Festival. There had never been a similar gathering in Australia. When the debauchery and meditation were over, most people returned to the cities. But a small number of committed visionaries stayed on, and modern-day Nimbin was born.

Most tourists come here to smoke plate-sized piles of grass. That's the truth of it. Getting wasted in Nimbin is as much a part of the backpacker trail as spotting dingoes on Fraser Island. Although people do take an earnest interest in the Hemp Embassy on Cullen Street, with its gospel of trying to change Australia's drug laws, Nimbin is essentially about losing your bearings. Thousands show up for the Mardi Grass campaigning street festival every year, filing away leaflets on permaculture, organic food and energy efficiency to take back into their regular lives.

You need to keep constant notes to pin down the Nimbin sensation. I lose mine in the Rainbow Café after accidentally going one hash flapjack too far down the road to delirium.

After Byron Bay and Nimbin, other rural towns in the region look tactfully straight-laced. In Ballina, this conservatism is manifested by the number of people who avert their eyes from us as we walk through town. Most are elderly. There are expansive Federation-era homesteads tucked away behind the highway, with privet-hedge-walled gardens. As we cross a bridge on the southern edge of Ballina, pelicans fly above to their nests on telegraph poles. On one side of the road is an industrial estate, on the other pasture in which cattle munch with egrets resting on their hides.

We give up walking at a truckers' bay outside the Big Prawn Roadhouse, which has a big pink prawn stuck on its roof. Comedy plastic models of the local produce are a feature of towns in the more fertile parts of Australia. Bananas, pineapples and melons are all inflated for passing motorists who might be feeling peckish as they drive through these otherwise anonymous settlements.

Ballina is heading for a coveted position in the top three crappest places to hitchhike from in Australia when a young woman in a large estate car stops. She lives out in the bush, behind a deserted band of beach in a beautiful house built by her rich husband.

"I can watch whales from our patio," she tells us.

When not taking separate holidays from her husband, she breeds Italian mastiffs. But once she was a hippy, she says. She talks about how Nimbin has gone downhill and is infiltrated by heroin dealers. The dealers go there daily to supply local users, who in turn sell cannabis to tourists to fund their habit. According to her, the good vibes are being spiked into people's veins. After turning a blind eye for years, plain-clothes cops now wander the streets.

She drops us off at a layby in front of a turning for her home near a place called Iluka. Her daughter gets off the school bus a few minutes later, and we board it for free to Grafton, at the woman's request. The bus goes the long way, through all the country towns. The children look athletic and well nourished but not tanned (on the whole Australian parents are paranoid about their kids being exposed to harmful sun rays).

When we hit Grafton, the sky is dark enough to start asking for directions to local motels. But a truck driver sees us at a roundabout and brakes courageously, narrowly avoiding a rear-end collision. He is likeable. The reason for such a contrast with Rick the roadtrain roadhog is clear: this guy used to drive a long-distance semi-trailer to Perth, but has given that lifestyle up for more manageable runs back and forth between Brisbane and Coffs Harbour, which is where he takes us.

He asks Katia if she finds Australians difficult to understand.

"Sorry, what was zat?" she replies.

In a coffee shop in Coffs Harbour, we meet a friendly German guy named Hans who wanders over for a chat. He's living in a hippy commune out in the bush. A few drinks later, he invites us to stay there. Why not?

Eventually, after buying Hans some barramundi and wine as a gift, we move towards Bundagen, twenty kilometres south of Coffs Harbour. The commune is so self-sufficient from society at large that it isn't even on the maps. When we get to the turning – deep in fern-carpeted paperbark forest – no sign indicates where the road leads.

As we approach the cooperative down a gravel track, I notice that small patches of state forest have been cleared for logging. A sign indicates a diversion is in place while the road is being mended. Manning the sign, and making sure all Bundagen's residents respect the diversion, is a hippy who looks cryogenically frozen from the 1967 Summer of Love. We stop to chat. He's reading a book on enlightenment and has nothing else on him for his eight-hour shift.

The grand entrance to Bundagen is a bus shelter structure with a noticeboard. On it are flyers for various events:

"Dancing with Josy on Friday" and "Learn physical movement therapy" are two of my favourites.

We reach Hans' suburb of Bundagen, called The
Bananas by its residents. A sign says, "This is a car/e free
community". We bump into a couple with hair down to
their waists who are moving across the valley – for a
shorter commute to their vegetable patch the man, Klaus,
says. When I tell them we are only staying for a few nights,
he adds, "We said that, and we've been here for over three
years."

Out of the thick undergrowth sprout little cabins, eccentric wooden-peaked constructions, each distinct from its
neighbours. This is too gorgeous to be real. All Katia and
I can do is talk over each other with meaningless super-
latives: amazing, beautiful, fantastic, the full thesaurus.

The pathways are ambiguous, through grass higher
than our knees. When we reach the house Hans is crash-
ing in it is a fairytale, like a cute rabbit den designed by
Beatrix Potter. The dwelling is a squat, two-storey building
made of dark wood. Next to the main structure is a hut, a
massage room that also contains a heated shower.
Bundagen is not connected to the mains, but many of the
houses obtain electricity by solar power. This one has ten
solar panels. Behind the main home is an outdoor com-
posting toilet, which is entirely visible to passers-by and
affords a privileged panorama across the whole commune.
Rain water is collected in a tank and then put through a
purifying filter.

Hans is keen that we walk down the private path to
Bundagen's own beach before sundown. The roar of the
Pacific waves – the only external noise in the community –

becomes louder as we approach. Surfboards belonging to commune children are stashed against mangrove trunks. The beach, initially empty of human beings, stretches for miles on both sides of us. A pony-tailed man emerges naked from the surf, sprints across the white sand and says "g'day" to us. Black-necked storks wade in rockpools. The sanguine ball of fire becomes a faint tangerine glow and then slowly steps aside for the Southern Cross and other twinkling constellations that I can't identify.

We meet a Dutch guy on the way back, trying to find out who has borrowed his axe.

"I get to watch sunrise and sunset here every day," he says. "I never get bored living here. There's always something new."

It's when we get back from the beach that I realise just how much the Bundagen cooperative members have achieved the perfect hidey-hole. The house we're in has all the convenience of modern existence, but is disturbed only by crickets, the cooing of fruit doves and the occasional foraging of red-necked wallabies at dusk. Oh, and the sound of people pissing on the ground.

At the entrance to Hans' house is an alcove containing a little table, obviously designed by someone with gentle reflection foremost in mind. The lounge area has three huge glass windows that open out onto the garden. Arched stained-glass windows have been fitted elsewhere. There is a compact dining space beneath a sloping bookcase. We climb a steep wooden staircase to the sleeping area, barefoot all the while.

Nowhere I've ever been has immediately made me feel "I want to live here forever" like this room. For me, someone with more interest in tents than interior decoration, it is the ideal I never knew existed. The octagonal turret-like space has a 360-degree scenic panorama to match anywhere in Australia, at eye level with cabbage palms, native pines and banana plant leaves dotted about the community. Hans tells us that when he first slept in the room, he woke in the night, looked at the milky night sky above, and assumed he was in heaven. In one corner is a desk, in the other a supplementary chill-out zone.

In the morning, Hans takes us on a tour of the garden, filling a basket with fruit *en route*. Orange, lemon and grapefruit trees droop with the weight of their fruit. He introduces us for the first time to lemonades, a chewable lemon–orange crossover, and custard apples. Chickens peck grass seeds at our feet and run across the sweet potato patch. Every herb and vegetable imaginable is here. Katia is intrigued.

As blissful, uncomplicated days slouch into one another, we get to know some people in the community. One woman – who's name sounds like Koala but isn't – has the most palatial home of all. It's a large bungalow on stilts, with rocking chairs on a wide veranda running right the way round. Her place is so well fitted it has an interior bathroom and a toilet attached to the building. The kitchen is straight out of a lifestyle brochure.

Koala is studying her bills when we meet, like any conventional householder. She has been here for years, and stays because she can't think of anywhere better to live.

"Bundagen is too perfect," she says. "I can study my own methods here undisturbed by the authorities. I have found paradise here in New South Wales. That's so far out."

"What methods are those?" I ask.

"I used to teach contemporary dance professionally, but now I am involved in teaching movement."

"Movement?" Katia enquires. She used to dance ballet, so knows a little about these matters.

"Yes, this is what I was talking to you about," Hans answers. "This is movement and positions to enhance your awareness of your body."

The conversation dances around its nebulous subject, and eventually Koala manages to explain, in her own woolly way, what the community is all about.

Bundagen has strict rules governing its daily life, she says. There are 210 members, all of whom have a say in cooperative life. Decisions are made on a consensus basis at open meetings held every week in the main house. Co-op markets are held to trade the produce of individual gardens and share meals. Bundagen's guiding principles are binding. They are environmental responsibility, social harmony and economic independence. It all starts to sound quite dull, like the drudgery of regular "square" life. Rules here are inflexible too.

Koala debates for so long on minor matters that this rapturous Arcadia starts to fray around the edges, lose some of its gloss. Does anyone ever do anything here without discussing it democratically first, I wonder.

No one is prepared to talk with us about the origins of the community, how the land was acquired, how these penniless abstainers obtained the finances to buy it. And they aren't entirely detached from the world outside, they go to Coffs Harbour to buy luxury provisions that can't be grown off the land and visit the nearest Post Office to collect mail. The perfect alternative society is only sustainable because of the rich soil and ideal climate in this part of Australia, I realise. It's far easier to be a dropout when you have a beach on your doorstep, a subtropical forest to call your own and sunshine most of the year.

One morning we make our move, having learned that a stay of any lengthy duration requires us to go before the commune council meeting and achieve consensus approval. It all starts to sound like Neighbourhood Watch, like a petty parish council. As visitors, we are not necessarily tolerated by all residents.

Koala's ideas about our best hitchhiking spot are so half-baked that it's not worthwhile demurring. She hasn't actually gone further than Coffs Harbour for two years, it transpires. Her memory of the Pacific Highway, like most certainties, is foggy at best. She mentions towns I can't see on the map.

I'm so impatient by lunchtime that my impressions of Bundagen founder still more. Katia has really had enough, reading her book on a rocking chair. When we got here I thought we had found the pot of gold at the end of the rainbow, the Holy Grail for our quest around Australia. But although Bundagen is the bush at its most hospitable, it's still tainted by human beings, however gentle they might be.

We stand outside a little bungalow in Uranga, back on the Pacific Highway. Net curtains twitch. Perhaps we've brought that hippy aroma with us. Koala waves and goes back to nature, back to bitching about neighbours living on the other side of Bundagen. For someone living in a commune, she certainly hates company.

13

The Lucky Country

Sydney is biting cold, hemmed in by freakish weather. For the first time in Australia I can see my breath. Katia pulls her sleeping bag hood over her head, also for the first time. The hostel we selected at random from the list of hundreds is shabby and unheated. It has two kitchens, one for the numerous Japanese guests residing here long term and one for anyone else - us. There is only one strict rule at this establishment: don't smoke dope at the dinner table. Anything else is acceptable.

Even backpackers' hostels have a sliding scale of comfort. Ours is one of the cheapest in town, and therefore we find ourselves a long walk from the city centre and a winding bus ride from the beaches.

But through our now well-practised method of sheer arbitrary fluke, our undesirable location is - astonishingly - appropriate. The bus we take from the city centre finishes up on Botany Bay, at the suburb of La Perouse. Our hostel is halfway between the two points. La Perouse is one of the few places in Australia to have taken a French name. It is there as a reminder, a cheeky dig at Britain's greatest imperial rival. That little inlet on the craggy natural harbour marks the exact spot where Australia became an English-speaking nation instead of a French one.

Following Cook's discovery of Australia's east coast, the first British fleet set sail for Botany Bay in 1787. Led by Captain Arthur Philip, this flotilla of eleven ships contained 1,400 people, of whom more than half were convicts. The British government had selected Botany Bay as an ideal site for a prison settlement, since its own jails were becoming too overcrowded. Cook had described the bay as "tolerably well sheltered from all winds". But when Philip arrived, he found the site unsuitable, as it had little fresh water supply. So, after some scouting around, Australia's first colony was moved north to Sydney Harbour – described by Philip as the "finest harbour in the world" – which Cook had managed to sail straight past.

And it was at this point that the renowned French explorer Jean-François de Galaup, Comte de la Pérouse, who had been dispatched to match Cook's achievements, missed his great opportunity. He arrived at Botany Bay just as Captain Philip guided his massive convoy a few miles up the coast. Instead of claiming new territory for Louis XVI, the aristocratic captain would be heading back landless. Yet although Britain and France were competing for supremacy in the South Pacific, records show la Pérouse and Philip dined together, and presumably came to some kind of finders-keepers arrangement over a glass of cognac.

That was the last confirmed sighting of la Pérouse, whose ship *La Boussole* – the compass – is thought to have broken up and sunk on a reef in the Solomon Islands. On his way to the guillotine, Louis XVI asked, "Is there any news of Monsieur de la Pérouse?"

Contrarily, Cook had got lucky when he hit the coral off Cape Tribulation; a large piece of coral that became wedged in one hole prevented the *Endeavour* from sinking. On such strokes of fortune Australia's fate changed forever. It wasn't "the lucky country" for every new arrival. Today, the only souvenir of la Pérouse's presence is the coastal suburb at the end of this street, which incidentally has long been looked down on by white residents as a grotty, no-go ghetto where much of Sydney's destitute indigenous population lives.

So this great adventure we've just had could have been so different. I would have been the one struggling to understand truck drivers with their mangled version of the French language. Perhaps at servos, refined dishes would be followed by a selection of cheeses, because there is no way descendants of Katia's compatriots could come up with the Chiko Roll. I can't even imagine what the outback Franco-Aussie attitude would be like. Would the stiff-upper-lip indifference, optimism and biting sarcasm of the bush have come through? What would be the French version of "g'day, mate"? We'll never know.

One thing's for sure: Philip's navigational judgement was spot on in picking Sydney Cove. The genius of the city is its majestic, sweeping harbour. Like all great metropolises, Sydney has secret pockets that dazzle the unsuspecting visitor.

When taking the ferry to Manly, the grandeur of Port Jackson Bay folds out piece by segmented piece. We watch a restored cutter, like the one Philip would have used, sail across the broad estuary. Fleets of yachts, the toys of the local élite, race around buoys in the bay. Sydney sprawls for ever, but its residential areas are split by patches of untempered virgin forest, surf beaches and uninhabitable headlands. On the way back the setting sun streaks the Manhattanesque city-centre skyline and then, past Potts Point, the welcoming iron arch that is Sydney Harbour Bridge – known as the "coat hanger" to locals – and the daring sails of the Opera House come into view.

"En fait, tu as raison," Katia says at Mrs Macquarie's Point, a brilliant vantage spot, the perfect place for stepping down on one knee and proposing marriage – although, being me, I don't do that.

I'm momentarily taken aback. What can I be right about?

"Well, zis is a great place. People living 'ere, *ils ont de la chance,"* she explains, adding in English, "people 'ere are lucky."

Sydney has everything one could want in a city; there's no point in me repeating what the guidebooks already describe perfectly tediously. No one could be bored by its nightlife, no one could be understimulated by the views, and no one could fail to appreciate its Olympian triumph from inauspicious beginnings. Not for nothing is Sydney is the place most European visitors decide to live in when they return on a migrant work visa.

One afternoon we get a bus through the leafy, elegant nineteenth-century terraces of Paddington to Bondi Beach, the semicircular sandy bay that is transformed into a sea of Union Jack swimming shorts on Christmas Day every year.

For me, Bondi is a place of pilgrimage. I spent the last four nights of my first trip to Australia sleeping rough on its finely raked sand. Bondi was my last resort after running out of money and being evicted from Centennial Park, where I had temporarily erected my tent. Every evening, I would sit on a bench on the grassy knoll at the beach's western tip and chat with a homeless bloke who came here every summer. We discussed the day's non-events before going our separate ways to crash out. There can be few better places in the world to be a work-experience vagabond.

As Katia and I stand facing out to sea, watching the proper wet-suited surfers get savaged by the waves and the *poseurs* compare boards, I sense a tap on my shoulder. No one's there.

"*Qu'est que c'est?*" Katia demands – what's up? "Are you cold?"

I start explaining: I have the impression of someone following me around, like that old cliché of someone stepping over my grave. I mention my tramp friend; he probably drowned in the Pacific. It could be the spirit of the outback calling me back. You see, I say, like most Australians our backs are turned to the brutal interior, but its brooding presence pursues us.

And as she has throughout our relationship whenever I suffer from one of my pretentious delusions of grandeur, Katia makes sure my feet are rooted firmly to the ground.

"*N'importe quoi,*" she murmurs. That's French for "what a load of crap".

But, I insist, my theory isn't complete crap. The same instinctive yearning towards the forbidding heart of Australia bewitched the first freed convicts as they fanned out from Sydney Cove. Emancipated from their chains, relieved of their debt to the Old World, they drifted one by one into the bush. These "emancipists" – a distinctive class, apart from the free "exclusives" – gradually established themselves as the go-getters of the new colony. Given a second chance in this lucky country at the opposite end of the globe, they did everything they could to cultivate parcels of land, to make the most of what it offered. Other immigrants preferred to eke out a living in the city.

As Sydney spread, settlers increasingly found they were blocked off by the deep chasms and steep peaks of the Blue Mountains.

In 1813, twenty-five years after Captain Philip landed with the first fleet, a group of men that included two convicts and several Aborigines forged a route across the range. They succeeded where seven previous attempts had failed, presumably in no small part thanks to the Aborigines' tracking know-how and the liberated prisoners' rugged determination to succeed. By following ridges instead of dipping into the gullies, Gregory Blaxland, William Lawson and William Wentworth – the men who led the troop – triumphed in crossing the Blue Mountains. On the western side were fertile grazing plains.

For me, the Blue Mountains are yet another part of Australia that I got drunk in on my first trip without taking proper notice. I saw the Three Sisters formation, the Blue Mountains signature landmark, with a hammer-blow hangover. So when we arrive at the Echo Point lookout, thanks to a ride with a Sydney student going to his parents' house in quaint Leura to have his clothes washed, I appreciate it afresh. The glow of the bush whisks me off my feet again.

In the case of the Blue Mountains, that glow is a purplish navy mist – the genuinely blue haze oozing off the abundant vegetation. You can see the eucalyptus vapour waft from the Mountain Blue gum trees that carpet the fortress-like barrier of knife-blade apexes and bottomless ravines. The air is much thinner than in Sydney, the kind of crisp, wintry air ailing people bottle for a cure. Night in Katoomba is so quiet we hear the trickle of the floodlit waterfall long before we reach it. Our cosy room is wood panelled, with a single-bar electric heater that we switch on.

A path from the car park at Govett's Leap lookout follows a straight line around the crescents of a giant abyss; vertical walls crash down into the greedy forest below. During a morning walk I pause and peer down. The drop makes me vertiginous. Only the branches of wispy gums stop us falling into the canyon. The track is slippery from melting frost.

Finally we get to the aptly named Pulpit Rock, a stage of flattened sandstone in the centre of a vast green chasm. The wilderness is unbounded, cinematically stunning. Cliffs slash into the sandstone plateau. There is total silence except for the calls of acrobatic, squawking black birds with yellow throat markings that dive into the space below.

We survey all this from a bench – probably one of the best-placed benches I've ever sat on. It's tempting to stay, we have spare sandwiches, but Katia, now taking charge of the hitchhiking agenda, reminds me it's getting late and we should head back. What a turnaround from our first morning on the road.

A forestry worker tells us he's going to Goulburn, the long way via partly surfaced minor roads. That will do.

"I think you guys are the first hitchhikers I've seen around here for over ten years," he says.

"That's strange," Katia says, "it's easy to get lifts."

"Yeah, but most people in these parts remember Ivan Milat, you see."

And then it's too late. I can't stop him telling Katia, who no longer has nagging doubts about the sanity of hitchhiking, about the one murder case I was really hoping to keep under wraps – the one that involves the deaths of eight hitchhikers.

Ivan Milat's gruesome killing spree first came to light during my previous trip. The bodies of British backpackers Caroline Clarke and Joanne Walters, who thumbed rides south from Sydney, were found in the Belanglo forest, not far from where we are now. They had been missing for five months. But I had known nothing about the fear stalking Australia's highways, pointing my thumb towards traffic regardless. The killer, however, was still at large. They found two more bodies a month after I returned to Britain.

Road worker Milat carried out the murders between December 1989 and April 1992. His victims were stabbed repeatedly or shot in the head. Some had been bound, gagged and sexually assaulted. One was beheaded with a cavalry sword. A total of eight bodies were found in the Belanglo forest 60 miles from Sydney. All were people whom Milat had stopped for on the Hume Highway.

Sentencing Milat to life in jail four years later, the judge said, "It is clear that the victims were subjected to behaviour which, for callous indifference and complete disregard to humanity, is almost beyond belief."

In a gap between gory details, none of which the driver spares, I notice that the land is aerated, freeze-dried. Odd clusters of sheep graze on high, yellowing grass. Solitary iron windmills on rusty stands tinkle in the gentle wind. Without warning, the smooth road suddenly becomes a gravel track. Our host slows down.

Jurors heard that Milat, a 49-year-old Yugoslavian immigrant, killed simply for the sake of it. His murderous binge began by picking up an Australian couple in his lorry, and he subsequently developed an incurable obsession. In fact, he had a history of targeting hitchhikers going back to the early 1970s, but police failed to check his record until too late in the investigation. When they raided his house, they recovered the firearm used to shoot Miss Clarke, and one of his German victims, concealed in a wall. A pillow case containing blood-stained sash cords was also found during the 1994 raid.

British hitchhiker Paul Onions, who escaped from Milat after being abducted on the Sydney to Melbourne road, eventually provided the key evidence that nailed the murderer. His traumatic experience in January 1990, when Milat fired shots at him, was pivotal in the conviction. Chillingly, the judge also declared, "In my view, it is inevitable that the prisoner was not alone in the criminal enterprise." But no one else has ever been convicted.

Before, I would have expected this tale to be the nail in the coffin for our intrepid expedition. I realise it does take a certain kind of pig-headedness to embark on a hitch-hiking journey around Australia knowing about the Milat murders.

"I'm sorry I didn't mention that," I tell Katia.

She shrugs her shoulders. "You wouldn't 'ave stopped anyway, would you? Even if I'd said no, you would 'ave made sure."

In turn, I shrug my shoulders. She knows me too well to protest.

In the dim illumination of the side lights we see a wombat on the now sandy road in front, transfixed by the blaring intrusion. The forestry worker tries to swerve out of the way, but not far enough. Beneath the front right tyre, we hear the crack of the wombat's spine. It's the first wombat we've seen.

"Zer poor sing," says Katia, already forgetting the hitch-hiking horror story. *"Il était carrément mignon."* This is a reference to the wombat's cuteness. After that neither of us says much. The forestry worker returns to the Milat topic every ten minutes, as though to test our mettle.

Hitchhiking is strongly discouraged in all the guidebooks. The last time I leafed through a Lonely Planet guide to Australia in a bookshop, it said, "Hitching is not a particularly safe practice in Australia and we don't recommend it. Even people hitching in pairs are not entirely safe." Naturally, and sensibly, the Milat case was given as one of the principal reasons for this. According to the guidance, modern-day travellers should be so suspicious that even notices offering lifts in hostels should be treated warily. "You can still never be too careful," the book implores.

Independent backpacking magazines I leafed through in Brisbane last time I was here also lectured budget travellers about the dangers of getting lifts with strangers. Take the bus, they implored. "Hitching not advised. There are plenty of other cheap ways to get around," one said. I considered this an affront. To me it was taking the excitement out of my big trip before I'd even started it. Safety was the last thing on my mind.

In any case, if one looks hard enough through newspaper archives one can find plentiful horrific crimes committed against hitchhikers, sufficient to put you off for life. For example, in 1998 a British couple travelling in Israel were shot by a gunman as they thumbed a lift to a kibbutz. The man died in the attack. A few years ago, a 75-year-old retired fruit-lorry driver was convicted of the 1979 murder of a woman hitchhiker in Kent, England. But the fact that these stories get mentioned at all proves they are exceptional. The same goes for airliner crashes: they are far more prominent than car smashes in news bulletins precisely because they occur more rarely.

But after all the fascinating, generous lifts we've had – perhaps except roadtrain Rick – maybe Katia has come to the same illogical conclusions as me. She's too sensible to have given up caring about her own welfare, but she accepts the fatalism of hitchhiking, the daily roll of the dice that makes it such a brilliant diversion from the straighter road. There are sick murderers in every walk of life, I say; hitchhikers are no more prone than anyone getting a late-night taxi, taking urban public transport or walking through a badly lit inner-city slum.

"'Itchiking 'as been easy, really. I sink zer Ossees are really nice," Katia says.

"What the hell are O-zies?" the logging worker says. "Is that a French thing?"

He drops us off at the dirt road turning for his timber camp. "Take good care of yerselves," he shouts down, overemphasising the word "good".

A pea-soup fog hangs over Canberra, Australia's purpose-built federal capital. Government buildings peer abruptly through the brittle white mist, unnaturally situated in balding, sallow bush. The streets too are abnormally clean. When we get dropped off outside a tourist information centre, we have to buy a map just to get away from the overbearing woman behind the information desk. She can't accept that we only want to know the best way out of here.

Canberra is a city of *apparatchiks*, lobbyists, civil servants and student interns. The site was chosen fastidiously after federalisation for its unspoilt virgin neutrality – a woop-woop capital where kangaroos could wander freely. An American architect won a prize to design it, with a futuristic model of concentric circles linked by broad Washington DC-style boulevards. To me, Canberra looks like a cardboard cut-out experimental film set. What a ridiculous idea, building a national capital from scratch out here. We walk straight past the ultra-modern 1988 Parliament building on our way to catch a bus to the southern city limits.

Political aides whisper over double skinny mochas in a coffee shop. In the toilet there is a poster for coffee-making classes. That confirms my memory of Canberra from my last visit – the least lively capital city in the world, night and day.

The waitress says, "You guys could take a look at some of the embassies. They're beaut."

When her back's turned, Katia says to me, *"Je m'en fous"* – I don't give a stuff.

The lift we do get is with a snowboarder heading to Thredbo in the Snowy Mountains. The brief month-long ski season is in full flow. He drives us through hostile terrain, where boulder screes lie unmoved in paddocks. Snow rests on mountain tops. The road gets really steep at the Kosciuko National Park entry station.

"You have to put chains on your wheels to drive through," the attendant tells us. "Sorry, it's a legal requirement."

So we go back to Jindabyne to look for wheel chains. But a woman in the information centre says there's no snow, it's no worries. Our host is appalled to hear of this: no snow means no snowboarding.

In fairness to the National Park attendant, the conditions further up are atrocious. A drizzly blizzard drowns Thredbo, a ski resort town full of Alpine chalets. There is snow on the mountains. The chairlifts are running and Katia spots skiers through the pines. She's is shocked, having never imagined skiing as one of Australia's attributes.

On the downhill road to Khancoban the bush puts on a farewell show. A herd of fifty or more bored kangaroos stare at us gormlessly; afterwards three baby emus linger on the tarmac in front before disappearing into the dark, lichen-encrusted forest. From there on our driver – a coast-bound farmhand – puts his foot down, ignoring speed limits through agricultural towns with their claim to fame emblazoned on a plaque. One place proclaims it was moved entirely in 1950. There is one last animal experience before blasting across Victoria on the straight highway – fried chicken at the Red Rooster fast-food restaurant in Wodonga.

In Melbourne we meet up with family friends, who emigrated from Britain in the 1980s. They live in Diamond Creek, a well-heeled suburb that is tastefully sculpted from the bush, a world away from urban hurly-burly. One has to listen hard for traffic. The gardens are the size of small public parks, the spacious homes, built from local stone, are not within hearing distance of neighbours, and the driveways are large enough for at least four cars. Their split-level home is on a slope, so the kitchen leads out to a veranda atop a green lawn surrounded by native Australian shrubs. Taking pride of place in the garden is the barbecue. Standing behind it affords the best view, which is no accident.

That's where we find Dan, with his barbie-mate tool in his hand, when we arrive.

"Well, g'day travellers," he says. "It's bloody good to see you. Shall I throw another snag on the barbie, mate?"

The last is a well-worn Aussie cliché, used for witty effect. Dan betrays barely a hint of the Midlands accent he used to speak with. It was his ambition to emigrate to Australia years ago and he is a willing convert to the lucky country. His profession, chartered surveying, remains the same, but he has happily swallowed the Aussie lifestyle whole. He's a great bloke, full of dry humour, always upbeat, cheerfully mocking. At nights he puts his rock CDs on so loud the house vibrates.

His wife Jenny, on the other hand, doesn't want to shrug off the old country. Her schoolteacher voice is intact. You wouldn't think she has been living in Australia for over fifteen years. It doesn't take long for her to be taking potshots at the country's education system while in conversation with Katia.

A few days into our stay, we go out in Dan's new flash sports car to Healesville, east of Melbourne. Healesville, they tell us, is the kind of place people go to for a picnic on a Sunday. On the way there we stop at picnic benches in a forest where red and blue rosellas tamely perch on our shoulders.

Kindness apart, I'm not sure why they're taking us to Healesville. We were more than happy to relax in our temporary idyll of home comforts.

"Blimey, not Healesville again," Dan said yesterday. "Can't we go to Mount Dandenong? These two would love it up there."

I find out in Katia's guidebook there's a wildlife sanctuary at Healesville, but that can't be it; we've already told them about encounters with marsupials during our journey.

Only when we reach the picturesque town and stand below the trees does it become clear. The leaves are golden, red-orange and hazel brown. The main street is lined with deciduous trees, beech and oak. Unlike everywhere else we've been to, in Healesville you can see the leaves fall in autumn. And that's something rarely visible in Australia. Gum trees don't lose their leaves in the same seasonal way.

"God, I miss England so much," Jenny says. "It's the little things, I suppose. Stupid memories like hearing church bells on a Sunday, or hedgerows around the fields."

The England she pangs for sounds very much like some long-lost Eden, like a John Betjeman poem.

"But most of England's not really like that," I reply.

These words do nothing to soothe the situation. I was making light of it. Jenny looks so downhearted.

The Black Spur road beyond is far more dramatic than Healesville, like the outback. This stretch is famous because it winds through a spectacularly tall forest of mountain ash trees and lush green ferns.

"What d'ya reckon?" Dan says. "Really amazing, isn't it? We never get to appreciate this country as much as we should do. But when you see this, you never regret coming over here."

The number of people of European extraction born in Australia first exceeded the number born abroad in the 1870s. Before then, many immigrants frowned on the new country, looking down on the alien landscape and still referring to Britain and Ireland as "home". Slowly a new Australian ethos evolved and white Australians came to appreciate the striking beauty of the outback that is so distinct from what is attractive in Europe.

Jenny, however, looks to be on auto-pilot behind the wheel, perhaps dreaming of country lanes back in England where oak trees stand guard in swaying barley fields; just as, perhaps, la Pérouse yearned for plantain-lined avenues in Provence after his confrontation with the lucky country.

14

Hopping to the Finishing Line

Them here are two obvious routes when hitchhiking from Melbourne to Adelaide. One is meandering, along the Great Ocean Road, through picturesque seaside towns like Lorne and past coastal marvels like the Twelve Apostles. The other is almost direct, through purposeful municipalities that serve the Victorian wheat belt and were once the route of gold diggers planning to ship their wares from Port Adelaide. We choose the latter as the people frequenting the scenic route would be tourists, people who stop to buy souvenirs and pause every ten kilometres. To go that way deliberately would be a total betrayal.

I want our last days on the road to be spent with locals, always more interesting for hitchhikers. It has been a privilege to sit on passenger seats next to Aussies we would otherwise rarely have bumped into. Thanks to thumbing rides, everything I hungrily anticipated in Australia has been reaffirmed.

I'm struggling with the knowledge that this will be the last chunk of our mammoth voyage. Katia is even more melancholy than me. She has transformed from a hitchhiking sceptic into a complete convert, an evangelist even. Nothing anyone said against hitchhiking now could change her view that it is a life-enriching, positive way of getting from *A* to *B*.

Dan drops us off by taking a detour to Melbourne's most westerly outlying suburb, Deer Park, on his way into work.

For once we're both quiet by the roadside. I don't even kick stones. I want to relish the sensation of being out here at this noisy, polluted, unremarkable slip road going out of Australia's second city. My introspection on what our shambling movements around this land might mean in the great scheme of things has almost reached the level of a spiritual epiphany when a car pulls up. The driver leans across as I run up to the passenger side. He's wearing a dog collar.

"You're more than welcome to put your baggage in the boot," he says. I almost flinch; he speaks with a hoarse, choking rasp. I look at him again and notice the dog collar is loose because he has a hole in his throat from a tracheotomy.

He's a United Church pastor, a long-serving member of the clergy. This is his first lone journey since the operation at a Melbourne hospital just over a month ago.

"How are you feeling now?" Katia asks.

"Oh, I reckon, she'll be right."

Most of the time he talks about street kids in Australia's big cities. "Streeties" they call them here. He's not in the slightest bit interested in talking about himself.

Ballarat is industrial looking from the periphery. The pastor deposits us by the pedestrianised mall, a ubiquitous feature of Australian town centres. Swarms of uniformed schoolgirls pour out of the Woolworths store with bags of sweets.

"May God be with you," he calls out as I get our rucksacks. When he departs, I realise God has played little role in our quest up till now. The Almighty could come in handy for the final stretch.

Ballarat was the scene of Victoria's most copious gold rush in 1851, shortly after the state separated from New South Wales. Word spread quickly down to Melbourne, then a week's walk away, creating a scene of total pandemonium as people downed tools to pan in the richest seam the country had ever known. Thousands of fortune hunters arrived from the United States, China and Europe. Ballarat brought immediate wealth to the new state and its population increased sevenfold. But like all gold rushes, the boom was short lived. A third of the optimistic diggers disappeared into the bush empty handed.

Discontent was fuelled by the cost of a government licence to pan for gold. Just before reaching Ballarat, we passed a sign for the site of the Eureka Stockade, where a bunch of miners revolted against the authorities in 1854. Led by a militant Irishman, they formed their own republic and mounted a homemade Southern Cross flag. When the army arrived to quash the uprising, twenty-two diggers died. Today, Eureka remains a potent symbol of Australian distrust of authority.

Ballarat's brief period of gold-laminated glamour remains visible in its elegant Victorian buildings, preserved for people who follow brown heritage signs. Banks, hotels and churches all date back to that time. Much of the rest of it looks mundane.

Amother and her inquisitive, pretty five-year-old daughter pick us up on the edge of Ballarat. At first the mum, Anne, is honest about her nervousness in stopping for hitchhikers.

"My husband told me I should never do that," she says, "but I thought, 'Why not?'"

Anne is as kind as anyone we've met. She worries over whether we've had enough to eat, where we're going to sleep tonight, how we wash our clothes. The existence of backpackers' hostels is totally new to her. This supports a theory I've had for a long time, that many ordinary Aussies living in the outback have practically no interaction with the thousands of foreigners moving up and down the east coast. The visiting community exists totally separate to them, in a vacuum.

Anne and Stacey live in Nhill, one of the bigger agricultural towns on the Western Highway. They are active members of the local Wesleyan church and have some flower arranging to do for a special service tomorrow. If more hitchhiking days had been like today, I'd start believing in God.

Stacey whispers something in her mum's ear. "Mummy and I would be very happy if you could stay at our house tonight," she announces.

After the Grampian mountain range, the bush bordering the highway is gently undulating wheat prairie. Fields are hedged by whispering gums. This is the Wimmera wheat belt, the bread basket of Victoria. The sparsely populated towns we roll through have mills and grain-storage barns. Before squatters moved out here to graze sheep in the nineteenth century, the area was covered in heath, tea trees and stringybarks. The squatters carved up their hold-ings into rectangular plots.

Just south of Nhill is the Little Desert National Park. I look out: the horizon is too full and the saltbush and grass too bushy to be the real desert we've left behind. But there are snakes and bearded dragons out there, Anne assures us. I like the idea of a Little Desert, a microcosm that is manageable enough for a day trip.

Nhill becomes visible on the horizon by virtue of its impressively tall grain silo, the largest single-bin silo in the southern hemisphere, Anne jokes. She mocks her home town, but when we get close her face lights up. She waves to people down the main street. The town has a homely quality to it. The frontier saloon pub is decorated with grape vines. They've made the broad central reservation into a park. Nhill is exactly the kind of unremarkable coun-try town that fails to get a mention in guidebooks.

Anne's house is cosy, decorated with doilies, vases of dried flowers and china cats. She makes a huge saucepan of pasta with tomato sauce. Before we eat, she says grace. I look across to Katia and note gladly that she's already got her fork in her hand, like me.

Listening from our downstairs bedroom window that night, I hear only an occasional passing tractor. Sheep bleat and wheat rustles. This may be farming country, but it's still the outback. I sleep wonderfully well under a thick, fresh-smelling duvet.

A rasping, 1970s-style Satsuma-orange Holden dents the rustic calm of Nhill before screeching to a clumsy halt in front of us. The butch woman behind the wheel apologises to us when we get close.

"Ah yeah, sorry, that was bloody unreal," she blurts out.

Neither of us knows what to say. The driver continues her flustered explanation. She shakes her head from side to side as she breathlessly talks us through her morning.

"Phew, unreal, I'm telling you. First my chooks escaped, and then my friend that was going to come to my farm, she broke down in Adelaide with four little kangaroos in the trunk." She sighs deeply and collects her breath. "Unreal. I've got two joeys to feed as well at my place."

I peer into the back. To squeeze our rucksacks in, I have to shift a large bag of animal feed across the rear seat. The interior of the car is evenly coated with an inch-thick layer of dust.

The woman's name is Melissa. She lives alone in an isolated farmhouse, down a gravel track from a village called Karoonda, which has about 250 inhabitants. I want to be alone, Melissa explains, adding, "Phew, the cities are just too crazy, really full on all the time."

It takes me a while to grasp that Melissa's social circle is made up entirely of animals. Each one is referred to by name, not species, and given a personality.

"Lee, he's eating everything at the moment," she says. "He's going to grow so big, I tell ya. Unreal. He's greedy about everything."

"Is this your child?" Katia asks.

"No, Lee's a little Chihuahua."

Despite a lack of professional training, Melissa makes it her business to provide a loving home for every dying, lame or mistreated animal in the vicinity of her home. She is a surrogate parent for subsequent offspring, feeding the babies with a bottle. Melissa is the ultimate obsessive animal lover. Her compassion is visible when she talks about defenceless creatures. The language she uses is excitable, childlike.

Katia mentions kangaroos just once and Melissa is off. "Oh it's terrible, unreal. We're the only country that kills its national emblem. People from the city come out with floodlights on their jeeps and shoot at them at night. It happened to my neighbour. I rescued two joeys from the pouches of their mums who were dead by the side of the road. Sometimes they're just like little tiny worms inside. There's a ten-dollar fee if you rescue one and hand it in..."

Melissa is stout and practical in appearance. She wears a blue sweatshirt and baggy jogging trousers. She has the physique of a rugby prop forward. Nothing about her is feminine except her massive bosom, so large one feels she might topple forward at any minute. She sports a schoolboy haircut, with bushy eyebrows below. When she fills her vehicle with LPG at the servo, I notice she is wearing sturdy boots and stomps like a building-site labourer. But despite the outer robustness, she looks bashful at the pump.

As she wrestles with the steering wheel, Melissa rolls rotund cigarettes. She smokes incessantly as we clatter through an anonymous-looking place called Bordertown, which takes its unoriginal name from being near the border of Victoria and South Australia. Bordertown was built as a stop-off point for the transportation of gold to Adelaide from Victoria, part of a sensible route to avoid the long-winded coast. The terrain is dominated by crop-covered plains and knee-high grass paddocks in which lumbering Merino sheep graze.

We get to Tailem Bend where roads fork north and south. I remember being stuck here on my first trip, coming the other way. Melissa mutters pitifully to herself about the pending evening feeding ritual, as if we're not there.

"How far away do you live?" I ask.

"Ah yeah, hum, unreal... hey, would you like to see my farm?"

Katia answers for us before I even have a chance to exchange raised eyebrows with her in the mirror. Now I feel like it's us doing Melissa a favour rather than the other way around. Our hitchhiking has come full circle. Australia has given us so much already; the least we can do is offer a little extra company to a lonely woman who talks to her animals.

"M*erde, oh la la.***"** Those are Katia's words as Melissa stops the car in the courtyard of her forlorn, untended farm; a scene of devastation, like a farm in a developing country trying to get back on its knees after a hurricane. There are creatures everywhere: goats, donkeys, a huge cow and some sheep eye us from the unkempt paddock. Inside the fence surrounding the house are scores of yapping Chihuahuas and Schnauzers, and diseased, balding cats. One that rubs its back on my leg has cataracts in its eyes and a hernia. There is a huge wire cage full of pink galahs and pigeons. Two peacocks strut on top of a water tank. The yard is thickly coated in excrement large and small, from foot-long splattered cowpats to rabbit droppings.

"Come in, come in," Melissa calls out, after chucking hay to the cow, the donkeys and the sheep.

As we cross the threshold, a powerful acrid stench nearly sends me flying. Katia momentarily walks back out before returning with her nose wrapped in a tissue. I am tempted to do a swift return and look for a lift. I have never smelled such a revolting pong. What the hell is it? I look around. The culprits are cowering in a corner of the front lounge room – two three-foot-high kangaroos.

"Sorry, I didn't do too much housework," Melissa says without the slightest hint of irony. "It's no palace, my place."

She stoops down to pick kangaroo droppings off the floor. "Jackie's done little poopsy-poo, hasn't she?" she says to one of the kangaroos in a playschool tone.

Afterwards, she wipes her shit-stained hands on her jumper. A brand new mop and bucket are conspicuously positioned in the corner of the kitchen. Noticing Katia, Melissa adds, "Phew, unreal. Ah yeah, the smell, that's my lovely little roos, and I've got a wombat in my bedroom too. He's incontinent, ay."

Melissa has been tending to the kangaroos for several months. They were orphans of their roadkill mothers. One is a central desert Big Red and the other a Western Grey. They sleep in synthetic pouches made of pink fabric, like babies' bouncers. Melissa lets them hop across the room, but they can't go out.

That's enough diplomacy for Katia.

"I'm sorry but I think we'll have to go now, Melissa. It's starting to get dark."

Melissa doesn't even pause while manhandling one of the kangaroos back into its pouch. "Phew, no way. No. Yous gotta be kidding. I've got to help two lame chooks tonight. Phew. Unreal, ay."

Katia leads me out forcefully to the summit of the little hill on which Melissa's squalid, tin-roofed house is perched. The farm is called Rainbow Hill, but under grey clouds it looks far from colourful. I suspect *chez* Melissa is a breach of Katia's endurance limit, like Mount Sorrow or the Great Barrier Reef boat trip. Perhaps I should have insisted Melissa left us at the highway.

But I'm wrong, too quick to judge, too presumptuous that I'm the tough one in our couple. Instead of whingeing, Katia shrugs her shoulders, like an Aussie swagman too far from the nearest town in the outback. I'm the one who moans on this occasion, a proper Pom.

"*Ça va?*" she asks. "You look sad."

"Yeah, I'm just thinking about finishing tomorrow."

Katia talks sensibly about how everything has to have an end. But she's more concerned about the present, the smell especially. That's symptomatic of our relationship: me with my head in the clouds while Katia considers immediate living conditions. It's made this trip a success.

When we get back inside, Melissa shows us to our sleeping quarters – a room at the back filled with shabby unused furniture, with a thin strip of soggy carpet for our sleeping bags. When she goes, we open the windows in a vain effort to dilute the smell. But this is a pointless gesture; the stench is engrained in the floorboards. Kangaroo piss is like a concentrated version of cat urine, possessing an all-pervading, unmistakeable tang. Most people are fortunate enough to travel around Australia without ever realising this, as they see kangaroos in their natural free state. I make a mental note to add this memorable night to the list of extraordinary experiences one can have as a direct result of hitchhiking.

We hear feeding time through the open window. Melissa's uses her baby voice, shouting, "Where are you, Pigsy? Come on Daisy, where are you?"

At night we are kept awake by the thud of kangaroos crossing the living room floor, looking around, and then turning back to where they started. The wombat, still unseen, makes little noise. We are only aware of its existence because, from time to time, we hear Melissa scream, "Ya bad wombat, you've pissed again. Phew."

We awake to what Australian forecasters term "a bit of weather"; that is, unseasonable blustery rain. Pulling back the dirty, translucent curtain, I see the Western Grey hop around the paddock, encircled by Chihuahuas. Melissa is chasing it. She wears a tight blue T-shirt, stained with mud. Her bowl haircut is punky after sleep.

In the kitchen, flies swarm around the rancid pile of washing-up. Melissa finds some stale bread in a cupboard. In another drawer is a jar of chicory coffee, years old, hardly used. She spends all her social security money on the animals, she explains. Once a year she picks grapes in the Barossa Valley. The extra funds go on chicken wire, wood for animal pens and cages.

"We should go," Katia implores. "You've been too kind already."

But her latest hint is so sugar-coated in good manners that Melissa misses it once again.

"Yeah, I'll take you back to Murray Bridge. That's on the way, isn't it? Hey, we could go on the paddle steamers. Yous tourists like that, I reckon, don't ya? They're unreal, massive, really unreal. Phew. But you're more like freaky tourists, hitchhiking and everything."

We drive back into Karoonda, past a concrete statue of a Merino sheep. Karoonda is also famous as the site of a meteorite fall in 1930, Melissa tells us. Restrained patches of mallee scrub that weren't cleared by early twentieth-century settlers remain between large, unfenced wheat fields. The vista is flat, interspersed with sandhills and dotted with sandalwood trees.

The majestic Murray River – Australia's Mississippi – comes into view just before we get to Murray Bridge. Along its banks are houseboats and lean-to shacks, the weekend retreats of wealthy Adelaide residents. The Murray is the river that stimulated the great explorers into piercing a route across the outback; the search for the inland sea started when Sturt navigated it in a whaleboat. Through the grime on the window, we watch an apprentice water skier tumble into the drink.

"Shall we go on the water? I've never done it. What d'ya reckon? Must be unreal, yeah."

Katia nods a split second before me. There is unspoken accord; we might as well delay the end of this trip as long as possible. Melissa looks so excited. Quite possibly, we're the first human friends she's had in years. In the Karoonda general store, there was smirking when we all walked in.

"Shall we find a boat?" Katia suggests.

Melissa jerks the gear stick in the same violent manner she picked the kangaroo out of its pouch. She slams her foot on the accelerator pedal. The spasmodic hum of the car motor – a never-ending asthma attack – suddenly cuts out.

"Ah shit, shit, shit," Melissa cries. "It must be the gas, I reckon."

"Don't worry about it," Katia says.

"I reckon it's the carby."

Melissa scampers breathlessly back and forth between the driver's seat and the bonnet, nodding nervously to herself and saying "unreal" a lot. She looks away whenever we make eye contact with her. When I finally convince her the car isn't going to start, she glumly tramps off to a Telstra phone box and calls her only sympathetic neighbour, Farmer Bert.

While we wait, she talks about one of her dogs that had pus on its intestine.

Farmer Bert is a sprightly 71-year-old. He used to farm sheep. He has just finished building a wooden-framed house for himself and his Filipino mail-order bride. The careful way he speaks reminds me of the cricket commentator Richie Benaud. Farmer Bert wears a hearing aid, but moves like a man half his age. He is the outback personified, the last vestige of the hardy Australian interior.

As he puts our luggage in his sparkling white 4×4, Bert shakes his head and tuts in Melissa's direction. He talks to her in a kindly, avuncular fashion.

"Did she feed you last night?" he asks us. "I thought she wouldn't have."

In a quiet moment, while Melissa is rambling on to Katia at the other end of the car, I ask if him if she has always been the same.

"She's got a big heart for those animals," he says. "Sometimes she ends up eating dog biscuits because she's already spent so much feeding them."

The Murray River cruise isn't mentioned again. Melissa is thinking ahead to the next feed.

"Bert, do you think the RAA will pick up my car?"

We're a bad omen for old bangers. That's two we've seen off now. Next time we'll make it a rule only to accept rides in properly serviced vehicles.

Farmer Bert drives right on to the highway and fearlessly stops on the emergency lane. He puts us where the three-lane freeway section of the Dukes Highway starts at Monarto.

"How's that for you kids?"

I look around; it's terrible. Farmer Bert has found us the worst hitchhiking location in Australia. At last, this is it. I knew it had to be somewhere. For once I admit we're a dangerous hazard to motorists. But neither of us says anything.

As we wave goodbye, a smile creeps back on Melissa's face. I promise to send her a copy of the group picture we asked Farmer Bert to take before leaving. I'm sure it's going to get pinned up next to the social security book and the chook-feed vouchers.

Katia and I have to yell to be heard. Passing trucks are worryingly close. We should have those fluorescent yellow jackets emergency services people wear at the scene of an accident. We're just over the brim of a hill where it's tricky for vehicles to stop. They race past, only noticing us at the last minute. We receive apologetic hand gestures from people seeing Katia's outstretched hand too late.

A police patrol car appears, almost launching off the rise. The siren is off but the blue lights are flashing. With expert dexterity, the police officer tears across the tarmac and deftly comes to a halt.

He surveys us in the mirror before stepping out. I hear the crackle of his radio above the traffic noise.

"G'day you two. We've had a few calls about you fellas standing here on the freeway. Have you any idea how dangerous this is? What are you doing here? Don't tell me you're hitchhiking."

I nod. My mouth is dry. Katia speaks up for us.

"Yes, we've 'itched everywhere. Why is zis a problem? We are not bozering anybody."

"You're allowed to hitch, that's no worries. But it's kind of illegal on the freeways, I gotta tell ya. This country's getting dangerous too for hitchhikers. I'm doing this for your own safety, guys."

I feel sulky. I can't believe we can't thumb a last ride.

"Where have you hitched so far then? Been up from Melbourne?"

Katia long-windedly describes the loop to the police officer. He is agape.

"Strewth, mate," he says to her. "I take my hat off to ya. That's ripper, that is. Good on ya."

And he does actually take his black police cap off, doffing it to the lady like a nobleman of old. His veneer of law-enforcing officiousness melts.

"Listen, kids, I shouldn't do this, but I'm going back towards Adelaide now. Why don't yous get in the back of the vehicle and I'll give yous a ride."

S o we hardly see Hahndorf or any of the settlements on the eastern periphery of Adelaide. The road tumbles away behind us at electrifying speed. We clutch the backs of the front seats as the car zooms down the fast lane (being in a police car, for once we both have to sit in the back). At such a high velocity, there's no place for conversation.

I look across to Katia.

"*Quoi?*" she demands.

"*C'est fini,*" I reply – it's over.

"Not now, I'm not feeling well."

So I keep quiet for our last ride in Australia. I don't want to distract Katia, who's concentrating on the white line rolling out in front of us. Throwing up in the back of a police car would be no way to finish our outback journey.

15
Stuart Highway Blues

Nearly back to where we started. If we ever had a mission - and I'm still not entirely sure - we have completed it.

This is literally the end of the road: the point where the tram from Adelaide city centre to the Victorian seaside resort of Glenelg clangs to a halt on the fringes of the beige sand beach. The pier is the only manmade route going further. It stretches a slender hitchhiking thumb out into the choppy Great Australian Bight, a reminder of the national desire to stay as far away from the outback as possible. The jetty says, "Look, we've been to the centre of Australia and it's a bloody desert, so we're reclaiming this bit of sea for ourselves." Fishermen down its length are furtively tying bait onto their lines. Guests from the Grand Hotel stroll along it, burning off calories from their breakfasts. Parents stop their toddlers climbing off it. Everyone is compelled to go to the end. But neither Katia nor I can be bothered.

We stride past the palm trees at the end of Glenelg's pedestrianised main square and down a ramp to the beach. A faint breeze licks off the ocean, quelled by the rapidity of the warming sun. I breathe in the saline tang of the sea air.

The sky is cobalt blue, sharply defining the formal, Anglicised contours of the town hall behind us. Adjacent to it is Hindmarsh Column, commemorating Adelaide's first governor Captain John Hindmarsh. He landed on this beach in 1836 and officially proclaimed the Province of South Australia. This very point was the state's tentative first base camp.

Sadly for us, it marks where our pioneering comes to a despondent, grinding halt. I haven't felt this deflated since... well, since living on a housing estate in Lincolnshire. I should keep my counsel on this. "Don't be so self-indulgent," a little voice says. After all, we have reached an end many times before: Darwin, Cairns, Sydney. At least we did it. But as the casuarina pines brush against the cloudless sky I sigh. Too loudly.

Katia carelessly chucks her rucksack onto the sand. Removing the pack was such a hassle before, but the manoeuvre has become effortless. She uses it as a pillow to rest her head on, as though second nature. Her sandals are ready for the bin, hanging together with thin strands of plastic. Both of us have our denim jackets tied around our waists for extra comfort against rubbing backpack belts while walking along the highway – surplus to requirements now.

"What's zer matter wiz you? You're on a beach and it's sunny. What can be wrong?"

"I dunno."

"*Tu es pénible*" – you're a pain. She adds, "I know exactly what's going on in your head."

"Really, you think you can read my mind?"

"Yes, I really do. You're saying to yourself, 'Oh no, zis is zer end of all my 'itchiking. Now I 'ave to go back to

England and get a job, because of Katia.' And you want to keep going because you're never 'appy zat somesing's finished. However good zis 'as been, you always want more. Am I right or am I right?"

"Yes, you're right."

"*Bah, moi*, I feel just zer same."

Lazy days in Adelaide reimmerse us into gentrified England, without the reality check. It is Australia's most refined, noble city, a crossing point between the museum of Europe and the glaringly bright New World, the "City of Churches". Named after King William IV's wife, the origins of Adelaide are evident in every grand old building. Spires are sentry beacons throughout the suburbs. St Peter's Cathedral could be in London if it weren't for the sun-bathed golden masonry, never stained by coal-burning smog. The city centre was arranged in an almost symmetrical grid by Colonel William Light, an engineer on Hindmarsh's first settler ship, and is surrounded by generous swathes of parkland beyond the River Torrens. Light chose the site fastidiously. Willows are planted along the river, like Stratford-upon-Avon.

The rattling tram into town is an archaic symbol of a bygone world. We overhear nimble, ripe-skinned pensioners in shorts talk about the effect of the expected heat on their flowers. After alighting, we cross Victoria Square to the statue of John McDouall Stuart, the final holy site in our pilgrimage. On a high plinth, the great man towers above the scurrying city workforce. He stares sternly into the distance, leaning against a tree, with his navigational tools in a bag around his neck. A plaque below commemorates both Stuart and his sponsors. I wonder what he would have made of being remembered here; cities were never really his thing.

Stuart returned to Adelaide a hero. In January 1863, he led a procession of the South Australian Great Northern Exploring Expedition down King William Street, the city's main artery. But the thrill of the achievement wasn't enough to sustain him for long. Poor health prevented further surveying and his backers James Chambers and William Finke died. Bored of pedestrian life in Adelaide, which could only ever be a poor relation to the wilderness, Stuart decided to return to Britain. After conquering the outback, everything else was too easy. His life's work was over. Why stay?

In a humbler way, I feel much the same. I like Adelaide, but I can't help but sense the remnants of untapped wasteland out there, beyond the back of Bourke, clouding my appreciation. Just like the last time I came to Australia, my thirst hasn't been totally quenched. Give it a few weeks and I'll probably want to start back into the unknown. This trip has come to an abrupt end too quickly. Here, we are just dots in an overhead dreamtime painting. Out there, opportunities are limitless.

As Stuart departed Port Adelaide, a ship set sail to establish a new town on the north coast, based on his recommendations. In June 1866, less than two years after his arrival back in Britain, he died. He was 50. Only seven people attended his funeral at London's Kensal Green Cemetery. He died an anonymous figure, still bearing the brunt of jealous criticism.

One day in a local bar, we again find ourselves talking about our now shared outback obsession. In a typically French way, Katia actually remembers some of those cuisine vacuum roadhouses by what food she ate there.

"*Tu te souviens, là où on a mangé...*" she begins – do you remember where we ate such and such?

I know we've been everywhere; yet at the same time we've only scraped our breathable fabric walking boots across the surface.

"*On était mieux dans l'outback*," Katia says, reaching the same conclusion I used to bore her with when we lived in Lincolnshire, that it's better in the outback. I've never felt freer than on my previous visit, and this trip has rekindled that belief completely. In my mind, I run over various schemes that could enable Katia to tear up her contract and not take that teaching job back home.

"Are you sure you want to go back?" I ask, with a leading edge.

"No, I'm not, but like zer Ossees say, 'No worries mate.'"

"That's Aussies, not Ossees."

A bloke in a singlet growls at the bank of television screens lining the far wall. On each is a different harness-racing event. These uniquely Australian races involve horse-drawn chariot contraptions on which the jockey sits. They call it "the trots". After one race draws to a close, the man throws his betting slip down on the bar and orders another schooner of draught beer. He's pissed.

"Where yous blokes from?" he asks Katia.

"I'm from France," she replies.

"I don't know French. What's the point?"

He ignores her completely and turns to a guy in the corner minding his own business.

"Rack off Phil, you old bastard," he yells, for no apparent reason. Then he turns back to Katia.

"Yous kids backpacking?"

"Yes," she says. "We've 'itchiked all the way around."

He almost spits out his beer.

"Yous are hitchhiking! Do people still do that? Mate, I reckon you're going to have heaps of problems. No one hitchhikes in Australia any more. You'll never even get out of bloody Adelaide."

"Actually, we already have."

"Well good on ya, mate," he replies, and turns his attention back to the trots.

In the other corner of the bar are the pokie machines. Occasionally a clatter of loose change spilling into the winnings tray resounds around the room, but mostly we just hear mumbled curses.

At the Botanical Gardens, the contrasting ecosystems of this amazing country are all there, in one manageable microcosm. Each tree is a memento for places we hitchhiked from over the last few months: the giant Queensland hardwoods, the bloodwood gums, the macadamias. I never thought for a second that trees could be so evocative. In a tacky souvenir shop at the exit, I buy a little bottle of eucalyptus oil, not for its medicinal benefits but for the bottled scent, so I can take a furtive sniff from the bathroom cabinet in years to come. Katia fills a plastic bag with furry toy koalas and kangaroos. She's been snared by the Australian outback. Next time *Crocodile Dundee* is on, we might both end up sitting through it.

The time comes for our reluctant return to our orderly, arranged-well-in-advance lives. I'm dreading it. The only comfort is that my girlfriend is now also my hitch-hiking buddy. We'll be able to go places... sometime soon. I'm sure we'll come back here again. What could possibly get in the way of another hitchhiking journey, a circle around Western Australia, for example? Jobs, children and marriage – those can all be put on hold, surely?

Katia's eyes fill with tears. Her brow becomes reddened. She gulps loudly. When she cries, it's as though a hidden fountain has just been dug up.

"What's the matter?"

"I don't want to go. I love it being just the two of us. I don't know if we can be so cool together if we're not 'itchiking."

I force one of my counterfeit smiles, remembering what a source of friction this expedition was when we packed our boxes in that little house.

"So what do we do now?"

She sniffs, breathes in deeply, sadly, like a baby after a bad dream. She won't let me wipe away the tears.

"Come on, let's 'itchike to the airport," she says.